TEMPORARY MONUMENTS

TEMPORARY MONUMENTS:
WORK BY ROSEMARY MAYER, 1977–1982

Edited by Marie Warsh and Max Warsh

Soberscove Press | Chicago

"PLEASURES AND POSSIBLE CELEBRATIONS":
ROSEMARY MAYER'S TEMPORARY MONUMENTS, 1977–1982

Gillian Sneed

"All men are into power," reads the opening line of a stream-of-consciousness text by the artist Rosemary Mayer.[1] The passage denounces the macho art system, epitomized in Mayer's mind by Richard Serra's then-recent monumental public sculptures. Written in May 1980, just one year before the controversy surrounding Serra's *Tilted Arc* (1981), Mayer's text likely references one of two earlier works by Serra, erected in lower Manhattan in the spring of 1980: *T.W.U.*, a construction of vertical slabs, or *St. John's Rotary Arc*, a curved horizontal wall similar to *Tilted Arc* (FIG. 1).[2] Both sculptures were Minimalist in style, both were made of corten steel, and both had been the objects of verbal and physical attack by the public. Viewing Serra's works as emblematic of broader problems in the art world, Mayer continues:

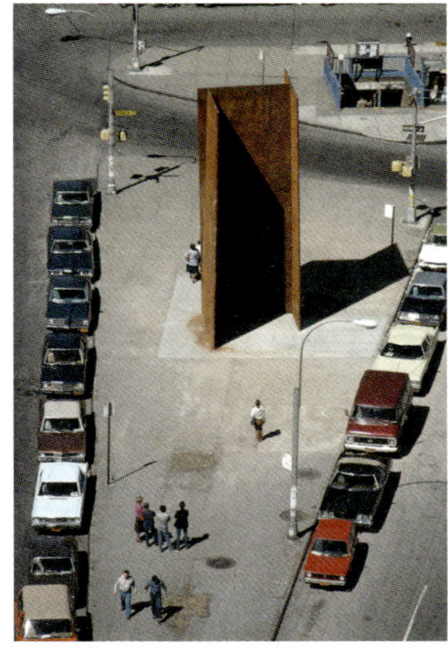

FIG. 1. Richard Serra, *T.W.U.*, 1980. Weatherproof steel. Three plates, each: 36 ft x 12 ft x 2¾ in (11 m x 3.7 m x 7 cm). Collection of the City of Hamburg, Germany. (Had been installed at West Broadway between Leonard and Franklin Streets, New York, 1980–81. Currently installed at the Deichtorhallen, Hamburg, Germany). Photo by Donna Svennevik. Courtesy the photographer.

> Not participating in a male system. . . . Power is evidence of inequality. . . . The Serra piece is CORTEN steel . . . [and is] not balanced, so it is a <u>sign</u> for other works of his. . . . Evidence of power manipulating the system. . . . Public art has to deal with people's opinion.[3]

At the heart of this passage, written from the perspective of a marginalized feminist sculptor as she looked toward the horizon of a new decade, is a reflection on the intersections between the patriarchal values undergirding the art world, and debates around the role of public art at the time. These are also the issues this essay addresses, specifically in relation to Mayer's site-specific and socially engaged public art projects of the late 1970s and early '80s.

Rosemary Mayer (1943–2014) was a pioneering feminist artist, and by the late 1970s, had gained recognition for her signature large-scale fabric sculptures and sensuous drawings from the earlier half of the decade. She began her art career in the late 1960s, studying painting at the School of Visual Arts, and collaborating with her then-husband, artist Vito Acconci, and her sister, poet Bernadette Mayer, on their conceptual art and poetry magazine, *0 TO 9*.[4] In the early 1970s, she became involved in a women's consciousness raising group led by artist Adrian Piper, an experience that propelled her art and interests in new directions. Becoming influenced by Renaissance, Mannerist, and Baroque art history and the lives of historical women who lived during those historical periods, she began producing sculptures using fabric as a primary material and exploring its formal properties (FIG. 2). Upon critic Lucy Lippard's recommendation, the fledging members of A.I.R. Gallery, the first all-female cooperative gallery in the United States, invited Mayer to join. Her first solo show there was a display of her early fabric sculptures, which ran from April to May 1973. This garnered the attention of critic Lawrence Alloway, who went on to champion her work throughout the 1970s and early '80s.[5]

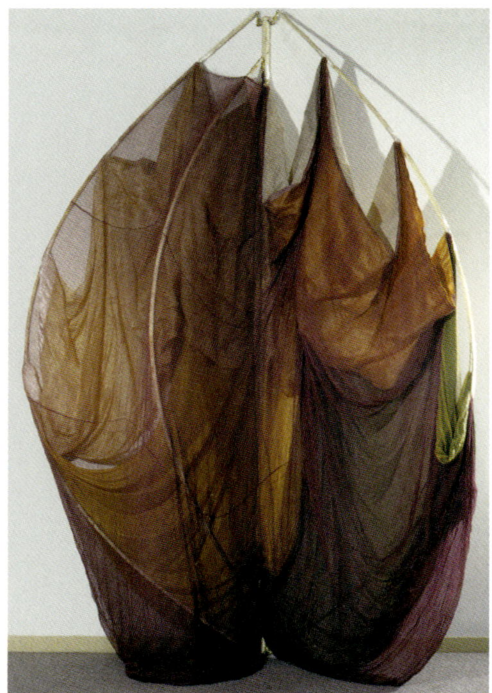

FIG. 2. *The Catherines*, 1973. Nylon, cheesecloth, pellon, fiberglass rayon, ribbon, dyes, wood, and acrylic paint. 116 x 48 x 48 in (295 x 122 x 122 cm).

Lippard has argued that many feminist artists of the 1970s used fabric, soft colors, decoration, and narrative in their art to counter the formal language of Minimalism, which they viewed as dehumanizing and oppressive, sentiments echoed in Mayer's text on Serra.[6] Art historian Anna Chave similarly proposed in her 1990 essay, "Minimalism and the Rhetoric of Power," that underlying Minimalist art was an authoritarian hyper-masculinity, which valued strength and rigor, and rejected softness.[7] It can certainly be argued that Mayer's commitment to feminism led to her fascination with fabric's sensuality. Yet, her early fabric sculptures were also influenced by the depictions of sumptuously draped cloth in late-Renaissance and Mannerist painting.

In the late 1970s and early '80s Mayer's artistic practice began to change. She became increasingly interested in the dissolution of the sculptural object and shifted away from the gallery setting. Though she was still informed by feminism, she transitioned from fabric sculptures to an entirely new genre of experimental and ephemeral installations she called "temporary monuments," which combined various forms of site specificity and audience engagement with an interest in commemorating and celebrating personal and public histories. While her work from the early-to-mid 1970s has recently received increased attention, these later more experimental and ephemeral art projects have remained virtually unexamined.[8] As the first comprehensive presentation of these works, this book addresses this gap in the literature.

The purpose of this essay is to situate these works within the historical framework of the New York art scene of the period, marked by the transition away from Post-Minimalist tendencies—and the proliferation of alternative spaces and public art grants in the '70s—to the era dominated by the rise of the East Village punk scene and the explosion of the art market in the '80s. It outlines and analyzes the three types of temporary monuments Mayer made between 1977 and 1982, broadly labeled "Balloons," "People," and "Tents." It argues that it was Mayer's feminist sensibilities that motivated her critiques of masculinist discourses in public art, and compelled her to memorialize and celebrate individuals, communities, and histories in her work. This essay analyzes Mayer's bookmaking and writing as supplements to these projects. It also examines her artistic dialogue with artist Ree Morton, who played a key role in Mayer's shift toward public art. It demonstrates that Mayer surpassed the types of installation art then in vogue—the earthworks and Post-Minimalist installations of the 1970s described by Rosalind Krauss as "sculpture in the expanded field"[9]—to innovate an entirely new genre of art that connected people and places with histories, both personal and public. I argue that in doing so, she helped pioneer the kinds of site-specific and socially engaged public art practices that are widespread today.

Balloons

Mayer's art practice first approached public space in the spring of 1977 with a work titled *Spell*. In 1976, she had received a Creative Arts Public Service (CAPS) grant from the New York State Council on the Arts that included a "public service" component intended to fund outdoor artworks. By that time, she had already begun to think of galleries as stifling and the wider public as a potential audience for art. She had also become interested in the elaborate spectacles of the Renaissance and Baroque eras, which consisted of multi-media pageants and performances, triumphal parades, and complex stage sets. She felt that such events achieved a total synthesis of the arts in time and space and involved the public. She wanted to emulate these historical forms of artistic celebration and the expanded roles they offered to artists as "decorators at festivities, memorializers of the dead, catchers, even of passing beauty."[10] Her interest in balloons developed in part from these

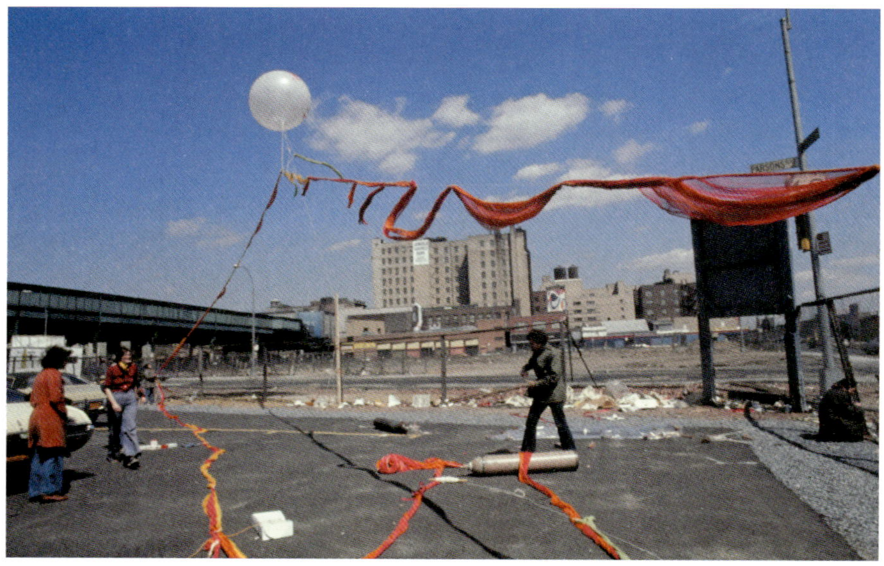

investigations into art historical spectacles, which she also associated with fairs, festivals, and carnivals. In a sketchbook, she listed different kinds of vernacular art forms related to such celebrations, including banners, kites, and "balloons and other sky things."[11] She had also become increasingly interested in the fleeting and ephemeral nature of time, epitomized in her mind by balloons.

The work that resulted from these reflections was *Spell* (FIG. 3), a public art project featuring large weather balloons and described in a promotional flyer as a "floating sculpture."[12] Intended to celebrate the re-opening of the Jamaica, Queens farmer's market, *Spell* comprised three enormous cream-colored balloons harnessed with nylon cords and draped with swathes of orange and red fabric. She wrote different phrases on each one in red block letters: "Iris Return," "Crocus Return," and "Hyacinth Return." She intended to set the balloons afloat over the flower stalls as a kind of symbolic resurrection, a "magic rite to ensure the arrival of spring, of flowers, fruit and vegetables," their upward movement evoking plants emerging from the ground.[13] However, it did not unfold as she had imagined. She thought the balloons would hold up the fabric, but the wind caused them to sway violently and break. Even so, it was not a complete failure. For Mayer, both the work's site specificity and her interactions with the public were crucial to its significance.[14]

As she reflected on *Spell* after its presentation, it began to take on other connotations related to memory and loss. She contemplated the location where it took place—Jamaica, Queens—a part of the city that she had often visited as a child because her father's family had lived there. The project revived her memory, taking on significance as a memorial to her family and deepening her sense of a personal connection to the place. She ultimately described *Spell* as an "attempt to connect a place, a time, and people to a sculpture . . . a first temporary monument, an evanescent public work."[15] She grappled with the newness of its form, and the fact that it was neither a sculpture nor a performance, but a hybrid of the two.[16] Her use of the term "temporary monument" to describe *Spell*, as well as her later ephemeral works, represented her effort to develop a vocabulary for a nascent genre of public art combining memorialization, site specificity, and audience engagement, for which there was not yet any terminology.

It also represented her attempt to redefine the role of both monuments and memorials. Throughout history, the functions and meanings of these two forms of public sculpture have been intertwined, although distinct characteristics differentiate them. While monuments are usually imagined as fixed, permanent, and didactic markers of historical figures or events, memorials are envisioned as emotional sites for paying tribute. Mayer blurs the distinctions between the two to express what art historian Erika Doss has described as the shift in 1970s memorialization from "official national narratives to . . . subjective symbolic expressions."[17] Like memorials and monuments, Mayer's *Spell* mediated memory. It functioned as both a marker of loss and the celebration of individual lives, histories, and places.

Spell also proposed a new kind of public art, emphasizing site specificity and social engagement.[18] In the 1960s, the most common kind of public sculpture was what is often referred to as "plop art"—large abstract sculptures "plopped" in urban plazas in front of corporate buildings with no real relationship to the site or the local community. However, by the late 1970s perceptions of public art had shifted. Funding organizations like the NEA that sponsored large-scale public art projects began to recommend that they facilitate community engagement and site specificity.[19] As critic Nancy Foote points out in her catalogue essay for the public art exhibition *Urban Encounters* (1980), artists of the '70s had demonstrated a renewed interest in site specificity, a trend epitomized by earthworks.[20] Yet, earthworks rarely achieved social engagement because they were often located in remote places.[21] In his essay for the *Urban Encounters* catalogue, Lawrence Alloway appeals to artists to make public sculpture in which participation takes the place of monumentality, a direction Mayer took with *Spell* and continued to explore in her other temporary monuments.[22]

Participation, or social engagement in art, has its own genealogy that intersects with the history of performance and conceptual art, and can count among its predecessors several experimental art forms including Allan Kaprow's happenings and Joseph Beuys's social sculpture. Art historian Grant Kester highlights the fact that conceptual and performance art of the 1970s by artists like Vito Acconci and Adrian Piper (both of whom were among Mayer's interlocutors) helped to propel a "subtle movement away from the

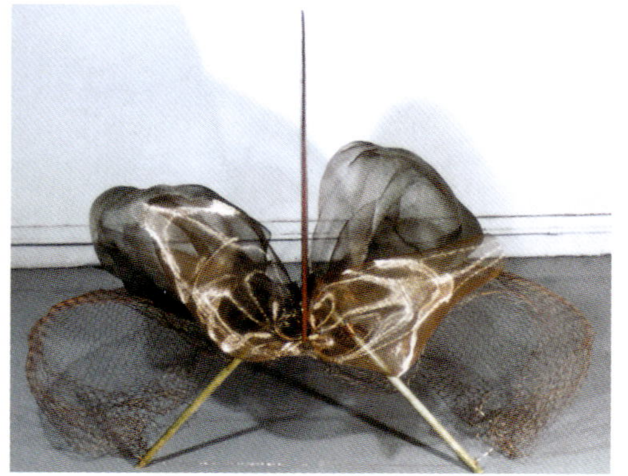

FIG. 4. *Ista II*, 1974. Wood, fiberglass, and paint. 60 x 60 x 48 in (152.5 x 152.5 x 122 cm).

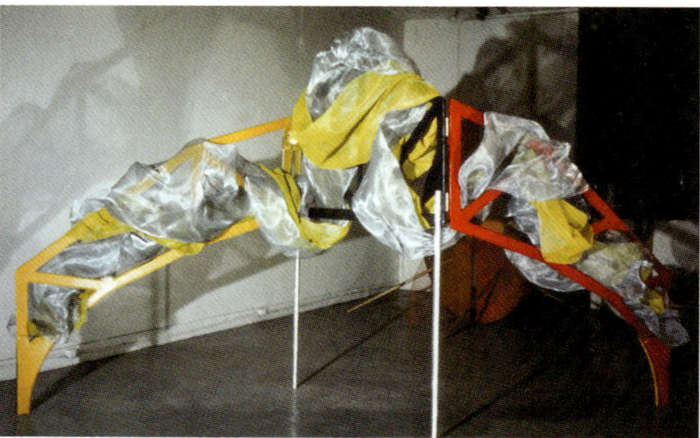

FIG. 5. *Portae*, 1974. Wood, aluminum, fiberglass, and oil paint. 105 x 204 x 69 in (266 x 518 x 175 cm).

FIG. 6. Ree Morton, *Signs of Love*, 1976. Mixed media. Installation view, Fine Arts Center, University of Rhode Island, Kingston, 1976. © Estate of Ree Morton. Courtesy Alexander and Bonin, New York.

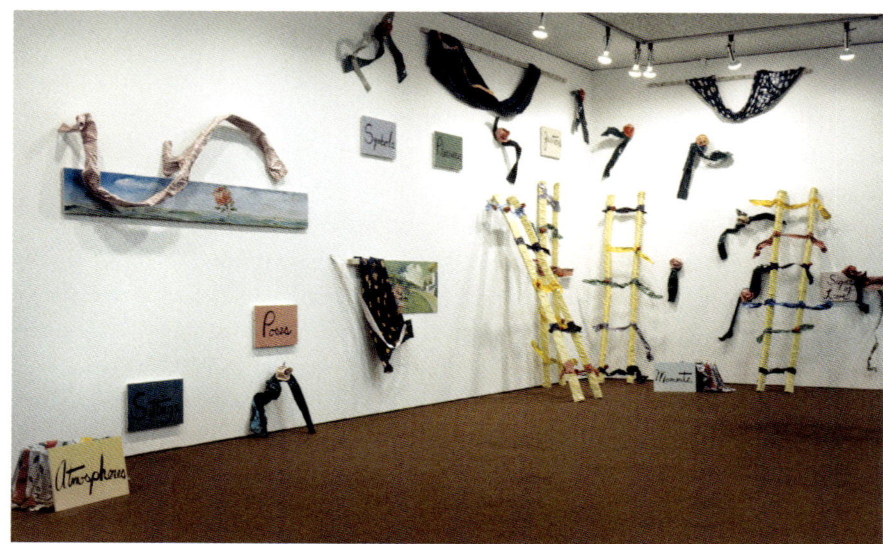

artwork as self-contained entity and toward a more dialogical relationship to the viewer."[23] Similarly, art historian Cara Jordan highlights the contributions to socially engaged art of another artist in Mayer's orbit: Gordon Matta-Clark. She argues that the alternative art spaces and co-op galleries that he helped organize provided the context for convivial artistic social gatherings that anticipated the socially engaged art of later decades.[24]

Another influence on the development of Mayer's temporary monuments like *Spell* was the work of her friend, Ree Morton. "We were always looking at each other's work," Mayer affirmed in an interview.[25] In fact, a close examination of the two artists' works between 1973 and 1976 suggests an intense dialogue and artistic give and take between them (FIGS. 4–6). For instance, Morton's decisive shift in 1974 to the medium of celastic (a fabric impregnated with plastic that is moldable when wet, but dries hard), as well as her emerging interest in draped fabric, bows, and flowers in works such as *Of Previous Dissipations* (1974), *Bake Sale* (1974), and *Signs of Love* (1976), echoes Mayer's earlier draped fabric sculptures of 1972 and 1973. The stiff fabric texture and feminine iconography of Morton's celastic works of 1974 also parallel Mayer's shift that year to using aluminum mesh to achieve a stiff fabric effect in works like *Istas I* and *II* (1974). Similarly, the draped fabric festoons in Morton's *Antidotes for Madness* (1974) evoke Mayer's fabric draped around a ladder structure in *Portae* (1974).[26]

Morton's public projects had a powerful impact on Mayer as well. In 1975, one year before Mayer had received the CAPS grant that funded *Spell*, Morton had also received a CAPS grant, and used it that summer to fund a public artwork at New York City's South Street Seaport. Titled *Something in the Wind*, the outdoor installation comprised one hundred hand-sewn nylon flags hung on a docked nineteenth-century schooner (FIG. 7). Morton appliquéd each flag with the names of family and friends, and painted a motif symbolic of each person—birds, clouds, kites, flags, or fans—all associated with the air.[27] Among the many individuals Morton honored in the work was Mayer, celebrated with a bright yellow flag bearing her name and accompanied by an image of a butterfly (FIG. 8). Morton's fascination with medieval heraldry, an interest Mayer also shared, inspired the flags and the emblematic symbols she used on them. In fact, Mayer likely played a role in the development of Morton's conceptualization of the work. In the summer of 1974 she and Morton had discussed heraldry, symbols, and coats of arms imagery. Mayer even lent her a book on the topic, which Morton seems to have used as a reference in the making of the flags.[28] As a part of their ongoing dialogue

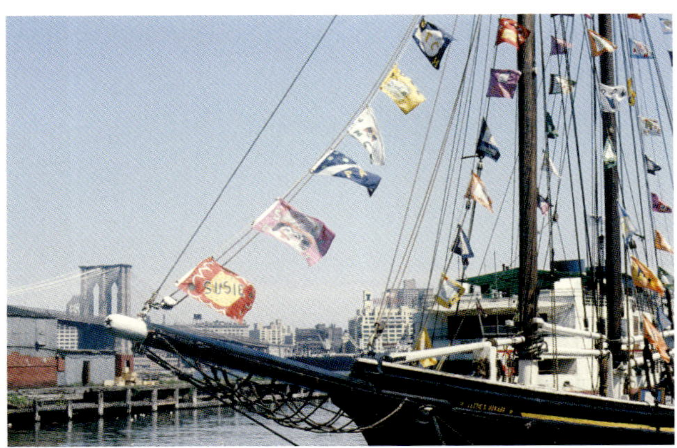

FIG. 7. Ree Morton, *Something in the Wind*, 1975. ca. 100 flags: acrylic and felt-tip pen on nylon. South Street Seaport Museum, New York, New York, 1975. © Estate of Ree Morton. Courtesy Alexander and Bonin, New York.

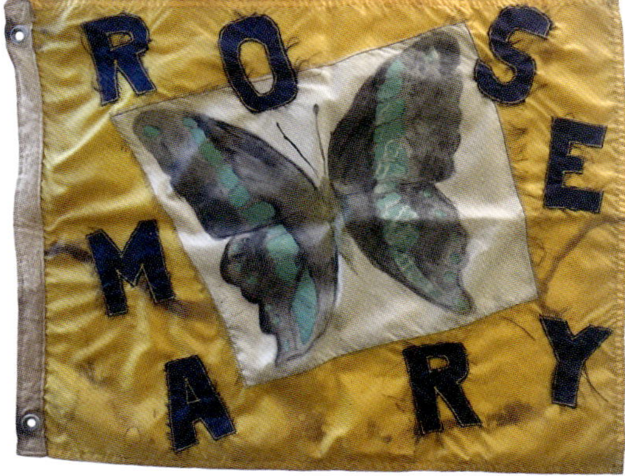

FIG. 8. Ree Morton, Flag for Mayer from *Something in the Wind*, 1975. Acrylic and felt-tip pen on nylon. 24½ x 39 in (62 x 79 cm). Collection of Rosemary Mayer.

and artistic exchange, it is probable then that Morton's *Something in the Wind* played a role in Mayer's shift in 1977 toward site-specific and socially engaged public art projects, particularly *Spell*. Like Morton's use of symbols associated with "air" and "wind" to celebrate people close to her in *Something in the Wind*, Mayer also associated the wind and floating with balloons and the celebration of individuals in her life in *Spell*.

In an essay published in *WhiteWalls*, a magazine of artists' writings, Mayer explored her family stories that had become connected to *Spell*, and the ways balloons came to symbolize for her the passing of time and lives. She writes: "I tr[ied] to flesh out the stories, bring them back, but this is their only existence, like the early balloons which . . . disappeared with their passengers or burst into flames in the sky."[29] Tragically, Morton died in a car accident in Chicago just a few weeks after Mayer presented *Spell*.[30] In a letter to a mutual friend, Mayer writes: "I went to her funeral, an experience I have yet to really absorb. It's hard to think about things. Ree floats in instead," a comment that seems to associate the loss of her friend with things that float, like balloons.[31]

Spell became another kind of hybrid, both a celebration and a memorial, which influenced Mayer's approach in her next balloon project. Thinking about her parents (who had both died when she was a teenager), Mayer realized that April had been the month of both their birthdays. Morton had also died in April. These reflections led to the next work in the balloon series, *Some Days in April*, which took place in April 1978, and was dedicated to her parents and Morton (FIG. 9). Installed in an empty field in upstate New York, it comprised seven red, yellow, and white advertising balloons tethered to stakes and festooned with bright ribbons at their base.[32] In addition to the names associated

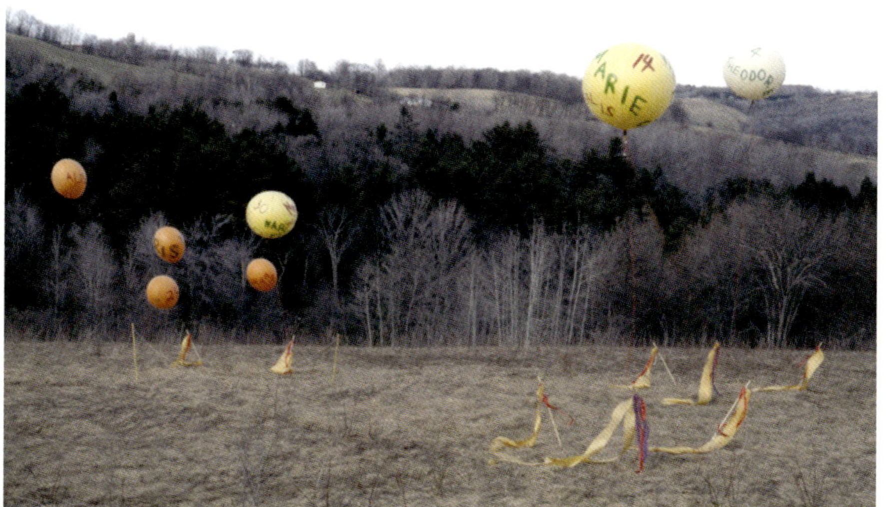

FIG. 9. *Some Days in April*, week of April 17, 1978. Balloons, helium, paint, fabric, rope, and wooden rods. Property of Bruce Kurtz, Hartwick, New York.

with the deceased, she wrote the name of a star and flowers that appeared in spring on each balloon, followed by a number (the day of each person's birth or death). For instance, a yellow balloon in honor of Morton read: "Arcturus" (star), "Narcissus" (flower), "30" (day she died), and "Helen / Catherine" (name).[33] Explaining her use of the names "Helen" and "Catherine" to identify Morton, Mayer clarified that Helen was Ree's actual first name, but that she never used it because it had also been her mother's name. Similarly, Mayer used the name Catherine, because it was a common name representing many great women throughout history.[34]

The color photographs documenting *Some Days in April* depict a still wintry landscape: a flat, barren field with rolling hills and wispy, leafless trees in the distance. In one, the bright balloons stand out against the muted background and appear to grow upward, like spring shoots erupting from the ground, their colorful ribbon tassels planting them to the earth. In another, we see Mayer herself in jeans and a sweater, a lone figure against the landscape, with ribbons flowing out of her back pocket as she wrangles the tether of a yellow balloon, gazing upward toward the sky beyond (FIG. 10). Though the work lasted several days, there was no audience, rendering it a private memorial that lived on only through its documentation (FIG. 11).

By contrast, the next work in the balloon series took place not in an isolated field in the country, but in the heart of the city. Mayer presented *Balloon for a Birthday* in November 1978 on the rooftop of 461 Park Avenue, a building that belonged to Mayer's friend, printer John Campione.[35] Unlike *Some Days in*

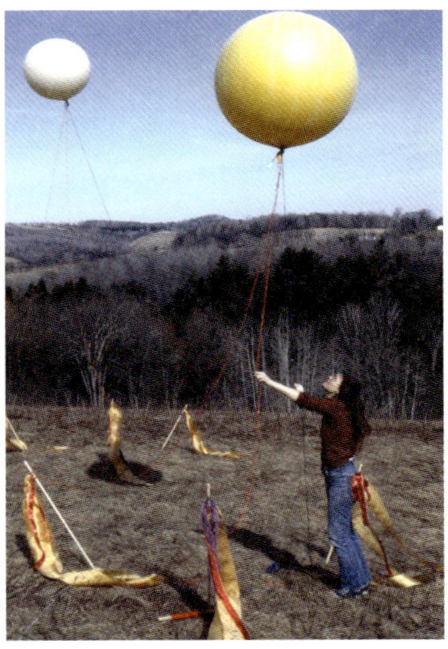

FIG. 10. Mayer installing *Some Days in April*, 1978.

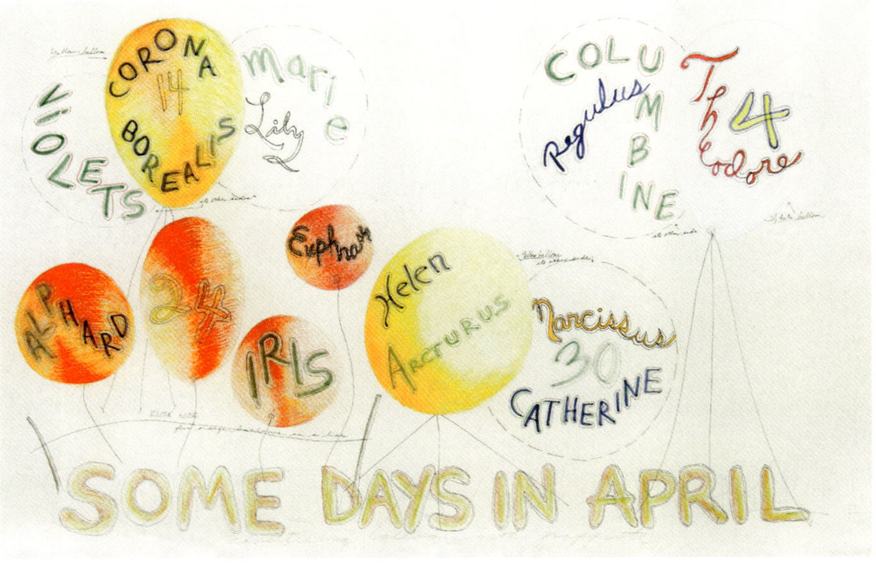

FIG. 11. *Some Days in April*, 1978. Colored pencil, pen, and graphic on paper. 26 x 40 in (66 x 101.5 cm).

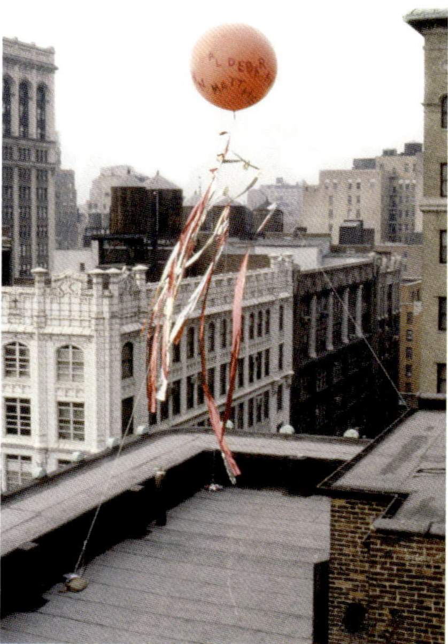

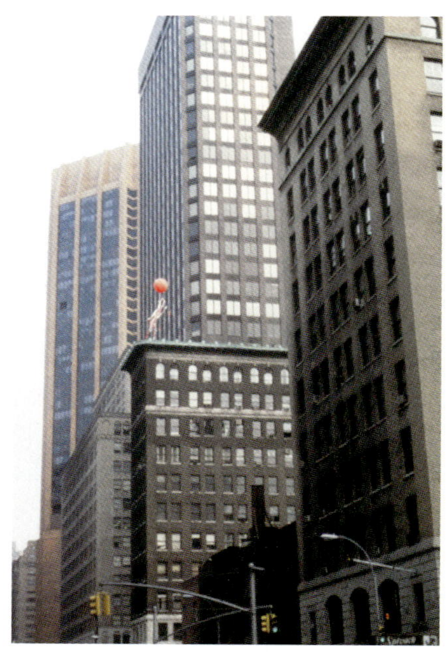

FIG. 12. *Balloon for a Birthday*, November 7, 1978. Balloon, helium, paint, rope, and metallic streamers. Rooftop of 461 Park Avenue, New York, New York.

FIG. 13. *Balloon for a Birthday*, view from Park Avenue.

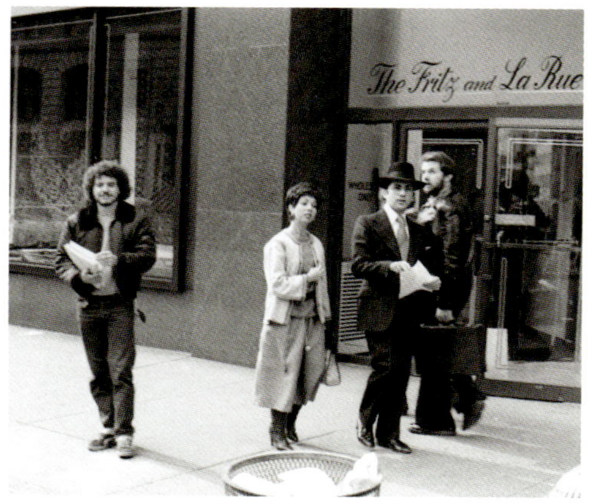

FIG. 14. Handing out flyers for *Balloon for a Birthday* on Park Avenue.

April, Balloon for a Birthday functioned not as a memorial for the loss of a loved one, but as a celebration for her friend, Campione, on the occasion of his birthday (FIG. 12). It consisted of a single red advertising balloon with streamers of ribbons flying like tails of a kite tethered to the building's roof where it remained for over a week. Like *Some Days in April*, Mayer made connections between time, seasons, and the cosmos. The work connected the date (November 7, 1978) with a flower that blooms in November (the chrysanthemum) and a reddish star that appears in the night sky during the month (Aldebaran). Assistants handed out pink flyers announcing the work to passersby on the street below as a way of inserting the artwork into the public's experience of daily life (FIGS. 13, 14). The mood was convivial and celebratory. "People in the street, in other buildings, stared, laughed, pointed," she explains.[36] In a text she wrote about the project titled, "Pleasures and Possible Celebrations," she highlights the joy she intended to evoke: "[T]he balloons and fabrics floating over buildings are ways to stay alive, pleasures to look up at while you're in the street."[37]

In addition to her realized balloon projects, Mayer also made plans for several unrealized projects between 1977 and 1978. The most developed of these was a work intended to take place in Castle Clinton, an old fort in New York City's Battery Park, which she titled *Connections* (FIG. 15). Mayer envisioned the project unfolding over several weeks. Each day she would invite children to come to the circular and roofless fort, where they could print the name of a person from their life, a date connected with that person, and a star and flower associated with them on a helium-filled advertising balloon. Most of the balloons would be moored inside the enclosure, their multi-colored orbs hovering above its walls, but some would be set free to float away each day. Underscoring its connection to place as well as its celebratory and participatory qualities, Mayer described it as: "[A]n attempt to ascribe meaning to points in time, to a place, to the meetings of participants . . . to make a community celebration."[38]

Mayer called *Connections* and her other unrealized balloon projects "impossible sculptures" comparing them to Claes Oldenburg's *Monuments*, unrealized anti-memorials depicting everyday objects blown up to colossal proportions, like an upside-down popsicle on Fifth Avenue (FIG. 16), made famous through a series of drawings of them that he published in *Proposals for Monuments and Buildings, 1965–69*.[39] In a letter to her sister, Bernadette, Mayer mentions that even if she is unable to realize the Castle Clinton project, "[A]t least . . . it will lead to some good drawings I'm sure. Most of Oldenburg's big sculptures started off first as just good drawings."[40]

Mayer extensively documented her balloon projects not just through drawings, but also in photographs and artists' books. Because of their role in capturing memories and events, she felt "photos don't belong on walls . . . but

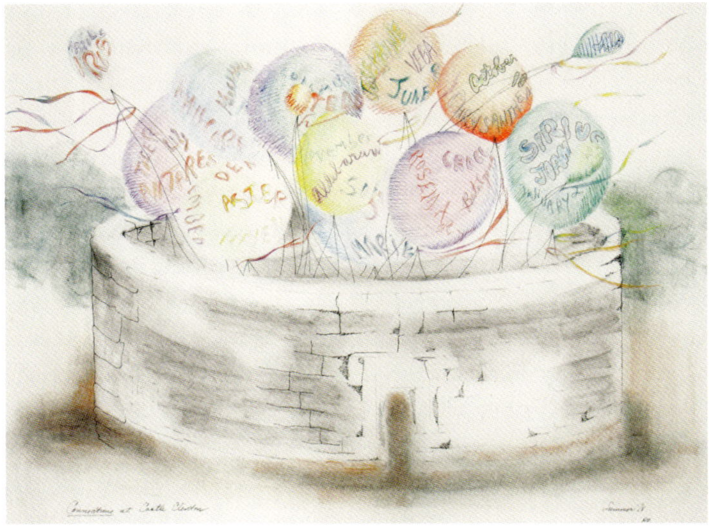

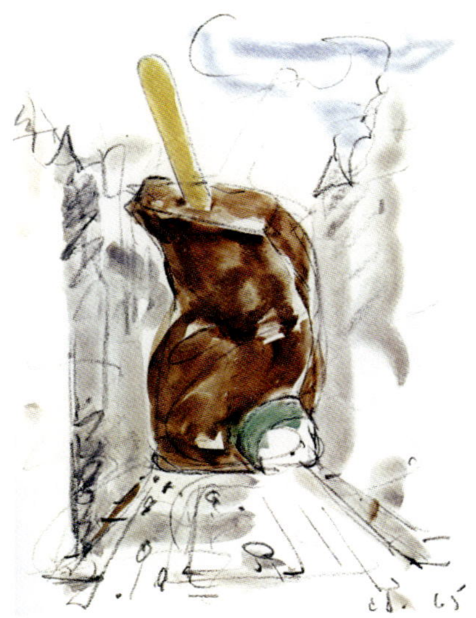

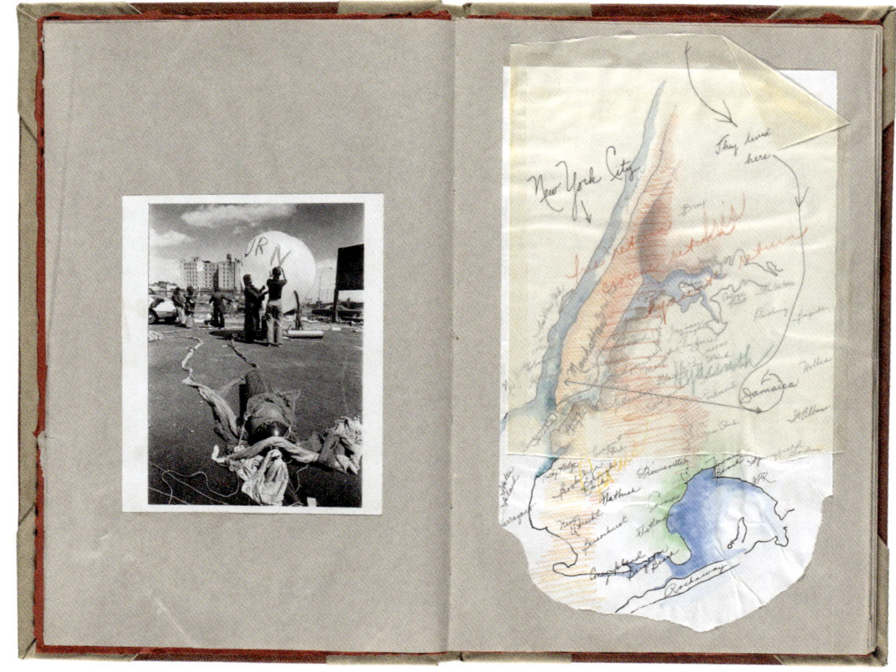

FIG. 17. Opening pages of *Spell*, 1977. Artist's book with 39 gelatin silver prints and cut-and-pasted transparentized papers with ink and pastel. Overall dimensions (closed): 20⅞ × 13⅜ × 1³⁄₁₆ in (53 × 34 × 3 cm). Collection of the Museum of Modern Art.

in books as illustrations."[41] All of the realized balloon projects had attendant handmade artists' books containing drawings, photographs, collages, and lyrical essays exploring the ideas and references underpinning the events and telling the stories of the people and histories she was memorializing. Like many other feminist artists of the period, Mayer also kept many journals and sketchbooks chronicling every aspect of her life, and made bookmaking an integral part of her broader artistic practice. Critic and curator Martha Barratt has described the impulse of women artists of the 1970s to document their lives and art projects through diaries and journals as a feminist desire to "auto-archive," demonstrating their need to testify to their own contributions in a neglectful, male-dominated art world.[42]

Mayer's practices of bookmaking and journaling also coincide with what feminist artists Miriam Schapiro and Melissa Meyer termed "femmage," art forms such as collage, assemblage, and découpage, which were historically associated with the decorative arts and practiced by women, and thus undervalued in patriarchal high art circles. According to Schapiro and Meyer, femmage was rooted in what they call "women's culture" and revolved around the use of disparate and often found or recycled elements. Though femmage is usually associated with the Pattern and Decoration Movement, in which Mayer was not involved, her bookmaking practice does fit many of its tenets, including saving and collecting, a diarist's personal point of view, collaging photographs or other printed matter, drawing or handwriting onto images, and most relevant to Mayer's books, "celebrat[ing] a private or public event."[43] This is particularly true of the books for *Spell* and *Some Days in April*. The former is a fabric-covered hardbound volume with layered transparent papers, the names of flowers written in cursive ("Iris," "Hyacinth"), and black and white photographic documentation of *Spell*, along with handwritten texts about her family (FIG. 17); the latter is a red-covered volume with gray pages onto which Mayer pasted photographic documentation of *Some Days in April*, with handwritten texts in block letters about her parents and Morton, overlaid with flowing pastel arabesques.

Mayer often showed these one-of-a-kind handmade books in exhibitions alongside her other more conventional artworks as a way to give gallery-going audiences access to the more ephemeral and site-specific works. She also published them as texts in artists' magazines in order to share the projects with even wider audiences. According to art historian Gwen Allen, in the 1970s, artists' magazines served as alternative exhibition spaces for artists like Mayer, who did not have steady gallery representation.[44] By the late 1970s, Mayer had circulated writings about these and other works along with images of them in some of the era's most celebrated artists' magazines—including *Art-Rite: Surroundings*; *Tracks: A Journal of Artists' Writings*; *WhiteWalls: A Magazine of Writings by Artists*; and the anthology *Individuals: Post-Movement Art in America* (which also included a contribution by Morton)—giving these artworks a great deal of visibility to her peers as well as contemporary art circles outside of New York.[45] Yet, beyond circulation and visibility, these writings—as well as her artists' books, photographs, and drawings—functioned as another form of memorialization, as ways to further tether these ephemeral projects to something concrete and material.

People

In many ways Mayer's works representing figurative forms and personal stories were a natural outgrowth of both her earlier fabric sculptures, which were dedicated to great women from history, and the increasing site specificity of her later balloon projects. By 1977, her once lush, full-bodied sculptures were becoming increasingly skeletal, as in *4 a.m.* (FIG. 18), a wooden dowel scaffolding minimally adorned with bits of crumpled paper. Her next work was titled *Scarecrow* (FIG. 19). Like *4 a.m.*, she made *Scarecrow* of wooden rods, structuring its dowels into a sort of triangular, tent-like form draped with colored fabric in such a way as to approximate a figure. As such, it represented a natural transition between the sculptures of 1977 and her People installations of 1978–80.

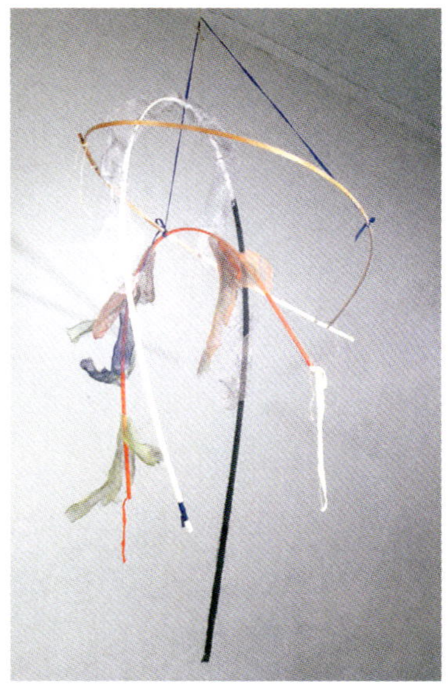

FIG. 18. *4 a.m.*, 1977. Wood and mixed media. 84 x 78 x 60 in (213 x 198 x 152.5 cm).

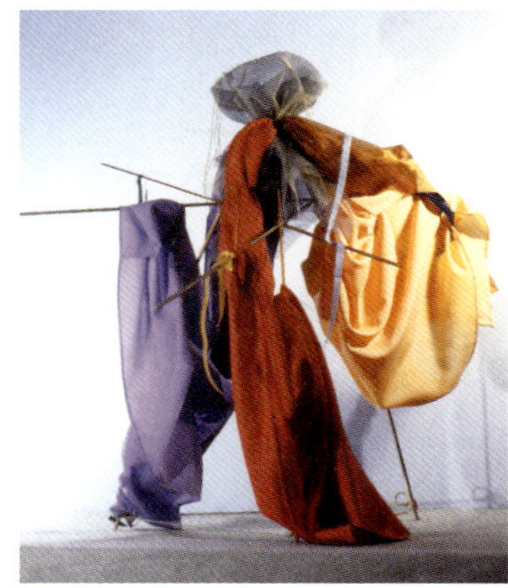

FIG. 19. *Scarecrow* (model), 1978–79. Wood, fabrics, and ribbons. 36 x 34 x 34 in (91.5 x 86 x 86 cm).

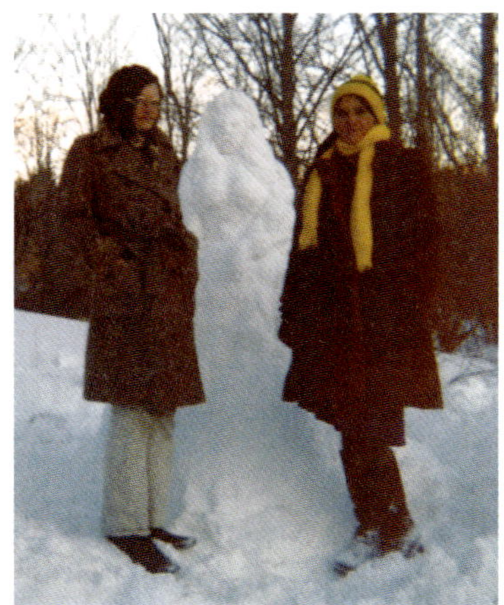

FIG. 20. Rosemary and Bernadette Mayer with the first "snowperson," Worthington, Massachusetts, January 1976. Photo by Lewis Warsh.

In the fall of 1978, Mayer began to develop *Snow People*, a group of figurative sculptures made of snow and located in a public outdoor site in Lenox, Massachusetts. The work was initially spurred by a visit with Mayer's sister, Bernadette, in the winter of 1976 in Worthington, Massachusetts, to meet her newborn daughter, Marie.[46] Following a snowstorm, Mayer constructed a large figure of a woman in snow outside of the house (FIG. 20). In 1977, Bernadette and her family moved to Lenox and during a visit there, Mayer came upon a monument in the town dedicated to Emma Stebbins (1815–82), a nineteenth-century female sculptor famous for her figurative sculpture *The Angel of the Waters* (1873), located at the Bethesda Terrace in New York's Central Park. Inspired by her earlier experiment using snow as a sculptural medium, as well as the town and this historical artist, Mayer proposed using a garden on the property of the local library as the site for an outdoor installation related to the town and its history.[47]

Like her earlier fabric sculptures and the balloon projects, Mayer dedicated *Snow People* to individuals from the past. In mid-February 1979, she built approximately fifteen figures out of snow, each one a different height and proportion so that they represented adults, children, men, and women, all of which had silhouettes that conformed to nineteenth-century clothing (FIG. 21).[48] In contrast to the figures memorialized by monumental public sculpture, these people were not famous figures from history. Rather, they were ordinary, even unknown, Lenox citizens from the past, underscoring the work's anti-monumentality. Mayer also researched the most common names used in Lenox during the nineteenth century. She then labeled each

FIG. 21. *Snow People*, February 1979. Sixteen life-size figures made of snow; signs of wood and paint. Garden of the Lenox Library, Lenox, Massachusetts.

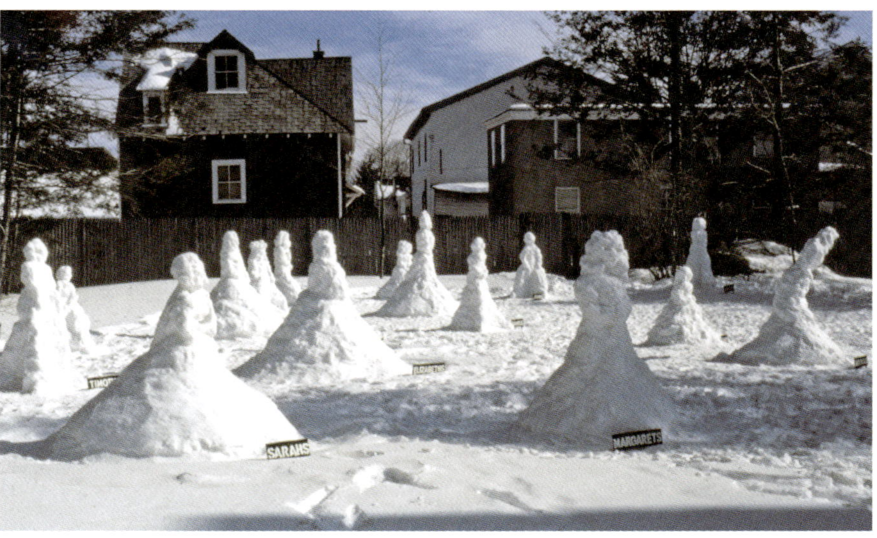

sculpture with a small plaque identifying it with a name (in the plural form) in capital letters: Sarahs, Elizabeths, Marys, Josephs, Ediths, Adelines, Carolines, Johns, Fannys, Annas, etc.

Like the balloons, *Snow People* also reflected on disappearance, transformation, and the cycles of renewal through the symbolism of the seasons. Because there were no armatures inside them, the figures slowly melted and eventually disappeared as the weather got warmer, revealing their ephemerality and their relationship to seasonal cycles. In "Those," an essay published in *White Walls*, Mayer describes the emotional impact of the figures: "You can hear the tones of their voices, familiar phrases connected to some particular place and time. . . . Sometimes they join hands and dance in a circle like a ring of seasons."[49] She also related them to the children's game of building "snow men," underscoring once again the significance of seasonal celebrations and pleasure in her work.

Ultimately, Mayer wanted to integrate the work into the town, making it truly public. She believed that public art projects such as this one, should both "make sense" to local audiences and have an emotional effect on them. It was especially important to her that townspeople could witness the work-in-progress as she built the figures—even interact with her or ask her questions—and that when it was finished, they could observe it from both the town's main street and the library, where she placed an explanatory text by a window. There was not only a connection to the site, but also to the community.

The use of melting snow and ice as a medium to reflect on time and seasonal cycles had been previously explored by Dennis Oppenheim in his earthwork *Annual Rings* (1968), in which he shoveled circular pathways in snow in reference to the growth rings of trees. However, Mayer's project was different in that she integrated it into the daily fabric of the town, and in this way it perhaps shares more in common with a project like Carl André's *Stone Field Sculpture* (1977), composed of 36 rocks arranged in rows on a public lawn in downtown Hartford, Connecticut (FIG. 22). It also relates to Ana Mendieta's *Silueta Series* (1973–78), but instead of leaving behind the indexical trace of a disappeared body imprinted in the earth as Mendieta did, Mayer erected bodies atop the earth in a natural substance that dissolved as time passed (FIG. 23).[50]

She later created a related work titled *Wax People* (1979–80) that was not a temporary monument, but rather a small-scale miniature of *Snow People* made of paraffin wax, a medium that "looks like snow and melts like snow,

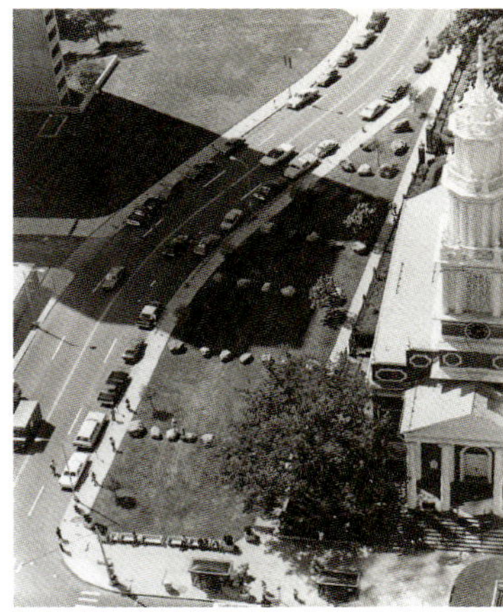

FIG. 22. Carl Andre, *Stone Field Sculpture*, 1977. Hartford, Connecticut. © 2018 Carl Andre / Licensed by VAGA, New York, New York. Courtesy Paula Cooper Gallery.

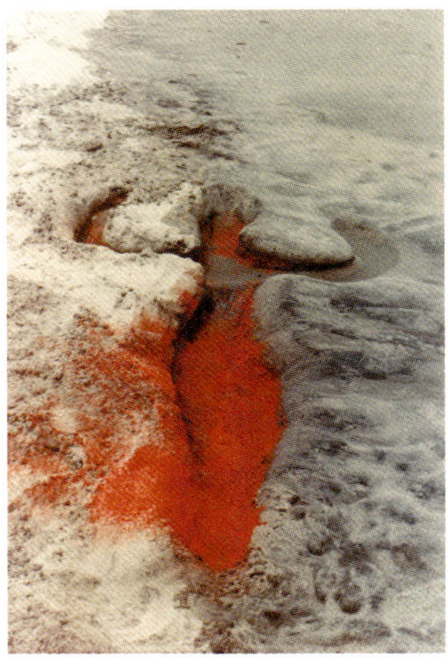

FIG. 23. Ana Mendieta, *Untitled: Silueta Series, Mexico*, 1976. Mexico. © The Estate of Ana Mendieta Collection, L.L.C. Courtesy Galerie Lelong & Co.

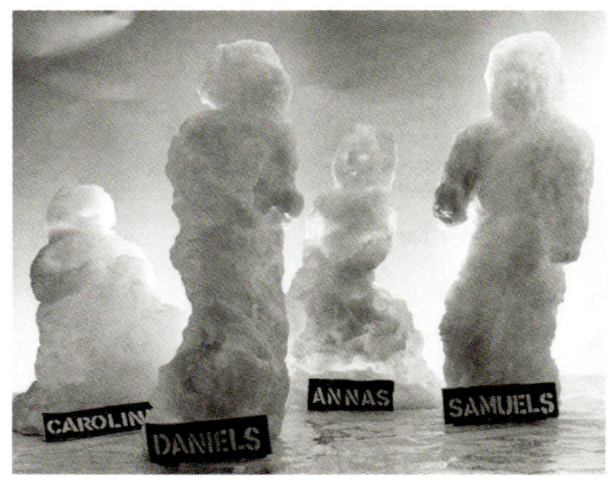

FIG. 24. Detail of *Wax People*, 1979. Sixteen figures, each approximately 18 in (46 cm) tall, made of paraffin wax.

but in a different season" (FIG. 24).[51] In an interview Mayer described *Snow People* as ghostly, because they vanished over time, a characteristic that became the focus of her subsequent projects. Her next project in the People series was aptly named the Ghosts. Begun in 1980, and hearkening back to *Scarecrow*, the Ghosts were fragile structures composed of wooden rods painted with metallic powders and draped with crumpled transparent papers. Concerned with light and dematerialization, Mayer intended the Ghosts to capture the "impermanence of a person, or a life."[52]

The first one, and the only site-specific example, was titled *Forty-First Street Ghost* (1980). It appeared in the *Times Square Show*, a landmark event that marked the decisive shift away from the Post-Minimalist trends of the 1970s toward the emerging punk and postmodern East Village art scene of the 1980s. Organized by artists John Ahearn and Tom Otterness with the art collectives Colab and Fashion Moda, the *Times Square Show* took place over the course of a month in June 1980 in a four-story tenement near Times Square, on the corner of Seventh Avenue and 41st Street that was a former massage parlor and bus depot. It boasted over one hundred artists, including young up-and-comers like Keith Haring, Kenny Scharf, Jenny Holzer, and Jean-Michel Basquiat, occupying different rooms throughout the building. In his review of the show in *Art in America* (FIG. 25), self-described investment advisor and art critic Jeffrey Deitch portrayed it as "a sort of funhouse," a "Day-Glo version of the

FIG. 25. Jeffrey Deitch, "Report from Time Square," originally published by *Art in America*, September 1980. © Art Media Holdings, LLC, New York. Courtesy Jeffrey Deitch, New York. Photos by Teri Slotkin and Wolfgang Staehle. Reproduced by permission.

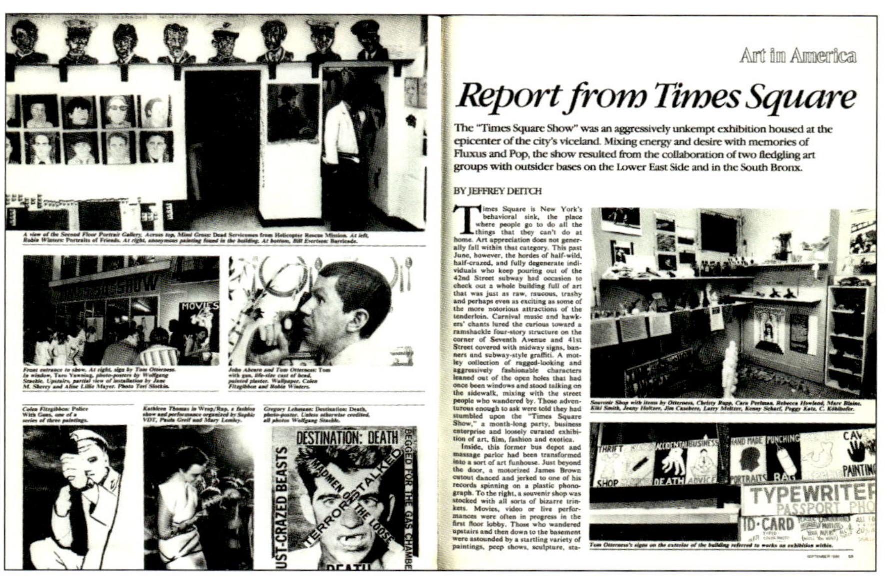

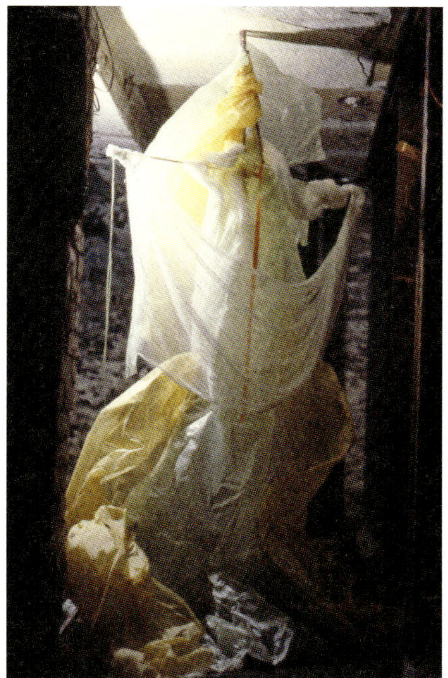 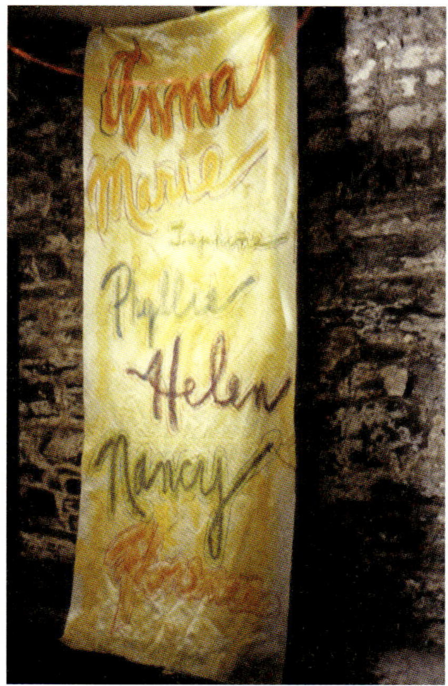

FIG. 26. *41st Street Ghost*, 1980. Sculpture: papers, wood, and ribbons, 78 in (198 cm) high. Installed at the Times Square Show, New York, New York, June, 1980.

FIG. 27. Banner for *41st Street Ghost*, 1980. Displayed on a wall to the right of the sculpture. Fabric and paint.

old Ripley's Believe It Or Not Museum," including "a startling variety of paintings, peep shows, sculpture, statues, model rooms, bundled clothing, and even a punching bag."[53]

Mayer was allotted a spot in the building's basement, a space she associated with ghosts (FIG. 26). Similarly, the building's history as a massage parlor sparked her interest in the untold stories of the lives of the long-dead and nameless prostitutes who had once inhabited the building.[54] She structured the resulting Ghost of dowel rods, and sumptuously draped it with ribbons, gauzy fabric, and swathes of crumpled yellow paper that gave it the appearance of a billowing gown, like a pared down version of her lush fabric sculptures of the early 1970s. Behind the sculpture, she hung a vertical yellow banner on a brick wall with the following names handwritten in cursive: "Anna, Marie, Josephine, Phyllis, Helen, Nancy, Florence," to evoke the possible names of the women who may have worked there (FIG. 27). Once again, she labored to make a connection between the site, its history, and the people who occupied that place in the past.

Yet, despite Mayer's inclusion in the *Times Square Show*, the exhibition ultimately made it clear that the art of the 1980s was taking a sharp detour from the process-based lyrical abstraction Mayer had been exploring throughout the

1970s. In his review, Deitch observed that the show indicated "a major Pop revival" and a shift away from Post-Minimalism's "celebration of space, light, materials, and reduced forms"—the very issues that concerned Mayer most—in favor of the new taste for pastiche, kitsch, and so-called "bad painting."[55] The Ghost that Mayer displayed in the *Times Square Show* did not fit in. In reviewing Mayer's work in the show, Lawrence Alloway wrote: "This [show] had some celebrity as the equivalent in visual art of Punk, but Mayer, though present, did not look at home."[56]

Mayer exhibited her later Ghost sculptures exclusively in gallery spaces (FIG. 28), including the Renaissance Society in Chicago (February 1981); the Tyler School of Art in Philadelphia (March 1981); the Minneapolis College of Art and Design (April 1981); and the Arnot Art Museum in Elmira, New York (Summer 1981). These exhibitions were mainly held in university art galleries in conjunction with visiting artist residencies. The works Mayer showed in them represented a regression from the more exper- imental and site-specific art that she had until that point been making, a result of the increas- ingly scarce grants and the circumstances of her position as a visiting artist. Even though the works were temporary and mutable (she re-used the same materials in different ways to create each one), and they resisted sculpture as a fixed form, they were still discrete objects on display in art galleries, and thus lost a connection to place and community.

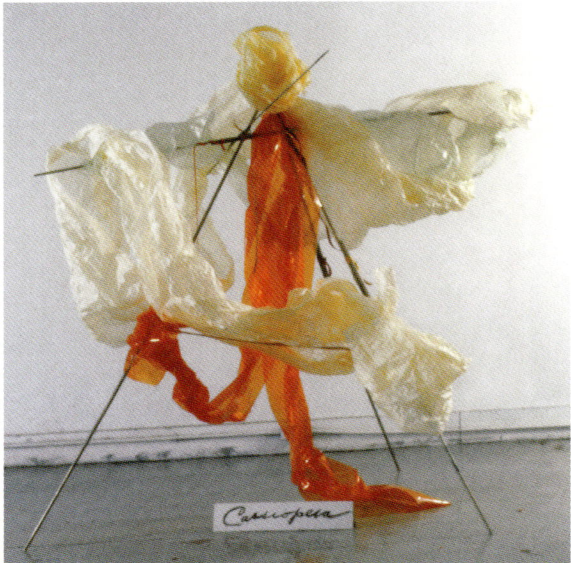

FIG. 28. *Cassiopea*, 1981. Wood, paper, and ribbons. 78 x 84 x 84 in (198 x 213 x 213 cm). Installed in the exhibition "Words and Images" at the Renaissance Society, Chicago, Illinois, February 1981.

Tents

The final series of Mayer's temporary monuments were her Tents. Like the People before them, they emerged from her interest in draping rod-like scaf- foldings with cloth or paper. As early as 1978, she was imagining tent-like structures, which went largely unrealized until 1982 (FIGS. 29, 30). Many of her sketches and drawings of tents also include flagpoles, which bear fluttering triangular pennant flags as part of their structures. Notes in her sketches of these tents and flagpoles reveal the extent to which Mayer was influenced by Morton's public artworks including *Something in the Wind* (1975) and *Maid of the Mist* (1976) and possibly also her drawings (FIG. 31).[57] Like Mayer's previ- ous sculptures, the tents she imagined incorporated structures composed of rods and poles upon which fabric is suspended, but they suggested a different

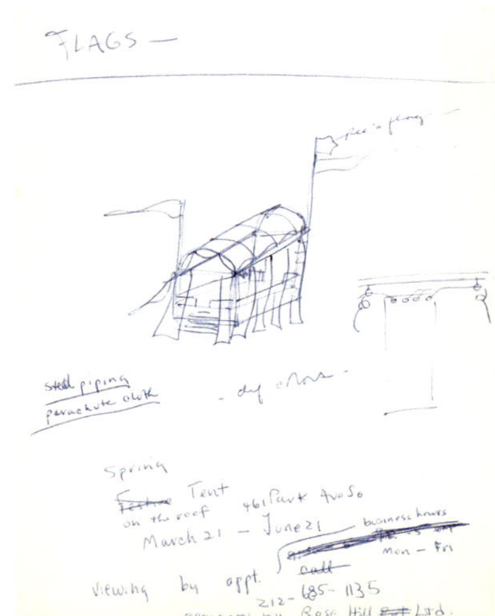

FIG. 29. Sketch of unrealized roof tent project, from 1978 notebook. Ballpoint pen on paper. 11 x 8½ in (28 x 21.5 cm).

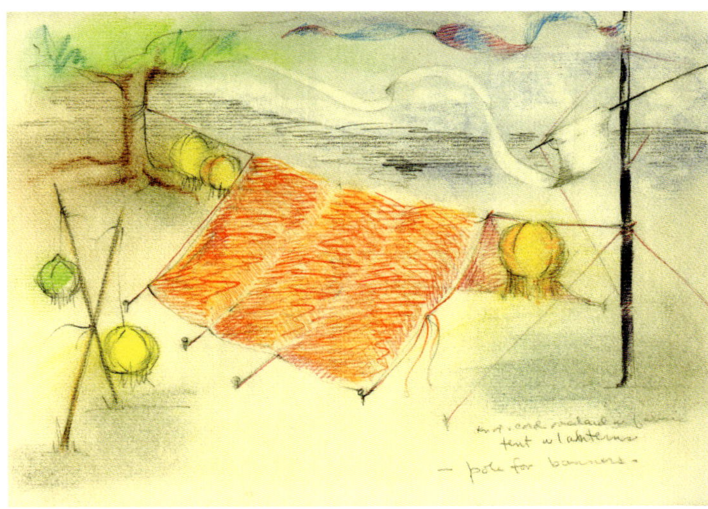

FIG. 30. Sketch of an unrealized tent with lanterns and banners, from a 1978 notebook. Colored pencil and graphite on paper. 12 x 9 in (31 x 23 cm).

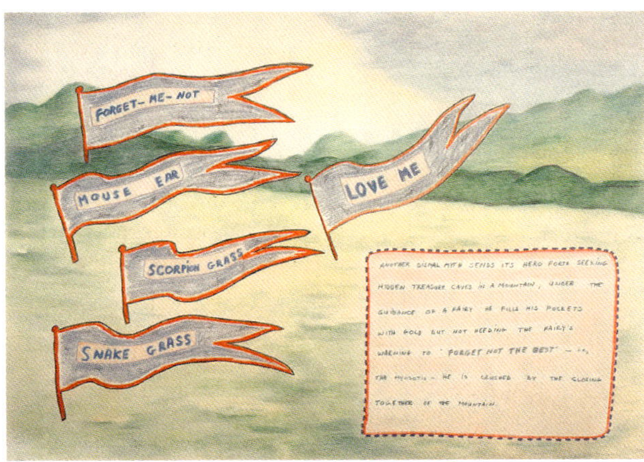

FIG. 31. Ree Morton, *Love Me*, 1974. Pencil, crayon, and chalk on paper. 29½ x 41½ in (74.9 x 105.4 cm). © Estate of Ree Morton. Courtesy Alexander and Bonin, New York.

connotation: tents are structures that house people, bring them together, and are often associated with festivities and celebrations.

Mayer's first sketches of tents appear just after she had presented *Balloon for a Birthday* on the roof of 461 Park Avenue. In a sketchbook, she imagines a future project, a "Spring Tent" on the same rooftop, a "tent-like structure on wheels" that would take place between March and June 1979.[58] In September 1980, she planned to create a rooftop tent with lanterns related to the Chinese Moon Festival.[59] In 1981, she threw "a moon festival party," a convivial get-together with friends on the roof of her loft in Tribeca. This was also based on traditional Chinese moon festivals, but it did not contain any sculptural elements.[60] The social atmosphere of this party recalls Food (1971–74), an artist-run

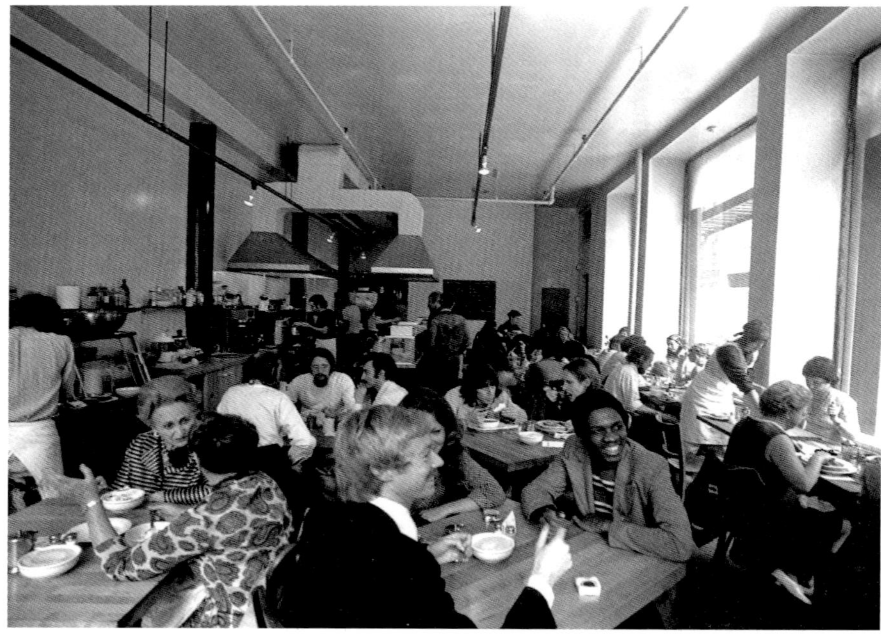

FIG. 32. Diners at Food, New York City, 1971–72. Courtesy The Estate of Gordon Matta-Clark and David Zwirner, New York/London/Hong Kong. Photo by Cosmos Andrew Sarchiapone.

restaurant and artistic intervention in SoHo founded by Gordon Matta-Clark, Carol Goodden, and Tina Girouard (FIG. 32).[61] Like Food, the artistic content of Mayer's party was not any one object on display, but rather, the social relations created by the gathering itself. The event also recalls *Balloon for a Birthday*, another rooftop celebration as art. Mayer seems to have found in rooftops—far from the dirty city streets below, and close to the cosmos above—a site of escape, of joy.[62]

She did not actually make any Tents until October 1982, when, with the support of a grant from the New York State Council of the Arts, she was finally able to create a rooftop tent, but not in Manhattan. Instead, she created the work on the rooftop pavilion of the private home of art historian Robert Hobbs, whom she had met when he curated an exhibition of her work at the Cornell University Art Gallery in April 1980. Having visited his newly constructed home, the "Hobbs House" in Lansing, New York, an icon of postmodern architecture designed by Simon Ungers and Laszlo Kiss, she was drawn to the "pavilion" on the roof, a gray structure shaped like the frame of a house that reminded her of the frame of her sculptures (FIG. 33). She instinctively wanted to wrap it.

This was the genesis of *Moon Tent*, in which she wound enormous swathes of crumpled glassine paper around the beams of the structure, in order to create a "tent" for a one-day event on the night of the full moon on October 3, 1982 (FIG. 34). In a 1983 text about the project that she published in *WhiteWalls*, she associates the tent with her Ghost sculptures by describing

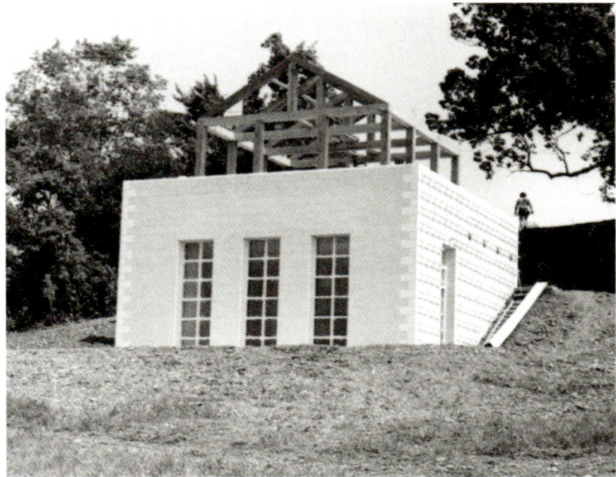

FIG. 33. House of art historian Robert Hobbs, with roof pavilion.

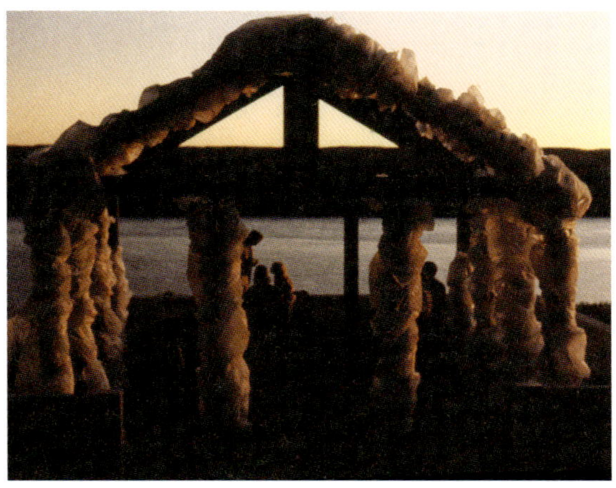

FIG. 34. *Moon Tent*, 1982. Installation with paper on the roof pavilion of the Hobbs House, Lansing, New York. Full moon celebration: October 2–3, 1982, 6:43 p.m. to 5:27 a.m.

it as, "a ghost tent, proliferating ghosts and the ghosts of tents in changes of light."[63] She also connects it to the themes of passing time and the cycles of life that she had tackled in her previous works, writing:

> To let the moon be seen, a moon tent can't have a roof. And its supports have to float, suggest the draped figures who would have been holding it up, caryatids and the dancing women who held the moon. People must . . . talk about the absent figures, the moon and its changing light . . . till morning when everything changes and the tent is dismantled, then gone like a tent moved on in the desert, melted snow figures, or last year's scarecrow.[64]

As in previous works, the mood of *Moon Tent* was celebratory and convivial: people brought food and instruments and "just sat around and had a party."[65] Mayer intended the work to evoke an ancient festival, linked like the unrealized roof tent of 1980 and her previous moon festival party of 1981 to Chinese moon festivals, as well as the Harvest Moon festival in the west, which involved a nightlong feast and celebration.[66]

Mayer's desire to create "homes and escapes, places of some respite" echoes the environments created by women artists in *Womanhouse*, a series of installations in an abandoned house in Los Angeles, organized by Judy Chicago and Miriam Schapiro as a part of their Feminist Art Program.[67] In particular, it recalls Faith Wilding's *Womb Room* (1972), a crocheted installation in *Womanhouse* that also functioned as a kind of feminine shelter

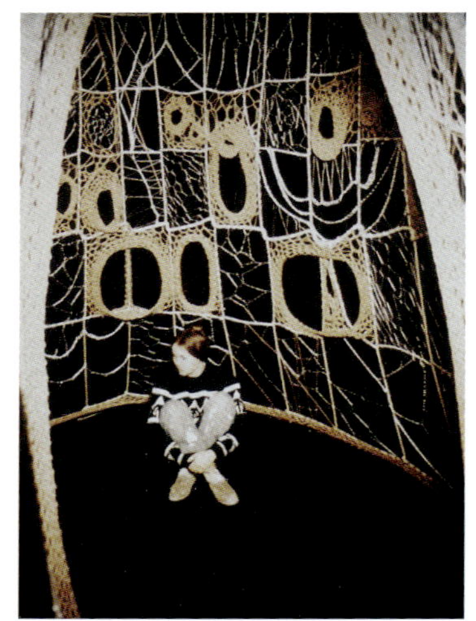

FIG. 35. Faith Wilding, *Crocheted Environment (Womb Room)*, 1972. Knitting wool and sisal rope. 9 x 9 x 9 ft. Courtesy the artist.

(FIG. 35).[68] Though both *Womanhouse* and *Moon Tent* presented sculptural spaces intended for dialogue and exchange, in *Womanhouse*, the artworks were the sculptural installations and performances housed inside, while in *Moon Tent* the convivial social gathering itself was the artwork, with the sculptural "tent" functioning as a site to host it.

Moon Tent was Mayer's last temporary monument. In many ways it represented the culmination of her desire to embrace affect and pleasure in order to develop a new genre of convivial public art. Like Morton, she rejected the austere hegemonies of Minimalism and the severe monumentality of public sculptures like Richard Serra's *Tilted Arc*, to embrace the then-disparaged language of celebration and joy. Also like Morton, whose *Signs of Love* (1976) has been described as a "willful pursuit of the decorative"[69] and a "joyous celebration . . . almost saccharine in its sentimentality,"[70] Mayer admitted that her temporary monuments were mainly intended to decorate and celebrate.

Curator Helen Molesworth has argued that while the mainstream art world of the 1970s was not very receptive to decorative or overtly personal art, Morton and her feminist approach to art making were central in developing the language of what would later be termed "installation art" in the 1980s and '90s. She contends that Morton pioneered installation art by embracing personal narrative and sentimentality, and by turning away from earthworks and Minimalist "environments" toward more theatrical tableaux.[71] Similarly, I contend that Mayer's interest in feeling, sentiment, and even pleasure stemmed from her feminist commitments, and propelled the development of her temporary monuments. I also argue that they comprise part of an unwritten history of socially engaged and site-specific art. While Morton played an important role in inspiring Mayer's temporary monuments, the former's own public art projects never fully surpassed installation or performance. By contrast, not only was Mayer able to connect with local sites through their past histories and material realities, but she was also able to relate to local audiences and communities through her celebratory and convivial interactions with them.

Artist Suzanne Lacy has outlined a history of socially engaged art from the 1960s to the 1990s that she terms "new genre public art," and which she defines as public art that maintained political commitments as activist, pedagogical, or community-oriented. Lacy includes as an example Judy Chicago's Feminist Art Programs of the early-to-mid 1970s, and she argues that feminism was at the heart of new genre public art because it was naturally rooted in activism.[72] Though Mayer's temporary monuments were based in feminism and took place outside of the confines of the gallery, unlike new genre public art, she did not intend her projects to be politically instrumentalized. Even so, they epitomize curator Allan Schwartzman's claim that the work of many women artists of the period *was* political, in its insistence on privileging women's subjectivities, histories, and experiences.[73]

Mayer wanted to honor the past, celebrate the present, and provide audiences with pleasurable communal experiences. In this way, she anticipated more recent strands of socially engaged art that curator Nicolas Bourriaud has termed "relational aesthetics," and has described as "convivial, user-friendly . . . festive, collective, and participatory."[74] Though these types of projects share much in common with Mayer's temporary monuments, they diverge in that they are usually staged within museums or galleries, and they are read as reflecting the shift from a goods to a service-based economy in the late twentieth and early twenty-first centuries. While Bourriaud himself has denied that relational art has any art historical precedents, curator Helena Reckitt has argued that such practices are rooted in the feminist art interventions of the 1970s, particularly in terms of their concern with affective and immaterial labor.[75] But, rather than draw a direct correlation between Mayer's temporary monuments and any one specific genre of contemporary art, what I want to underscore instead, is the role and influence of 1970s feminist art generally, and the relevance of Mayer's temporary monuments specifically, on the range of socially engaged, participatory, and site-specific public art practices prevalent across today's cultural landscape.

In 1978, Mayer wrote that in art "no <u>new</u> moves are possible—only hybrids."[76] Indeed, in their memorializing, historical research, and celebratory audience engagement, Mayer's temporary monuments anticipated the installation and performance hybrids of contemporary relational artists like Rirkrit Tiravanija, who famously turned a gallery into an open curry kitchen, and Thomas Hirschhorn, who creates DIY cardboard and duct tape "monuments" dedicated to philosophers that function as sites for community involvement in low-income housing projects (FIGS. 36, 37). They also laid the groundwork for

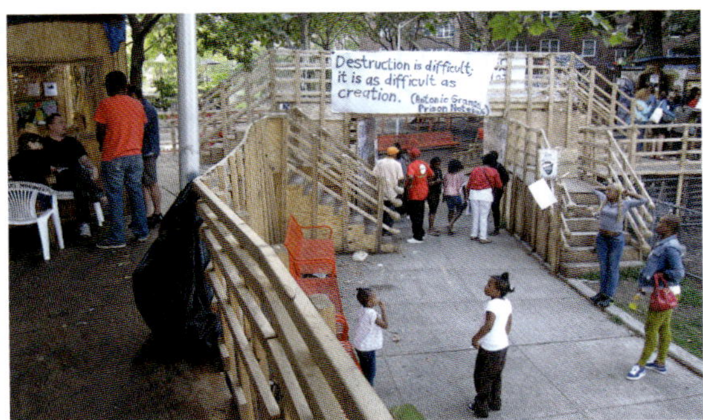

FIG. 36. Thomas Hirschhorn, *Gramsci Monument*, 2013. Forest Houses, Bronx, New York. Courtesy Dia Art Foundation, New York. Photo by Romain Lopez.

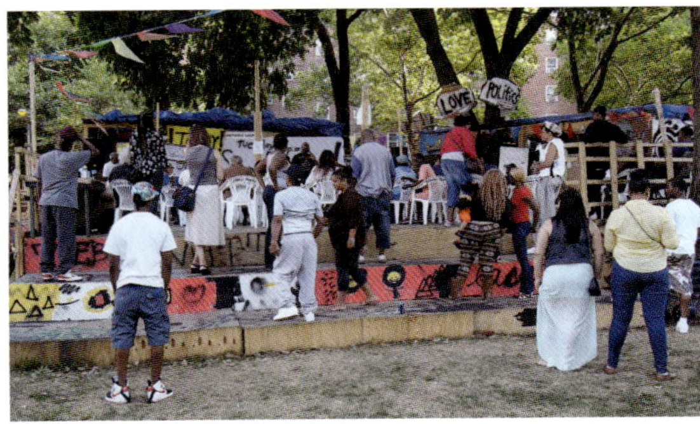

FIG. 37. Thomas Hirschhorn, *Gramsci Monument*, 2013. Open Microphone, Forest Houses, Bronx, New York. Courtesy Dia Art Foundation, New York. Photo by Romain Lopez.

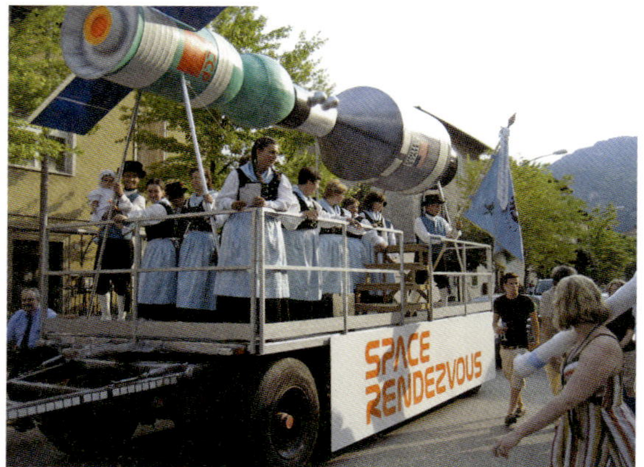

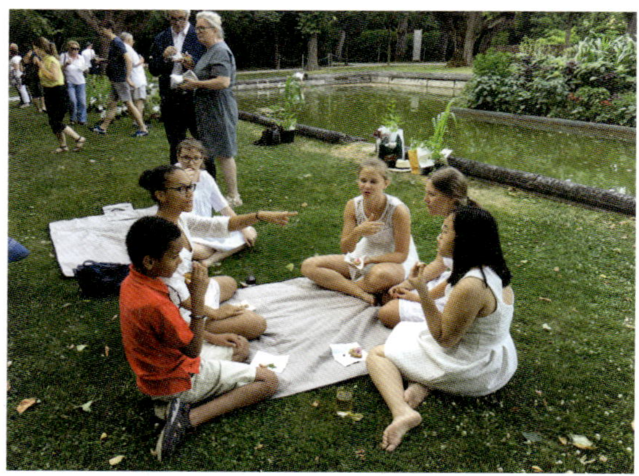

FIG. 38. Christian Philipp Müller, *Space Rendezvous, Carro Largo*, 2008. Manifesta7, Rovereto, Italy. Courtesy the artist. Photo by Christian Philipp Müller.

FIG. 39. Christian Philipp Müller, *The New World*, installed 2006, ongoing. Plant sculpture in the water basin, Melk Monastery, Monastery Park, Austria. Picnic, Summer 2017. Courtesy the artist. Photo by Christian Philipp Müller.

the types of research-driven and community based projects that celebrate individuals and local histories by artists like Jeremy Deller and Christian Philipp Müller, whose collaborative, interdisciplinary, and site-specific practices have included historical re-enactments, elaborate meals, and tours and parades (FIGS. 38, 39). These, and other examples, attest to Mayer's visionary—if experimental and sometimes uneven—art practice in the late 1970s and early '80s, and the important contributions she made, achievements deserving of continued inquiry and research.

Coda

Though Mayer had garnered visibility in feminist art circles and the alternative art spaces scene, and her writings and images of her temporary monuments had circulated in some of the era's most celebrated artists' magazines, by the late 1970s she struggled to make ends meet, stringing together an income from freelance writing, editing, and arts grants. Due to the changing economic environment in the art world of the early 1980s, Mayer was forced to procure full-time employment. In a September 1982 letter to a friend written on the stationary of her new employer (an advertising agency), she writes:

> I had hoped to ditch [this job] this fall, but money is impossible to come by in the free-lance market, in fact, I would say that right now there is no free-lance market, just starving free-lancers giving up in droves and going back to 9 to 5, if they can find it. This job is a pretty ok job. . . . However, it's still all day 5 days that I'm not in the studio.[77]

By the early 1980s, alternative spaces and co-op galleries were shuttering their doors as SoHo rents increased. By contrast, galleries and dealers were proliferating as corporate and private investments in the art market were on the rise. Artistic tastes were also changing as demonstrated by the kinds of works on view in the *Times Square Show*.

Lawrence Alloway commented on this in a December 1980 article, in which he laments an unacknowledged problem in the art world, namely that of "alternative space artists," who are talented and show widely, but are unaffiliated with commercial galleries. He uses Mayer as a case study of this phenomenon. "Not being regularly affiliated to a commercial gallery," he explains, "her work had been largely overlooked by critics, and so she was typical of an artist in her thirties with a solid record of work, but without a gallery at which it can be consulted."[78] Mayer was also beginning to detect fundamental shifts in the art world that did not bode well for her approach to art making. While the art scene of the 1970s had seemed "genial," by the late 1970s and early '80s, "it seemed very cruel, competitive, cutthroat."[79]

Even so, as I have shown, it was during this very period between 1977 and 1982, that Mayer made some of her most exciting artistic breakthroughs. Yet, as the art world evolved in the 1980s and became increasingly market-driven, Mayer was forced to continue working full-time, and as public arts funding was depleted, she ceased making temporary monuments (FIG. 40). Though she had thrived artistically (if not monetarily) with the support of grants and alternative spaces in the 1970s, the atmosphere of the 1980s stifled her experiments in socially engaged and site-specific public art. However, looking back on her work today, at a moment in which there is a resurgence in personal narrative, site specificity, and social engagement in art, her temporary monuments are more relevant than ever before, suggesting a model for public art that is more poignant, more human.

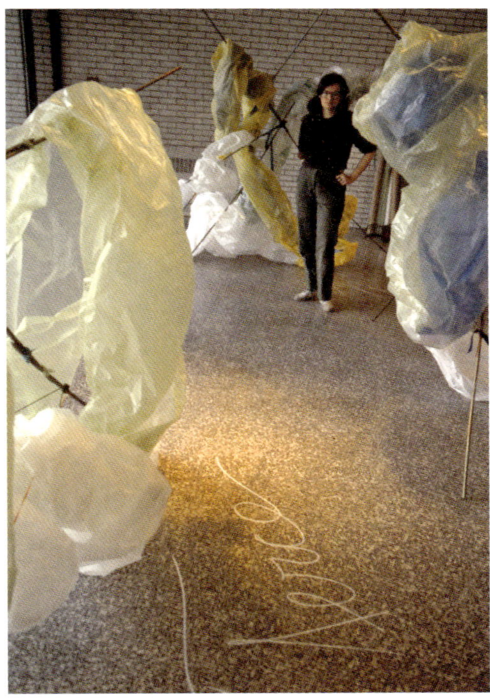

FIG. 40. Mayer with *Ghosts* installation at the Minneapolis College of Art and Design, 1982.

Endnotes

I want to thank Marie Warsh for her generous and collaborative spirit, and for her ample feedback on several early drafts of this essay. I also thank Julia Klein, Max Warsh, Cara Jordan, Farrar Fitzgerald, and Ricardo Valentim for their input, feedback, and support of this project.

1 Rosemary Mayer, notebook, April 1980, Rosemary Mayer Estate/Archives, New York, NY.

2 Harriet Senie, *The Tilted Arc Controversy: Dangerous Precedent?* (Minneapolis: University of Minnesota Press, 2002), 14–19.

3 Mayer, notebook, April 1980, RM Archives.

4 Mayer married Acconci in 1962 at the age of 19. They divorced in 1969, but maintained a strained friendship that eventually ended in the late 1970s.

5 Mayer was a member of A.I.R. from 1972 to 1974. Alloway and his wife, artist Sylvia Sleigh, also a member of A.I.R., became close friends with Mayer.

6 Lucy Lippard, "From Eccentric to Sensuous Abstraction: An Interview with Lucy Lippard," in *More Than Minimal: Feminism and Abstraction in the '70's*, ed. Susan Stoops (Waltham, MA: Rose Art Museum/Brandeis University, 1996), 29.

7 Anna Chave, "Minimalism and the Rhetoric of Power," *Arts Magazine* 64, no. 5 (1990): 44–63.

8 Claire Barliant has recently written on Mayer's fabric sculptures. See Barliant, "Invisible Presence: The Work of Rosemary Mayer from 1966–1973," in *Rosemary Mayer: Beware of all Definitions, Selected Works, 1966–1973* (Athens, GA: Lamar Dodd School of Art, University of Georgia, 2017), 4–8. Previous writing on Mayer includes Maureen Connor, "The Pleasure of Necessity: The Work of Rosemary Mayer," *Woman's Art Journal* 6, no. 2 (Autumn, 1985–Winter, 1986), 35–40; Christine Wilson, "Recalling Mannerism in the Works of Rosemary Mayer" (master's thesis, University of Oklahoma, Norman, OK, 1989), 60–71; and Marie Warsh and Gillian Sneed, "Diaries of an Artist: The Art and Writing of Rosemary Mayer," *The Brooklyn Rail*, April 2016, accessed December 6, 2017, https://brooklynrail.org/2016/04/criticspage/art-and-writing-of-rosemary-mayer.

9 Rosalind Krauss, "Sculpture in the Expanded Field," *October* 8 (Spring 1979): 30–44. Mayer's notes show that she read Krauss's writings. Mayer, notebook entry, October 3, 1977, RM Archives.

10 Mayer, "Passing Thoughts," unpublished text, November 4, 1978, 7. RM Archives.

11 Mayer, "Time and Light," sketchbook, February 5, 1977, RM Archives.

12 Connor, "The Pleasure of Necessity," 36.

13 Mayer, "On Balloons," unpublished text, RM Archives.

14 Mayer, "Notes for a Slide Lecture," 1980, RM Archives.

15 Mayer, "Spell," 55 Mercer Street, press release (January 15–February 16, 1979), RM Archives.

16 Mayer, diary entry, April 15, 1978, 53. RM Archives.

17 Erika Doss, *Memorial Mania: Public Feeling in America* (Chicago: University of Chicago Press, 2012), 43.

18 Mayer had been thinking about these issues as early as 1972, as evidenced by a review of a sculpture exhibition at 10 Bleecker Street that she wrote under the nom de plume, Rosemary Matthias, exploring public art and participation. See Matthias, "Indoor-Outdoor: Space and Materials, Six Young Sculptors," *Arts Magazine* (September–October 1972): 27–29.

19 Suzanne Lacy, introduction to *Mapping the Terrain: New Genre Public Art* (Seattle: Bay Press, 1996), 23–24; Miwon Kwon, *One Place After Another: Site-Specific Art and Locational Identity* (Cambridge, MA: MIT Press, 2004), 60, 67–68.

20 Foote suggests that this interest was "renewed" because as Krauss points out, historically, public monuments were site-specific. Krauss argues that it was with the advent of modernism that sculpture began to refuse the logic of the sited monument in favor

of site-lessness. Krauss, "Sculpture in the Expanded Field," 33–34. See Nancy Foote, "Sightings on Siting," in *Urban Encounters: Art, Architecture, Audience*, ed. Janet Kardon (Philadelphia: University of Pennsylvania Institute of Contemporary Art, 1980), 25.

21   Foote, "Monument—Sculpture—Earthwork," *Artforum* 18, no. 2 (October 1979): 32–37.

22   Lawrence Alloway, "Problems of Iconography and Style," in *Urban Encounters*, 20.

23   Grant Kester, *Conversation Pieces: Community and Communication in Modern Art* (Berkeley: University of California Press, 2004), 61. In 1972 Mayer wrote an essay on Acconci (her ex-husband) and Piper (her friend) exploring the socially engaged aspects of their performative works. See Mayer, "Performance & Experience," *Arts Magazine* (December–January 1972): 33–36.

24   Cara Jordan, "Directing Energy: Gordon Matta-Clark's Pursuit of Social Sculpture," in *Gordon Matta-Clark: Anarchitect*, ed. Antonio Sergio Bessa and Jessamyn Fiore (New Haven: Bronx Museum in association with Yale University Press, 2017), 37–39, 41–46. In 1970, Jeffrey Lew, along with Matta-Clark and Alan Seret, founded the alternative space 112 Greene Street. Mayer participated in a group exhibition there in September 1975. She also attended events, and reviewed exhibitions there, including a Matta-Clark exhibition in the autumn of 1972. See Mayer, "Gordon Matta," *Arts Magazine* (February 1973): 74. See also Robyn Bretano and Mark Savitt, eds., *112 Workshop, 112 Greene Street* (New York: NYU Press, 1981).

25   Rosemary Mayer, unpublished interview with the author, July 12, 2013, Brooklyn, NY. Morton had moved to New York in the summer of 1972, and Mayer befriended her sometime between 1973 and 1974. In an unpublished text from 1974, Mayer cites Morton as an important artistic influence. Mayer, "Passing Thoughts," 4.

26   Morton's use of a festooned ladder in her *Maid of the Mist* performance presented in the summer of 1976 at Artpark, an upstate New York sculpture park, also appeared two years after Mayer began exploring ladder structures as a visual motif, stemming from her study of Mannerist painting, in 1974. A more detailed comparative study of the two artists' works is beyond the scope of this essay, but deserves further scholarly research.

27   Sabine Folie, ed., *Ree Morton: Works 1971–1977* (Vienna: Generali Foundation, 2009), 133–137.

28   Mayer, letter to Ilse Lafer, September 26, 2008, cited in Sabine Folie, ed., *Ree Morton*, 184.

29   Mayer, "Spell," *WhiteWalls*, no. 2 (Winter/Spring 1979): 9.

30   Mayer presented *Spell* on April 8, 1977, and Morton died on April 30, 1977.

31   Mayer letter to Nancy Kitschel, May 6, 1977, RM Archives.

32   *Some Days in April* took place the week of April 17, 1978. The field was located on a property in Hartwick, upstate New York, belonging to her friend, art critic Bruce Kurtz, who taught art and art history at Hartwick College in Oneonta, NY, from 1969 to 1985. Marie Warsh, email to the author, December 7, 2017.

33   Mayer, "Some Days in April, Hartwick NY, Week of April 17, 1978," notebook, February 1977, RM Archives.

34   Mayer, "Some Days in April," unpublished text, 1979, RM Archives.

35   John Campione ran Rose Hill Editions, located at 461 Park Avenue, where he produced print editions for artists including Sol Lewitt, Hans Haacke, Robert Mangold, and Dennis Oppenheim. "From 461 (Park Avenue South)," Richard Kirk Mills website, accessed December 5, 2017, http://richardkirkmills.net/artwork/3439722-From-461-Park-Avenue-South.html.

36   Mayer, 55 Mercer Street press release (January 15–February 16, 1979), RM Archives.

37   Mayer, "Pleasures and Possible Celebrations, Connections in Context," 461 Park Avenue press release (January 15–February 16, 1979), RM Archives.

38   Mayer, "Projects: Connections," 2. RM Archives.

39   *Claes Oldenburg: Proposals for Monuments and Buildings 1965–69* (Chicago: Big Table Publishing Company, 1969).

40   Rosemary Mayer, letter to Bernadette Mayer, August 17, 1978, 2. RM Archives.

41   Mayer, "Passing Thoughts," 6.

42   Barratt uses this term in relation to the sketchbooks and diaries of artist Carolee Schneemann. Martha Barratt, "Autobiography, Time, and Documentation in the Performances and Auto-Archives of Carolee Schneemann," *Visual Resources* 32, nos. 3–4 (2016): 283, 299–301.

43   Miriam Schapiro and Melissa Meyer, "Waste Not, Want Not: An Inquiry into What Women Saved and Assembled – Femmage," *Heresies: A Feminist Publication on Art and Politics* 1, no. 4 (Winter 1978): 69.

44   Allen points out that Howardena Pindell originally proposed this idea in her article: "Alternative Space: Artists' Periodicals," *The Print Collectors Newsletter* VIII, no. 4 (September–October, 1977): 96-121. See Gwen Allen, *Artists' Magazines: An Alternative Space for Art* (Cambridge, MA: MIT Press, 2015), 122–123.

45   Most of these writings are re-printed in this book, the first time they have appeared together in one publication.

46   Bernadette Mayer's then-husband was poet Lewis Warsh. Their first child is Marie Warsh, co-executor with her brother, Max Warsh, and sister, Sophia Warsh, of the Rosemary Mayer Estate/Archives.

47   Mayer, "A Proposal for the Lenox Library Garden," unpublished text, Fall 1978, RM Archives.

48   Mayer, "Snow People Proposal," Fall 1978, RM Archives.

49   Mayer, "Those," *WhiteWalls*, no. 5 (Winter 1981): 55–57.

50   Mayer mentions liking the work of Oppenheim and André in her diary, so it is possible that she was aware of these works. Mayer, diary entry, April 28, 1974, 32. RM Archives. Mendieta joined A.I.R. gallery in 1978 (after Mayer had already left), so it is likely Mayer was aware of her work. Another possible connection is an undocumented work by Gordon Matta-Clark. Mayer told Marie Warsh that Matta-Clark had once used a tractor to move snow around into artistic forms in an empty lot across the street from her loft on Leonard Street sometime in the early-to-mid 1970s. Warsh, email to the author, December 28, 2017.

51   Like *Snow People*, *Wax People* comprised male and female figures with the same names as the Lenox figures, but they were only 14–19 inches tall. The small scale of the work allowed her to "bring" *Snow People* into the studio so she could continue to ponder the ideas presented by the larger sculpture. Mayer, "Snow People, Wax People," unpublished text, February 1980, RM Archives.

52   Mayer, notebook, June 30, 1980, RM Archives, New York, NY; Mayer, notebook, September 29, 1980, RM Archives.

53   Jeffrey Deitch, "Report from Times Square," *Art in America* (September 1980): 59–60.

54   Mayer, interview.

55   Deitch, "Report from Times Square," 61–62.

56   Alloway, "Art," 621.

57   For instance, in a drawing of a maypole in one sketchbook, Mayer includes an image of a wreath, writing beside it "like Ree's wreath in the water at Artpark." Mayer, sketchbook, April 24, 1978, RM Archives. In another sketch, she includes a drawing of a tent structure that includes poles and flags, one labeled, "Ree's Flag." Mayer, sketchbook, November 12, 1978, RM Archives.

58   Mayer, sketchbook, November 12, 1978, RM Archives.

59   Mayer, "Plans," unpublished text, 1980, RM Archives.

60   Mayer, interview.

61   It is unknown if Mayer ever went to Food, but according to her sister Bernadette, who went several times, it is likely she did. Marie Warsh, email to the author, January 11, 2018.

62   Mayer's interest in roofs also recalls Trisha Brown's 1971 performance piece, *Roof Piece*, consisting of dancers performing on rooftops in SoHo, a work Mayer may have been aware of given her interest in experimental dance.

63   Mayer, "A Moon Tent," *WhiteWalls*, no. 8 (Summer 1983): 76.

64   Mayer, "A Moon Tent," 81.

65   Mayer, interview.

66   Mayer, interview.

67   Mayer, "A Moon Tent," 80.

68   In a diary entry, Mayer mentions attending a screening of *Womanhouse* (1974), a documentary by Johanna Demetrakas chronicling the project and the artists involved. It includes documentation of Faith Wilding's performance *Waiting* (1972), and the *Womb Room* installation where she performed it. Mayer, diary entry, May 7, 1974, 34. RM Archives.

69   Helen Molesworth, "Sentiment and Sentimentality: Ree Morton and Installation Art," in *Ree Morton: Works 1971–1977*, ed. Sabine Folie (Vienna: Generali Foundation, 2009), 16.

70   Allan Schwartzman and Kathleen Thomas, "Ree Morton: A Critical Overview," in *Ree Morton: Retrospective, 1971–1977*, ed. Schwartzman and Thomas (New York: New Museum, 1980), 65.

71   Molesworth, "Sentiment and Sentimentality," 14–15.

72   Lacy, *Mapping the Terrain*, 25–27.

73   Allan Schwartzman, "Cornelia H. Butler, João Ribas, and Allan Schwartzman in Conversation, June 2009," in Ree Morton: *At the Still Point of the Turning World*, ed. João Ribas (New York: Drawing Center, 2009), 32.

74   Nicolas Bourriaud, *Relational Aesthetics* (Paris: Presses du réel, 2010), 61. Despite its widespread impact, relational aesthetics has been highly contested. The most prominent critique is articulated in Claire Bishop's "Antagonism and Relational Aesthetics," *October*, no. 110 (Fall 2004): 51–79.

75   Helena Reckitt, "Forgotten Relations: Feminist Artists and Relational Aesthetics," in *Politics in a Glass: Case Feminism, Exhibition Cultures and Curatorial Transgressions*, ed. Angela Dimitrakaki and Lara Perry (Liverpool: Liverpool University Press, 2015), 138–140.

76   Mayer, diary entry, May 12, 1978, RM Archives.

77   Mayer, letter to Clara Oleson, September 10, 1982, 1. RM Archives.

78   Alloway, "Art," 621.

79   Mayer, interview.

SPELL

Installed on April 8, 1977
Balloons, helium, paint, fabric, and rope
Farmer's Market, Jamaica, New York

Photographs, text, flyers, artist's book

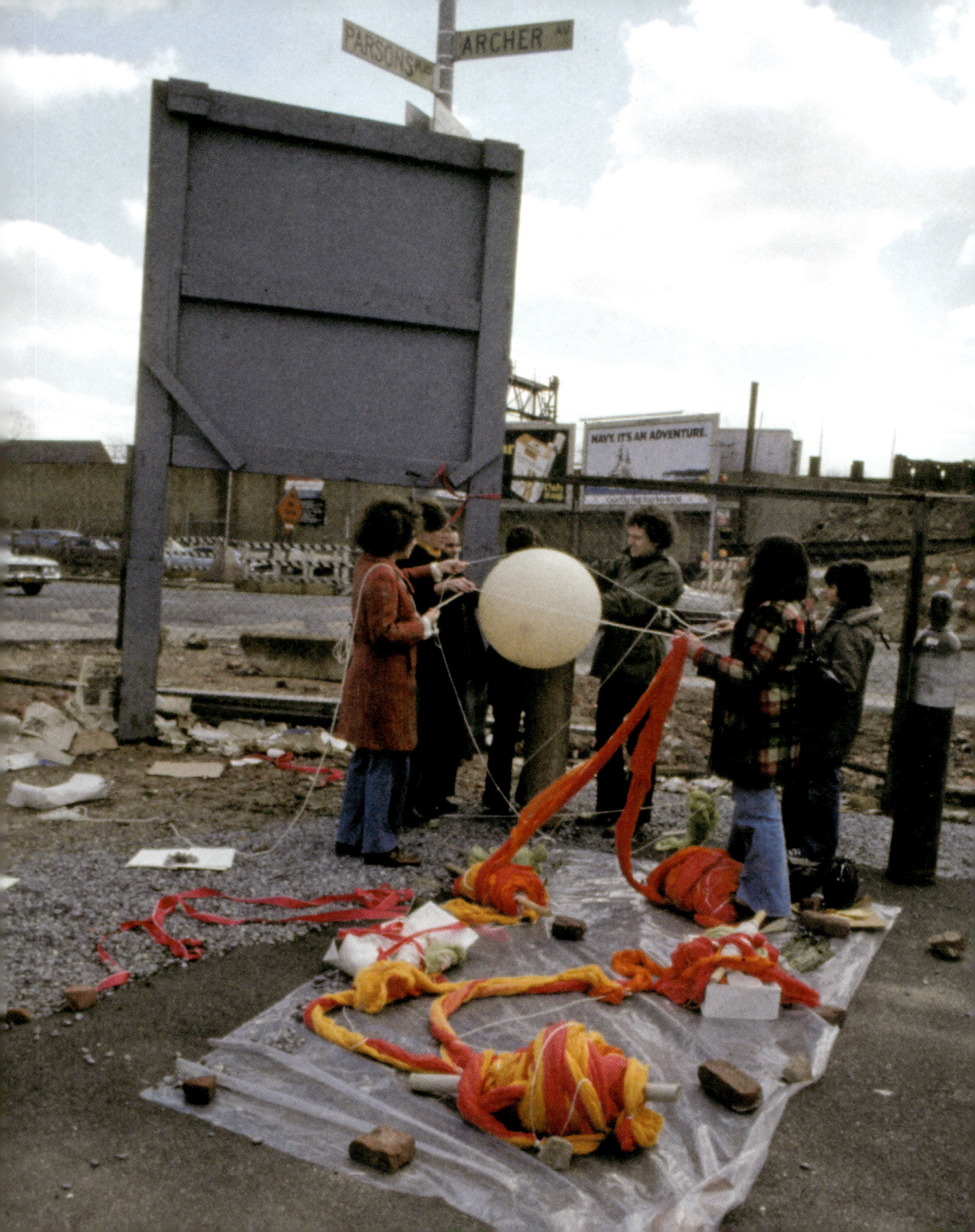

PARSONS
ARCHER AV
NAVY, IT'S AN ADVENTURE.

SPELL

Text from artist's book, 1977.
Published in *WhiteWalls: A Magazine of Writings by Artists*,
No. 2, Winter–Spring 1979.

Iris return, hyacinth return, crocus return.

Madelaine on the porch when we climbed in the tree and onto the slanted cellar door; George in the cellar between sacks of vegetables, empty birdcages; Teddy telling George how to grow more apples.

The phrases would be painted in red on inflated white weather balloons. Nets of gold-colored cord would contain the balloons, hold transparent reds, orange-yellows and greens floating between and down from the balloons. Other green and yellow cords would be moorings. All the colors would be unrolled when the balloons rose. They and the balloons with words would float over the stalls and displays at the opening of a flowers market in Jamaica in early April, 1977.

Weeds grow on some edges of cities, when stems can manage the sun, lift leaves, colors, up over pavements, fences, come up again through cracks in cement. Neighborhoods like these on the ways to schools, to movies or buying records. Garden flowers are different.

George's cheeks pushed out wider when he laughed. Sometimes double grey and black whiskers angled out different lengths from his face and neck. His pants were browns and greys. They sagged under his stomach and knees, were lower in back than in front. His shirts were dull, his shoes worn. He laughed when he rolled on the carpet with children. Then the flesh shook on his turning body. He lived near here in Jamaica.

Katherine
Madelaine
George
Madelaine
Florence
Catherine
Teddy

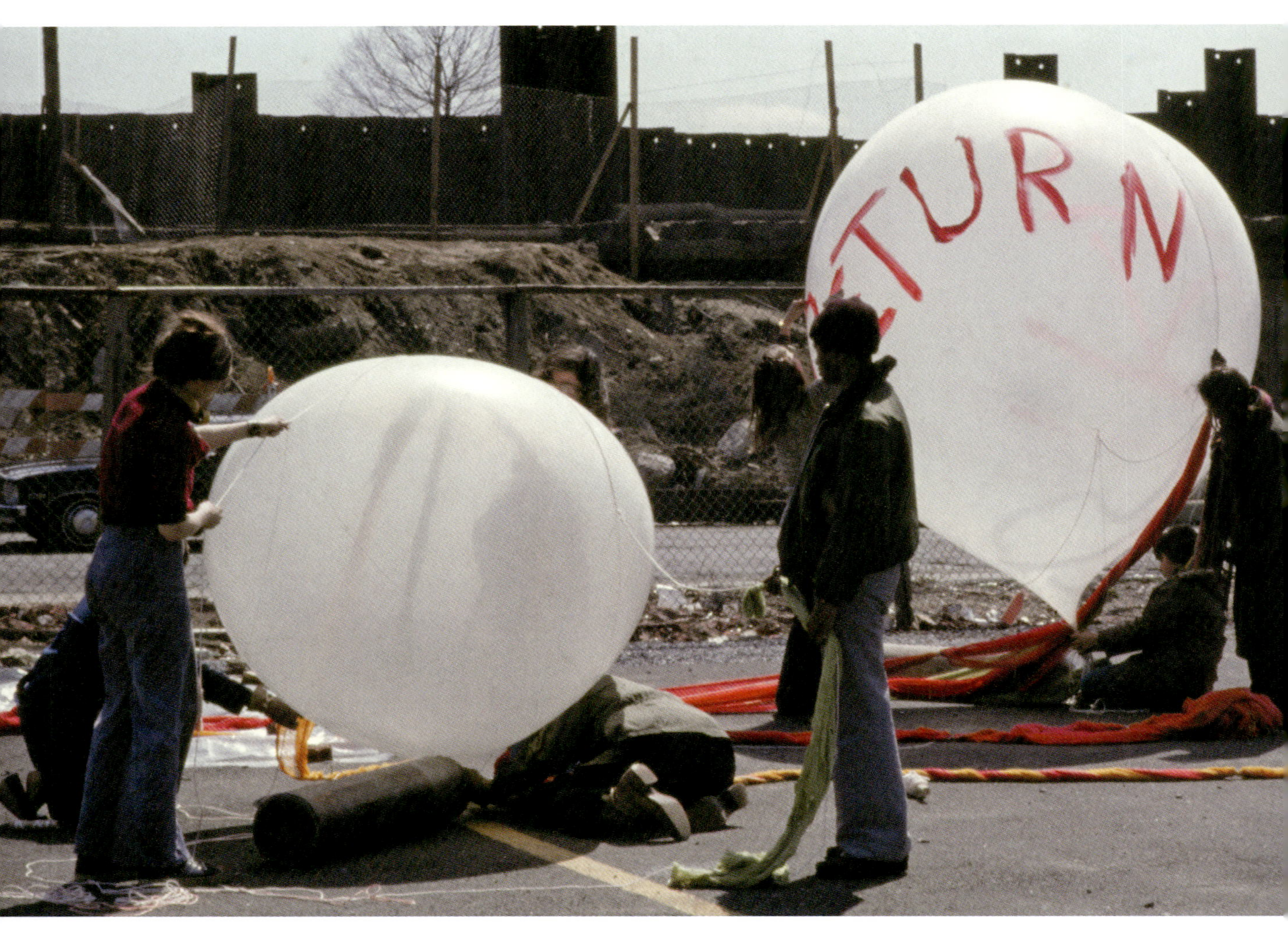
TUR N

They had a dull cast to their skin and strong, dark hair. They never went to high school.

I am trying to flesh out the stories, bring them back. They discussed their apple tree. From the swing in its branches you saw beds of flowering bulbs in Spring.

George could have been Santa Claus and they gave every New Year's Eve party. Even the one in the Winter after Teddy died there were the same foods and homemade wine. Then I never saw the enameled table for limburger, herring, translucent berry preserves.

I try to flesh out the stories, bring them back, but this is their only existence, like the early balloons which I tell you disappeared with their passengers or burst into flames in the sky. They slipped out of their rope nets, or squeezed out, or the wind blew them out, and they floated up to dots and out of sight. Then the rope nets fell like shrouds around the little cars with their passengers.

Madelaine sat near her birdcages. She laughed a lot in her living room, wore shiny blue fabrics with pearls sewn in floral patterns across her wide arms, fat breasts.

When Madelaine died George frightened his family. The house was silent. He didn't shave or bother to have his pants pressed.

There are several possible attitudes. I can tell you here that I know it was clearly impossible but it can be a kind of magic to make an effort so parallel to a problem especially if in the doing you produce simulacrums, or shadows, or even any kind of existence in some mind.

Then there is the further aspect, the pretense of hope, which could be considered one of anyone's jobs.

Consider that, every now and then one of them manages like this, then escapes.

That's what I'm doing here when I tell you that the painted wood house in Jamaica was covered with shingles, had lawns with evergreens, flowers, single fruit trees. Different assortments of factory workers, nurses, and salespeople, or they were plumbers, housepainters, waitresses, managed between parents and brothers, maiden aunts, wives and husbands and children. They had meat stews and ironed clothes. They bowled and went to church.

The first balloons amused well dressed crowds. They were thin silk varnished with elastic gum, were slowly inflated over fires. They entertained the court and terrified farmers and village people who sometimes tore them to shreds when they landed. Or they escaped. It could have been different but now it's the way I describe it, the way you see it in pictures. Madelaine kept caged birds, but they said that she let them escape all in one day when the house was empty, after her daughters married, in the time when they heard her talking to herself.

It's different with gardens. Teddy was the expert at caring for gardens and soils. His cellar had sacks of fertilizers next to the baskets of onions, squash, and potatoes. He knew which bulbs to cover, which bushes to wrap, when to rake, and what to add to soil. He could change the colors of flowers and grow more fruit from a tree. Once he was dead they never came back as many, and thick, and colored.

There were taffeta balloons and others colored with ornate rococo patterns painted in oils.

There were other stories of Madelaine's madness—how she put lamb or beef in the lighted hot oven but without a pot; of not bathing for weeks, refusing to eat, then getting sick from too much food; how she stopped speaking and then came her funeral.

Everyone had a yard. Remember that Teddy and George's mother Katherine kept chickens, but her sons grew flowers and George had a fruit tree with many tiny, tart green apples no one ever ate. They fell on the grass. If you played under the tree you stepped on them. If you climbed the tree, in some seasons, they fell in showers.

Her birds were ordinary canaries. Their cages were in the living room and in the kitchen and dining room. They would stop singing if anyone but Madelaine came in. She sat in a stuffed green chair. The dull yellow canary in the cage just above would watch you listen to her slow words. There were three daughters but there's no need to describe them. They are probably still alive.

Wind can tangle cords or twist the stems of flowers. Even dull flowers only bend, lose petals, but balloons burst on cement like knees and

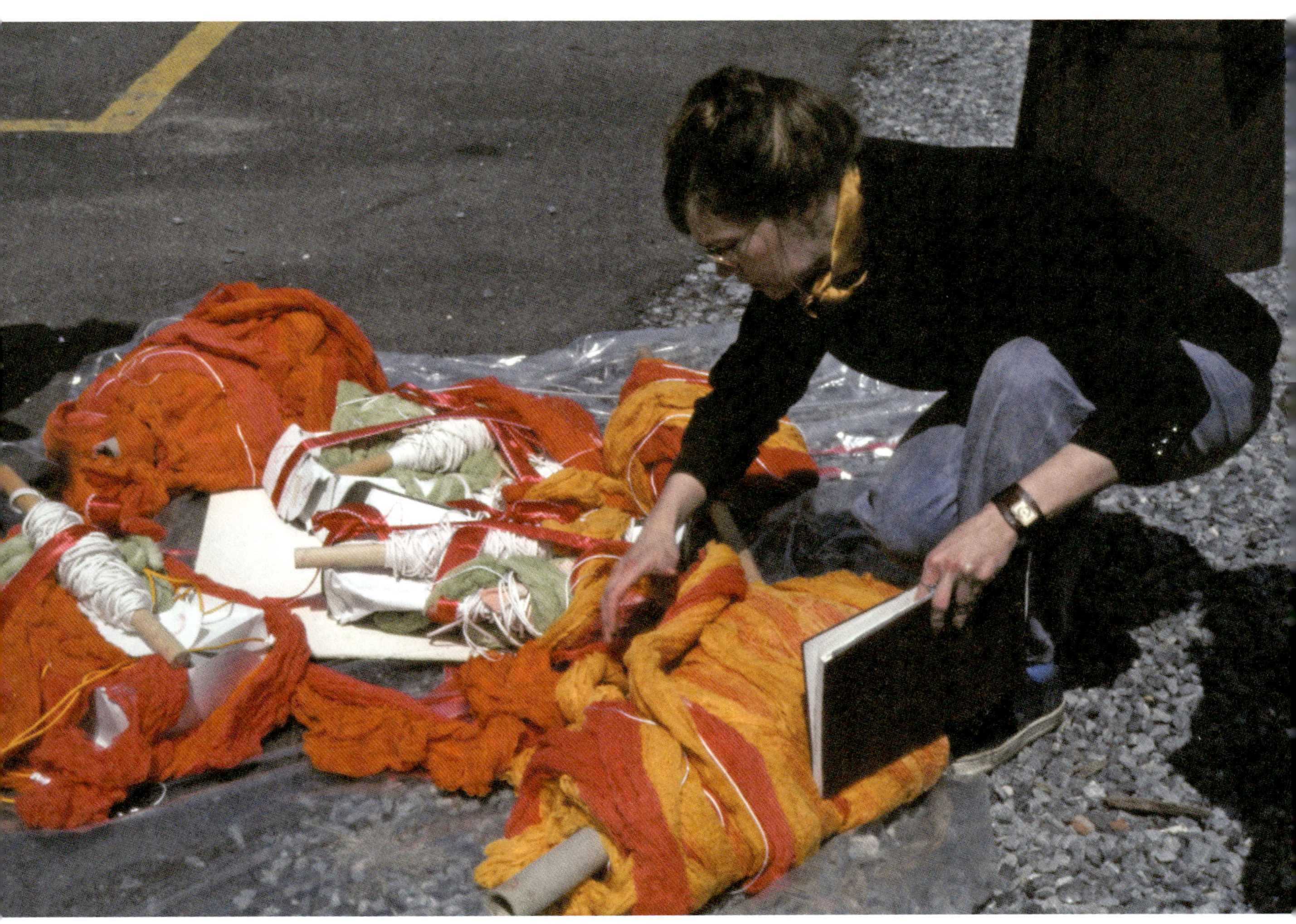

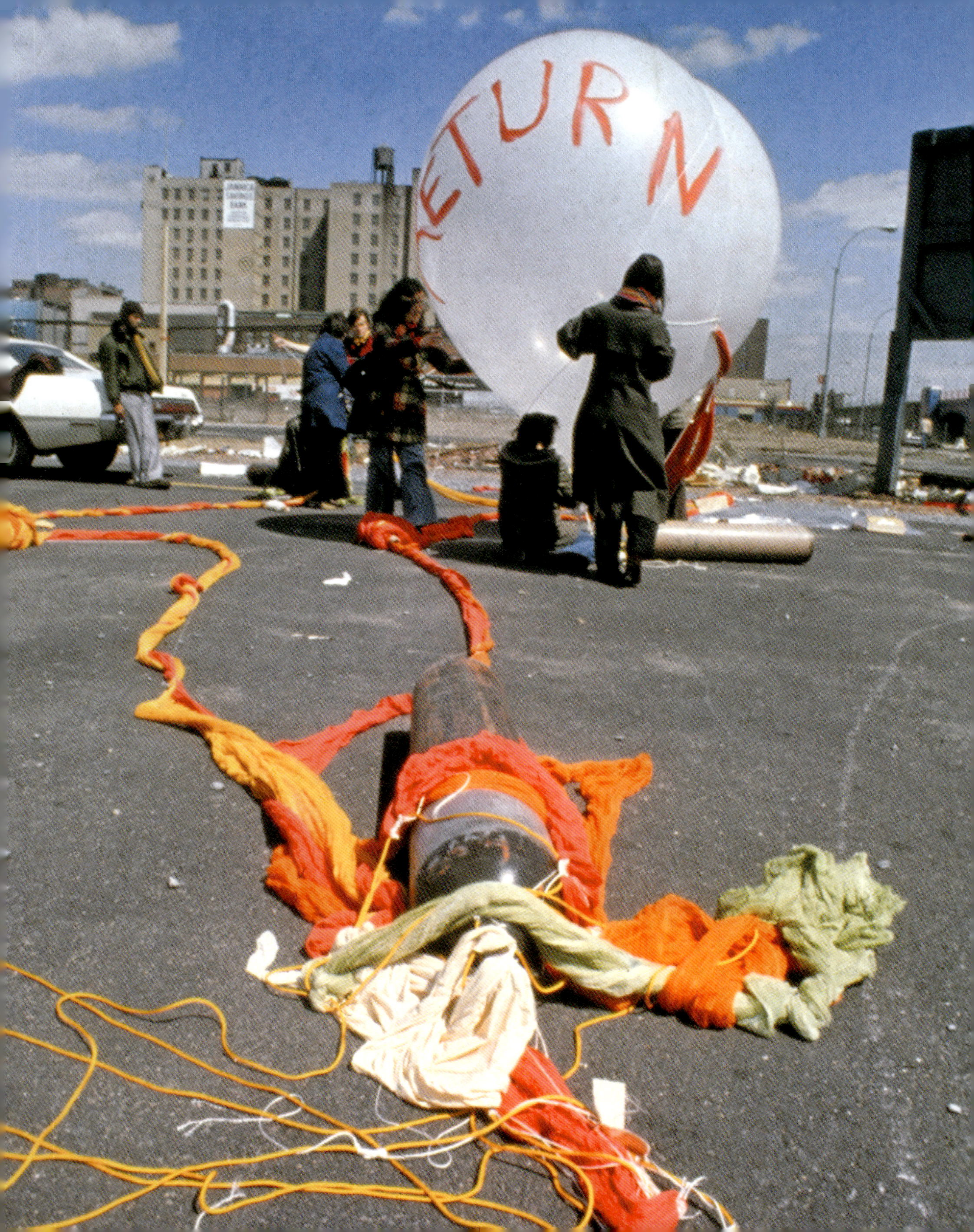
RETURN
JAMAICA SAVINGS BANK

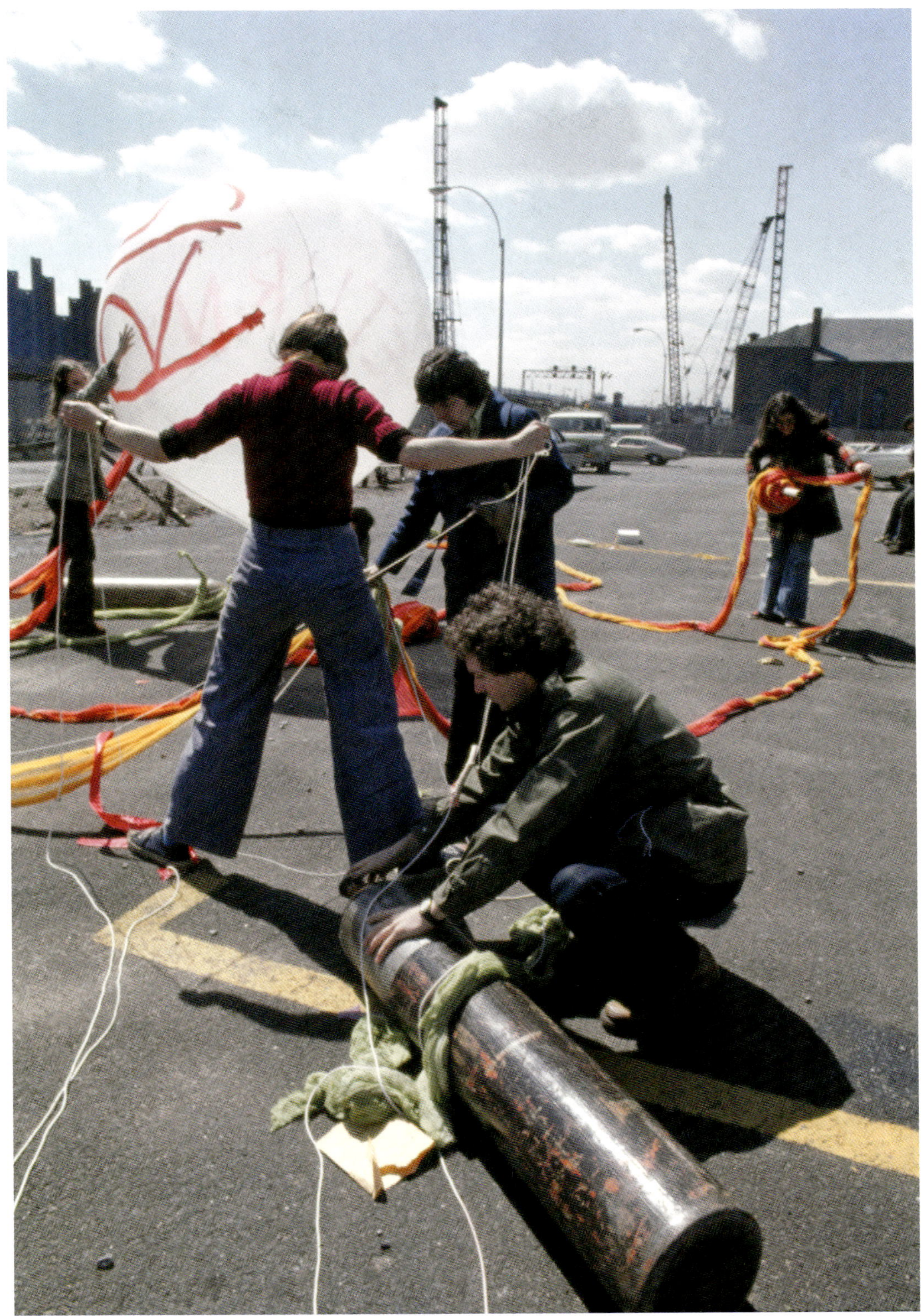

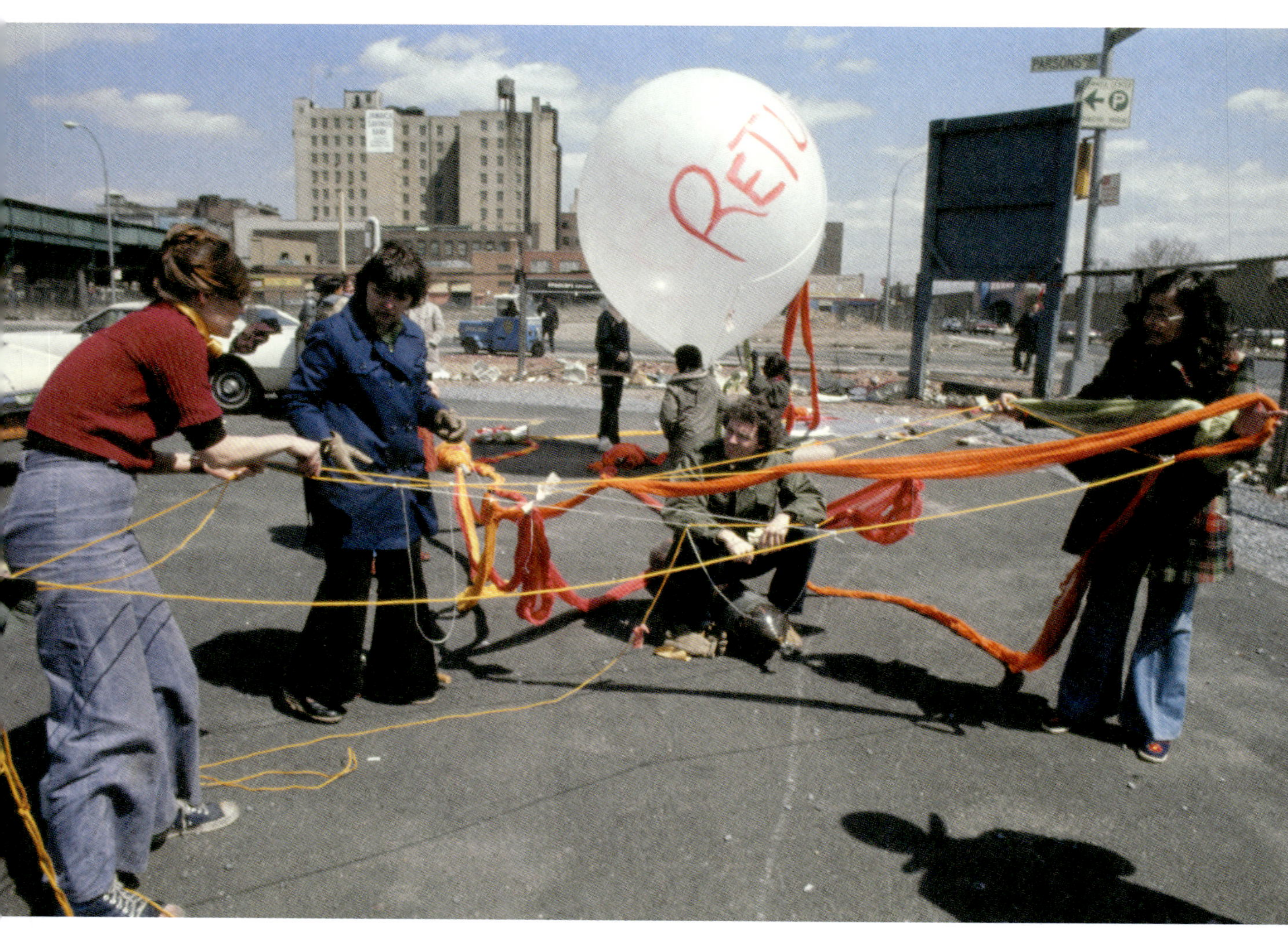
RETU
PARSONS

elbows, palms of hands bloodied by pavements and stone. The matter is does it matter that it exists in memory or in how many memories? How is that different, is that different than how it existed and in what time? Now you see some of George and the others, the flowers, and Jamaica, and balloons. I thought how they could have existed. We each have our images and you have the words and pictures.

What if a Spring had no colors or it stopped coming the way people stop eating and breathing? Gardeners tend buried bulbs through Fall and Winter, wait for crocus, hyacinth, and iris. Teddy told George how to grow more apples, give them some flowers.

There were two sisters and three brothers, the people they married and children. George was the fat elder brother. Madelaine his wife was even fatter than he and Teddy was thin. They all had a yellow-brown cast to their skin and thick, dark hair. Madelaine had hair on her arms. I have hair like Teddy's on my fingers and toes. They never went to high school. George had pointed ears and would make them perk up like the ears of wolves and cats and dogs.

The pictures are the tricks and turns in knots and how to hold onto things until the threads blow off, the scraps of phrases and images disappear with colors in the minds of Madelaine and Theodore and George.

I could say this work was as fragile or possible as breathing, mind, as managing, silence, any understanding of full variety in time, and that that was a reason to do it.

When Madelaine died George frightened his family. His house was silent. He didn't shave or bother to have his shirts pressed. He stopped bowling. Little Madelaine tried to talk to him. They said he had lost his grip on things.

This is an edge between real time and images long in mind, between sculpture and celebration, private magic.

Teddy kept sacks of fertilizers in the cellar. He could change the colors of flowers or get a tree to grow more fruit.

We are elaborate like weeds, those rarely flowering in different forms than the ones before, on empty lots, after the last office buildings. You see them on the edges of cities.

They had an apple tree he would discuss with other gardeners. It was so enormous that even the fattest of their daughters, any of the cousins, could swing from it or climb in it. Swinging feet sailed up in curves over the beds of flowering bulbs.

If they outguess the wind weeds grow huge on the edges of cities. The stems manage the sun, lift leaves, colors, up over pavements and fences. Then they come up again through cracks in cement.

I don't know anything to tell you about Madelaine from the time before she married George. She had her birdcages. And you'll also know that she laughed a lot but slowly, that she wore shiny blue fabrics with pearls sewn in floral patterns across her wide arms, fat breasts.

Iris is written in red. Orange-reds and greens hang from the balloon. Others are spread on the blacktop. The wind moves them less as the rough ground catches more of their surface, tangles the colors in pebbles and fences.

She put a chicken in the oven without a pot and sometimes she didn't bathe for weeks. Then she let the canaries escape.

There were many tiny, tart green apples no one ever ate. They fell on the grass and you walked on them. In some seasons, they fell in showers.

He made wine between the old birdcages. They served it at every New Year's party.

When the daughters were married and the house was empty, she sat with her birds and talked to herself.

Then she stopped speaking. She sat in her stuffed green chair.

There were taffeta balloons and others colored with ornate rococo patterns painted in oils.

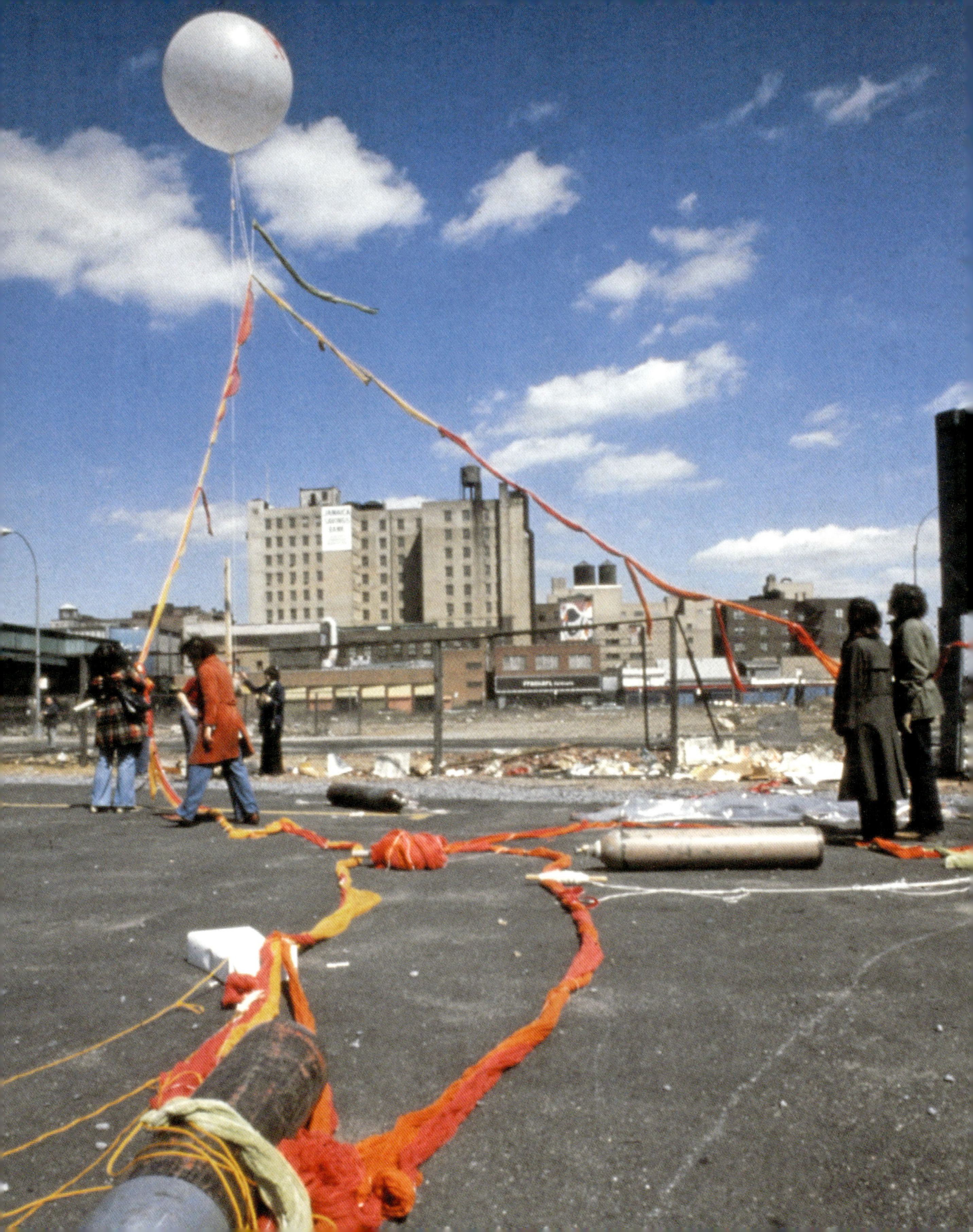

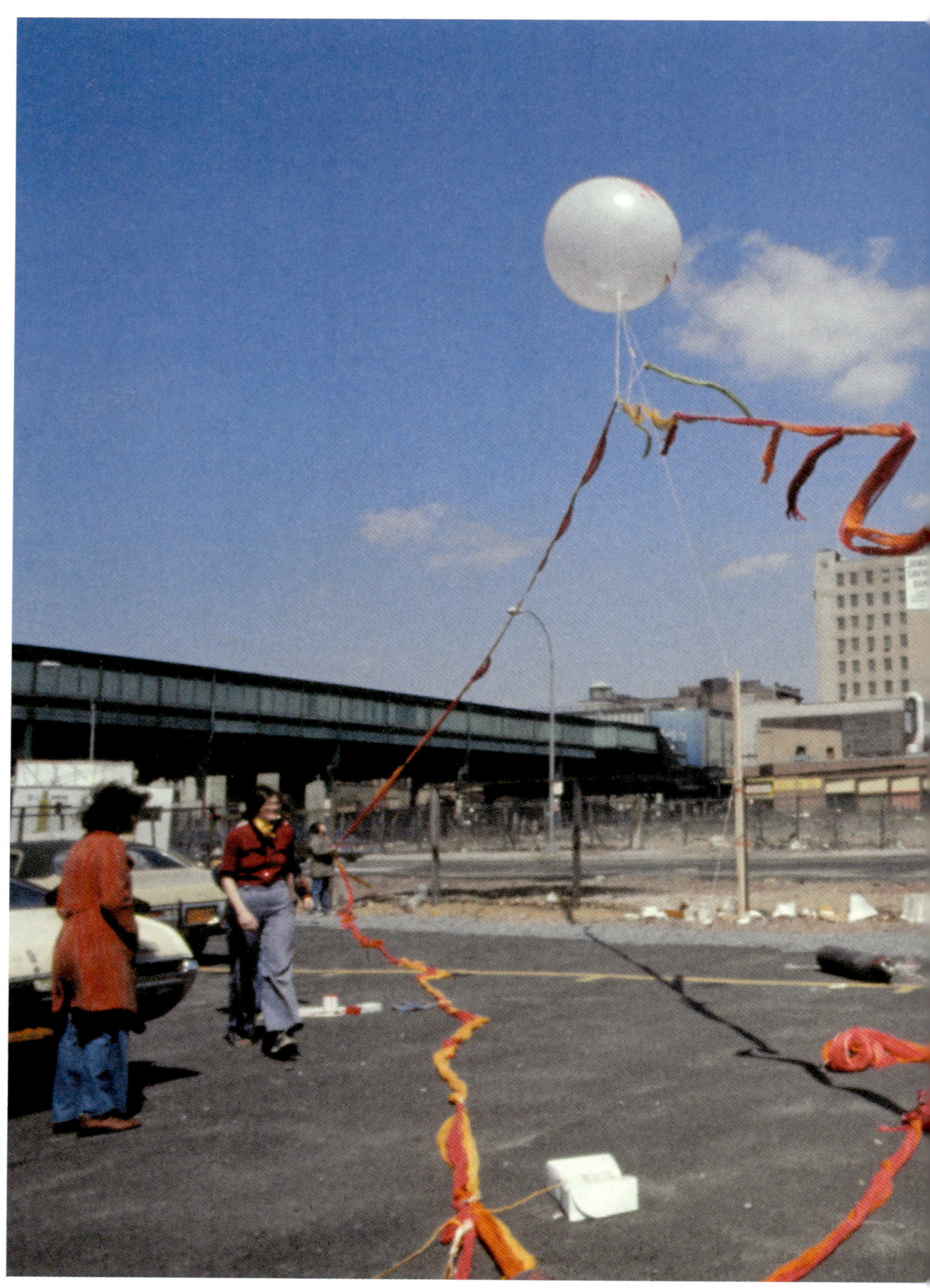

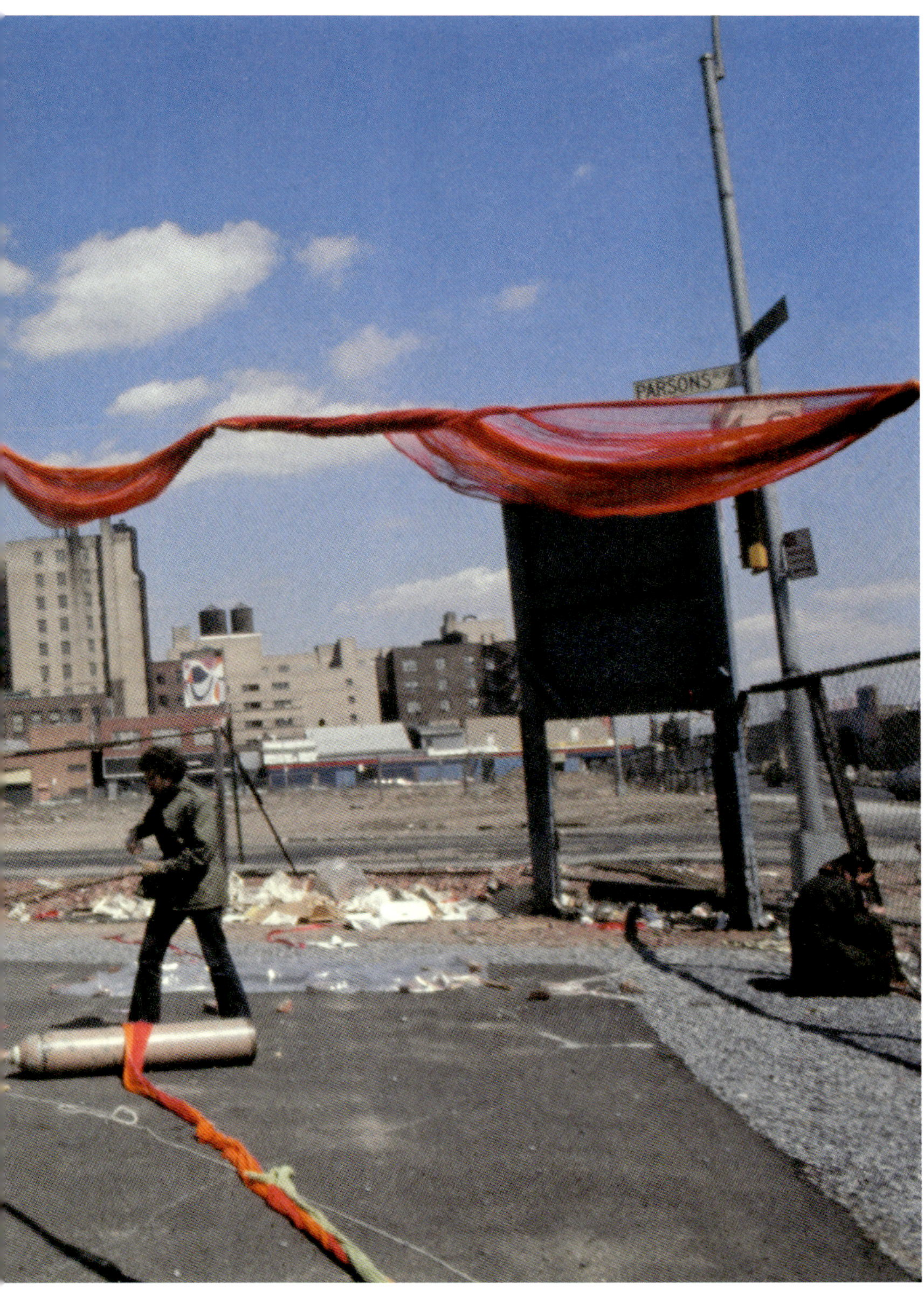

PARSONS

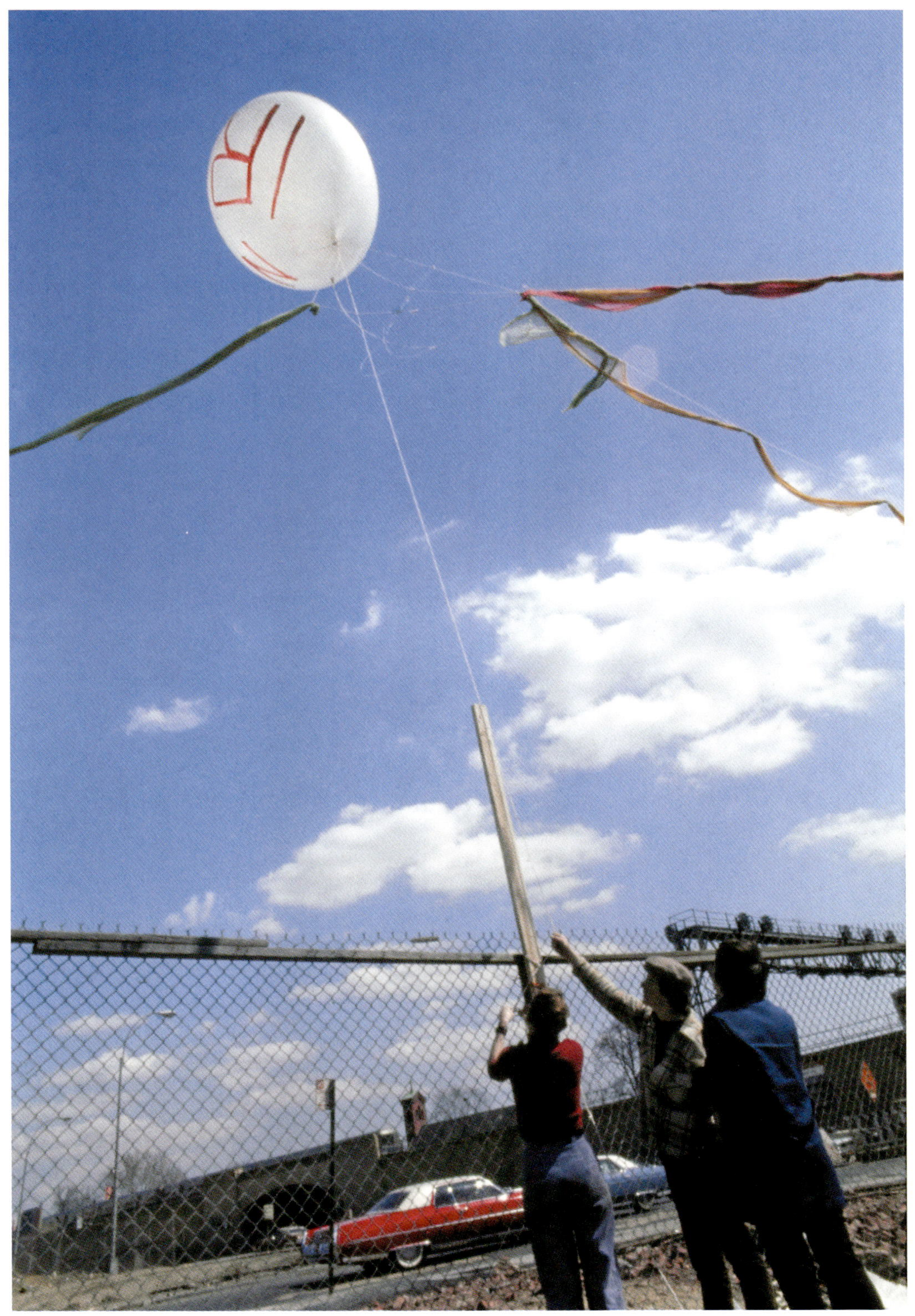

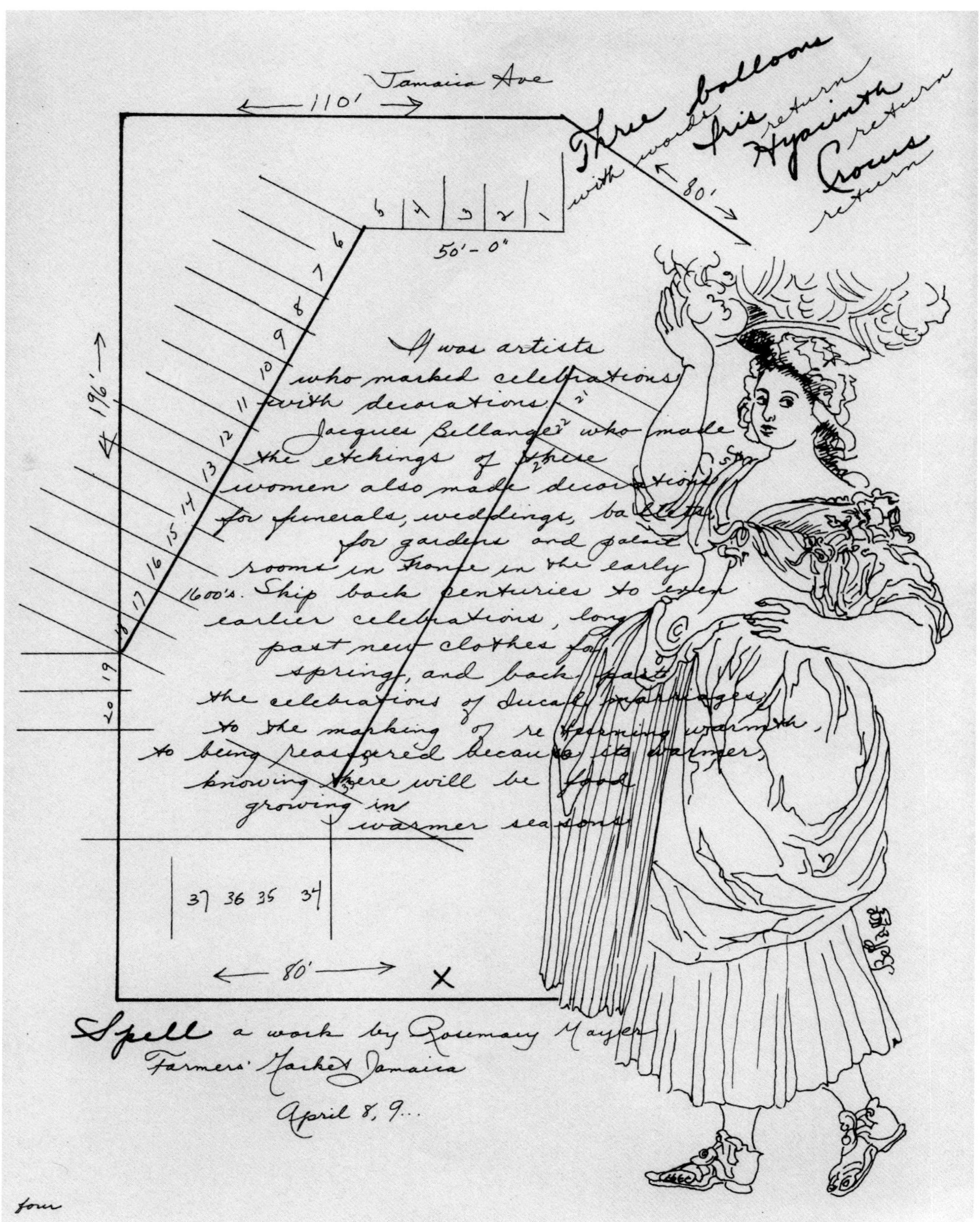

Jamaica Ave
110'
Three balloons
with marble tiles
Iris return
Hyacinth return
Crocus return
80'
50'-0"
196'
It was artists
who marked celebrations
with decorations.
Jacques Bellange² who made
the etchings of these
women also made decorations
for funerals, weddings, ballets
for gardens and palace
rooms in France in the early
1600's. Ship back centuries to even
earlier celebrations, long
past new clothes for
spring, and back past
the celebrations of ducal marriages,
to the marking of returning warmth,
to being reassured because its warmer,
knowing there will be food
growing in
warmer seasons
37 36 35 34
80'
X
Spell a work by Rosemary Mayer
Farmers' Market Jamaica
April 8, 9...
Bellange

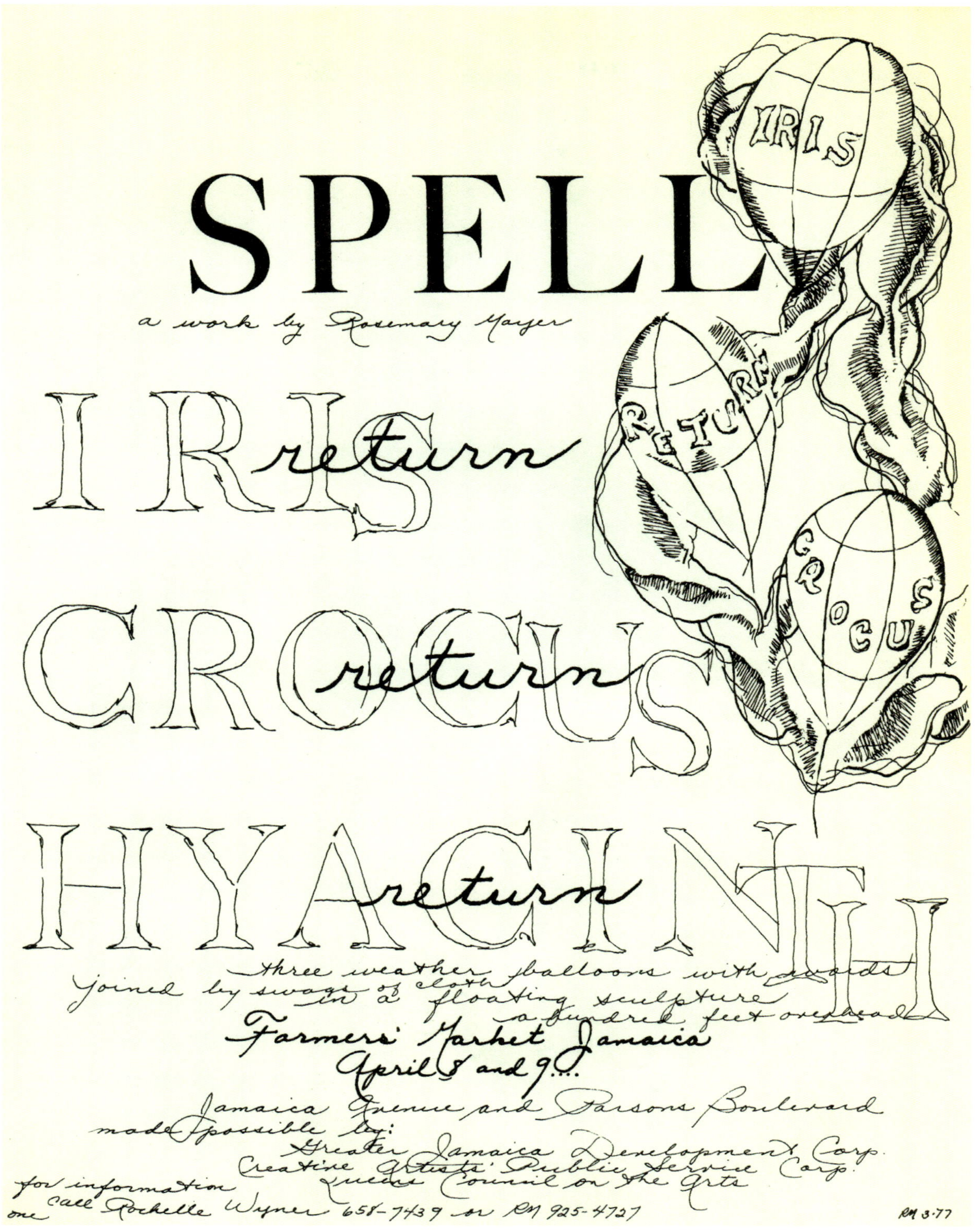

SPELL
a work by Rosemary Mayer
IRIS
IRIS return
CROCUS return
HYACINTH return
RETURN
CROCUS
three weather balloons with words
joined by swags of cloth
in a floating sculpture
a hundred feet overhead
Farmers' Market Jamaica
April 8 and 9....
Jamaica Avenue and Parsons Boulevard
made possible by:
Greater Jamaica Development Corp.
Creative Artists' Public Service Corp.
Queens Council on the Arts
for information
call Rochelle Wyner 658-7439 or RM 925-4727
one
RM 3·77

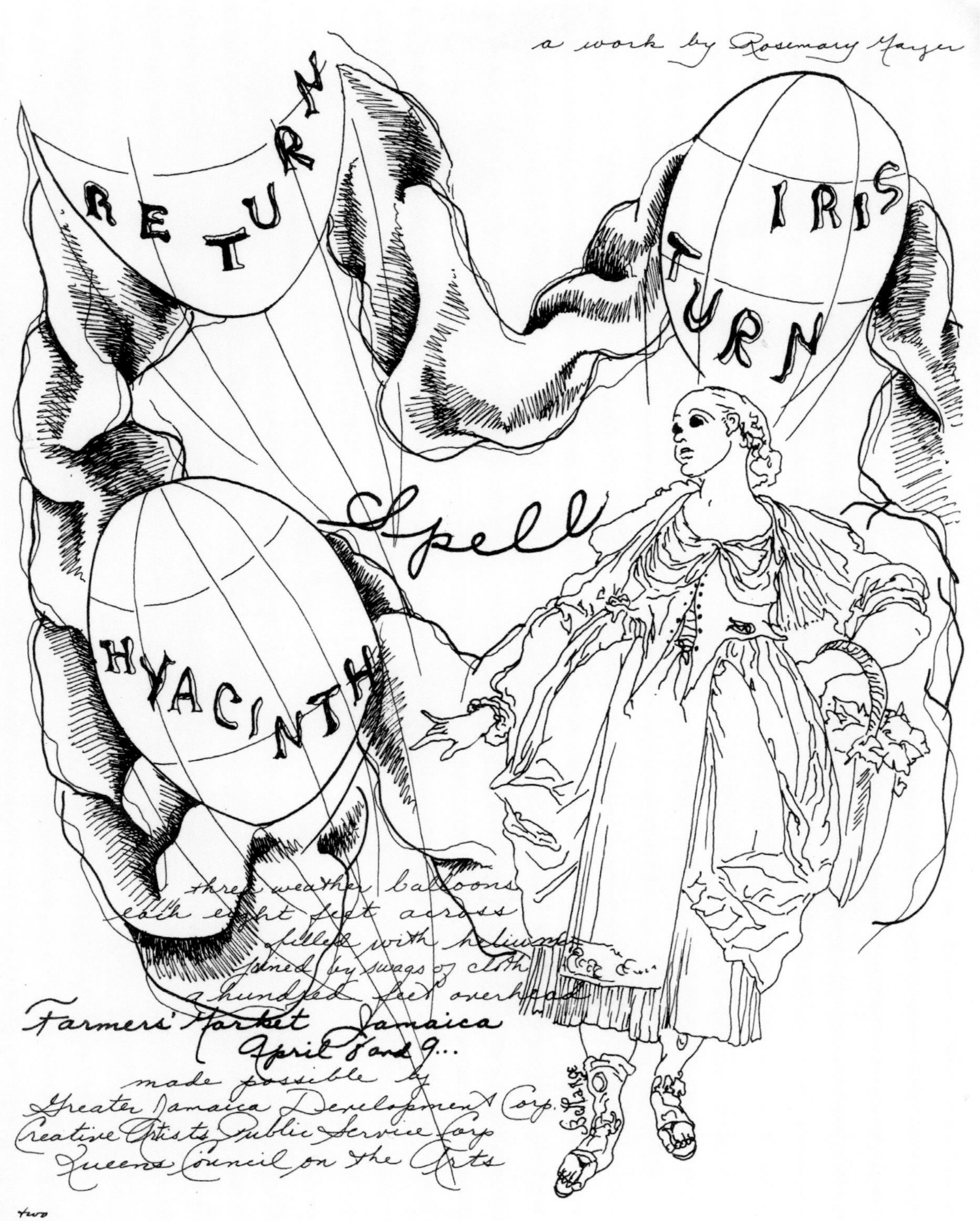

a work by Rosemary Mayer
RETURN
IRIS TURN
HYACINTH
Spell
three weather balloons
each eight feet across
filled with helium
joined by swags of cloth
a hundred feet overhead
Farmers' Market Jamaica
April 8 and 9...
made possible by
Greater Jamaica Development Corp.
Creative Artists Public Service Corp
Queens Council on the Arts

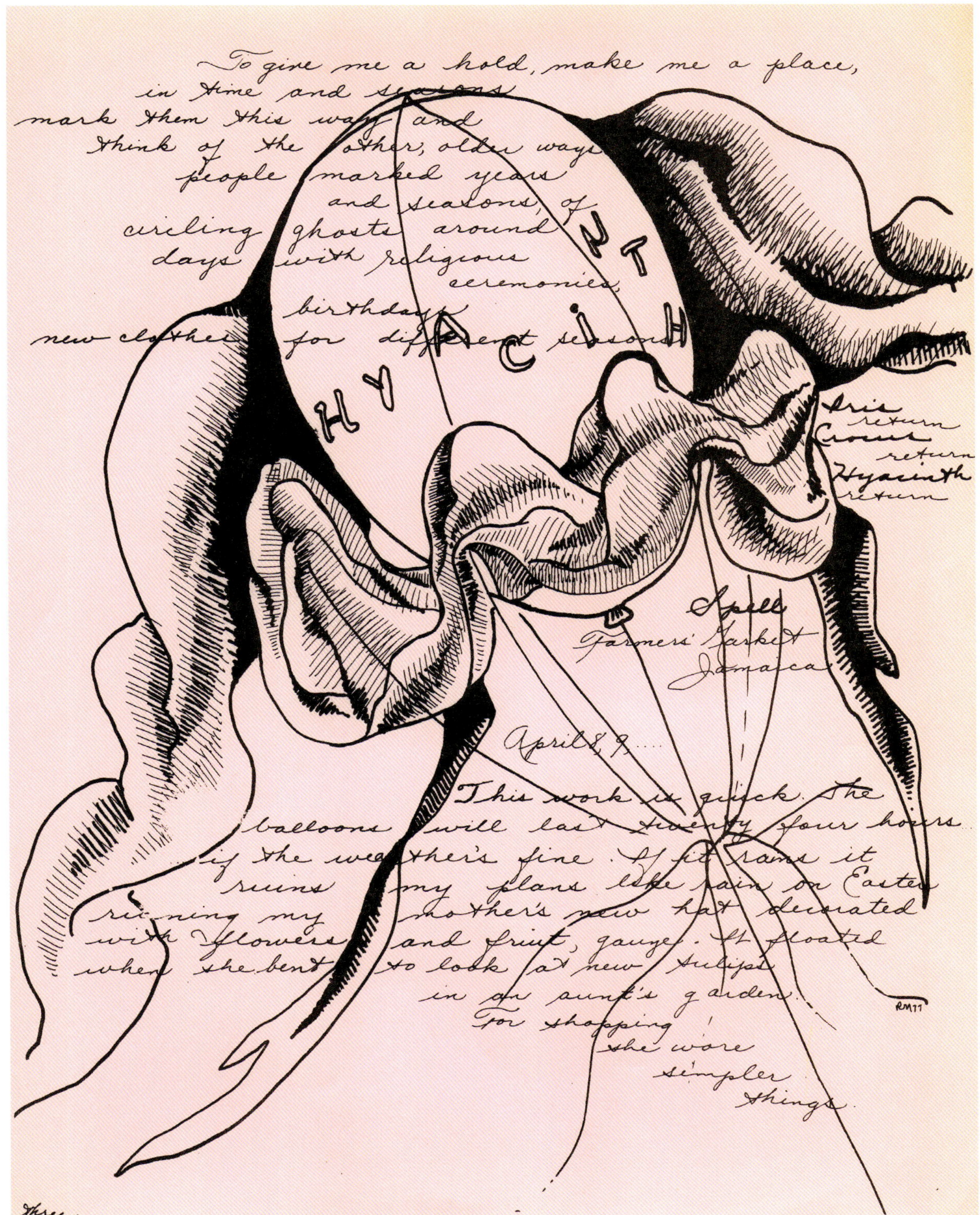

To give me a hold, make me a place,
in time and seasons,
mark them this way and
think of the other, older ways
people marked years
and seasons, of
circling ghosts around
days with religious
ceremonies,
birthdays
new clothes for different seasons

HYACINTH

Iris
return
Crocus
return
Hyacinth
return

Spell
Farmers' Market
Jamaica

April 8, 9.....

This work is quick. The
balloons will last twenty-four hours
if the weather's fine. If it rains it
ruins my plans like rain on Easter
ruining my mother's new hat decorated
with flowers and fruit, gauze. It floated
when she bent to look at new tulips
in an aunt's garden.
For shopping
she wore
simpler
things.

RM 77

Three

I try to flesh out the stories, bring them
back, but this is their only existence,
like the early balloons which I tell
you disappeared with their passengers
or burst into flames in the sky.
They slipped out of their rope nets,
or squeezed out, or the wind blew
them out, and they floated up
to dots and out of sight. Then
the rope nets fell like shrouds
around the little cars with
their passengers

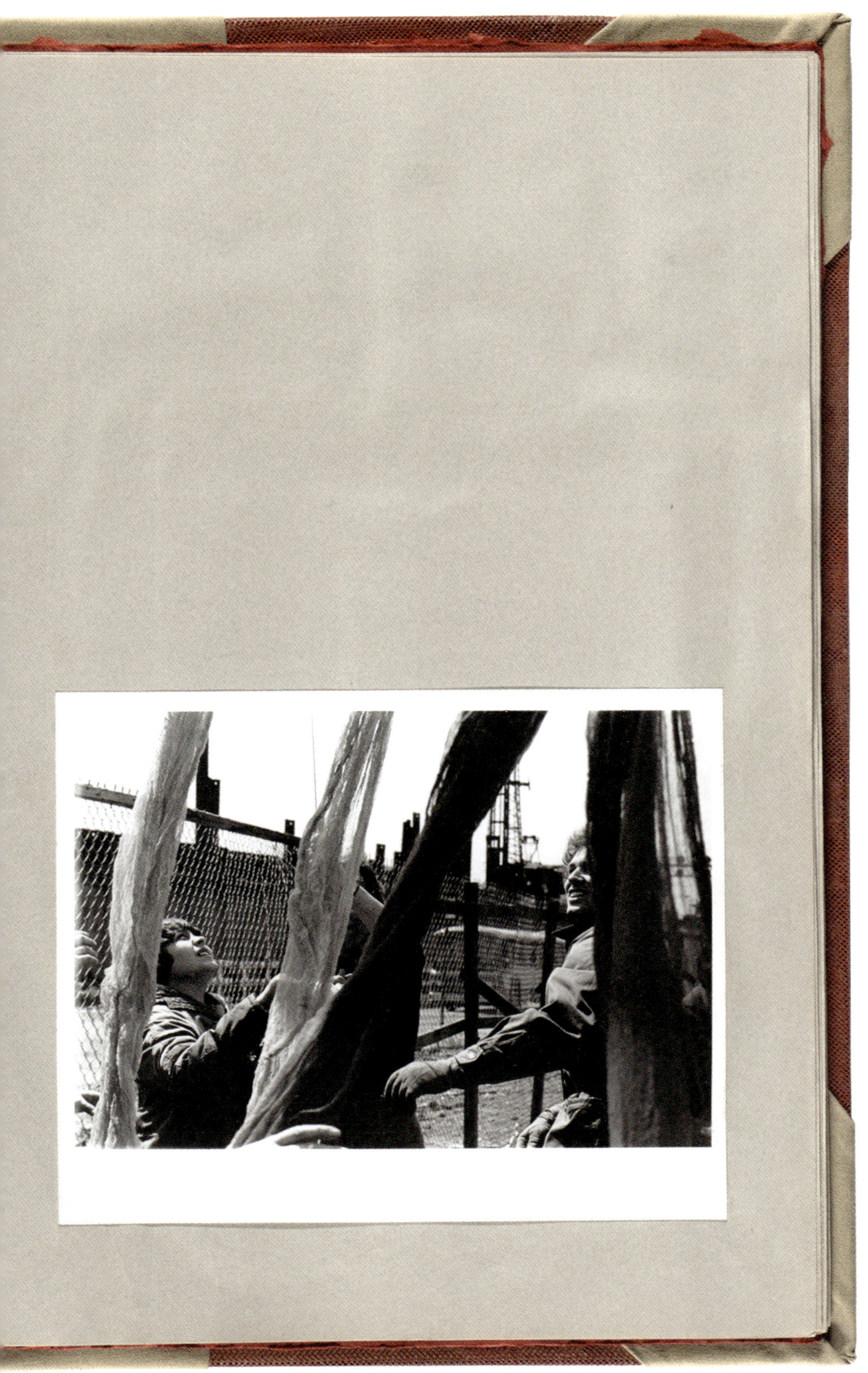

He made wine between
the old birdcages. They
served it at every New
Year's party.

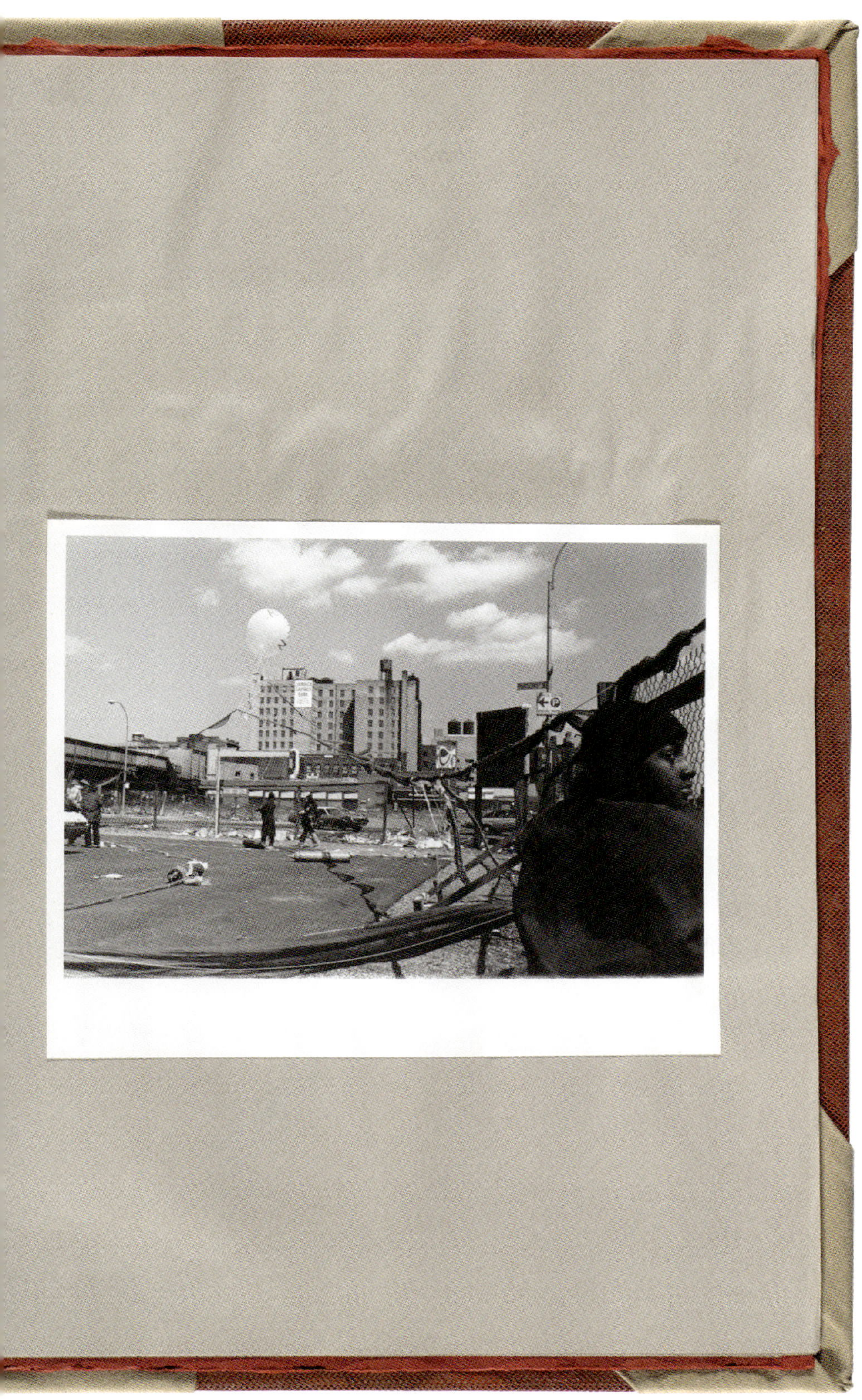

There were taffetta
balloons and others
colored with ornate
rococo patterns
painted in oils

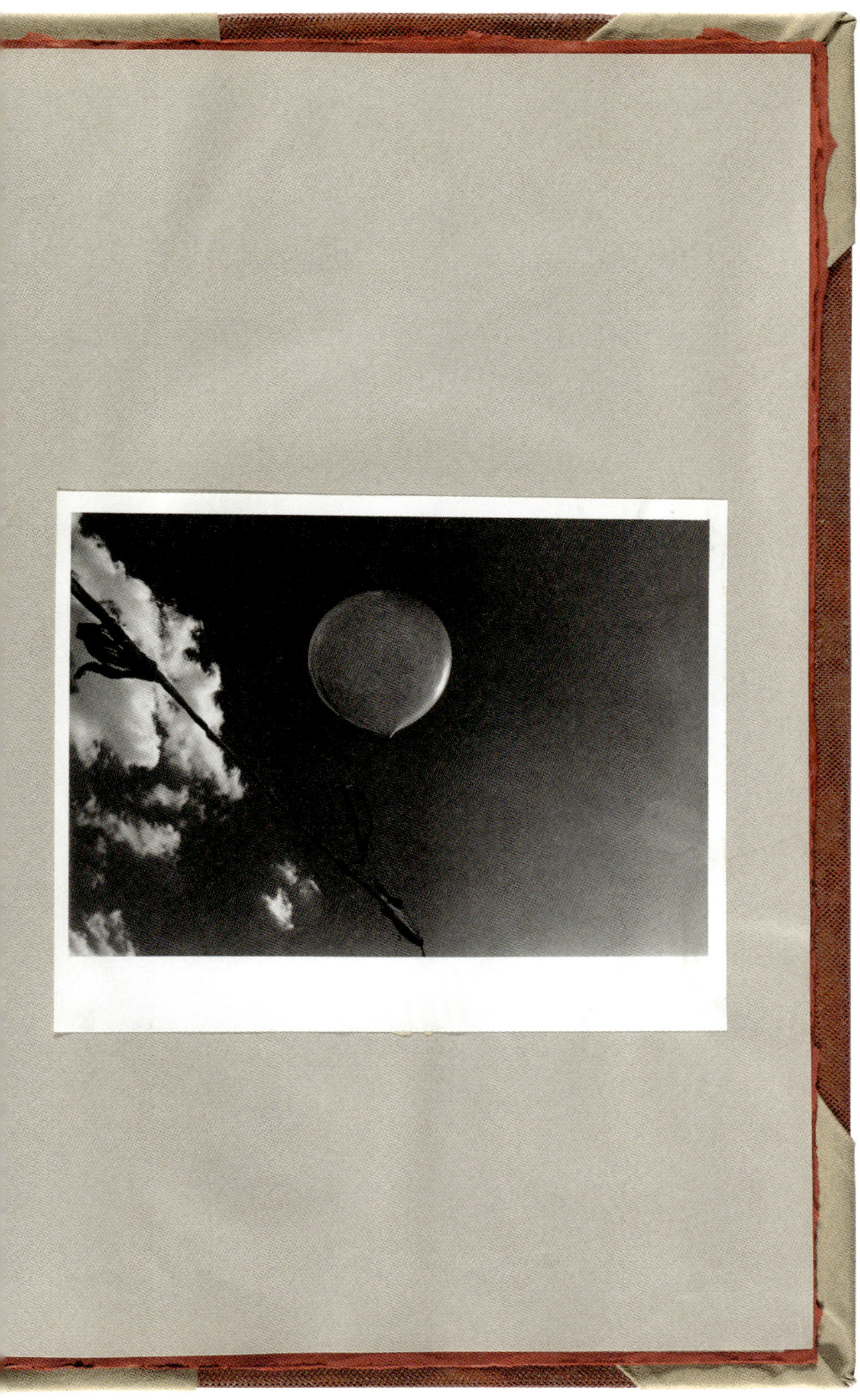

SOME DAYS IN APRIL

Installed during the week of April 17, 1978
Balloons, helium, paint, fabric, rope, and wooden rods
Property of Bruce Kurtz, Hartwick, New York

Photographs, text, drawings, artist's book

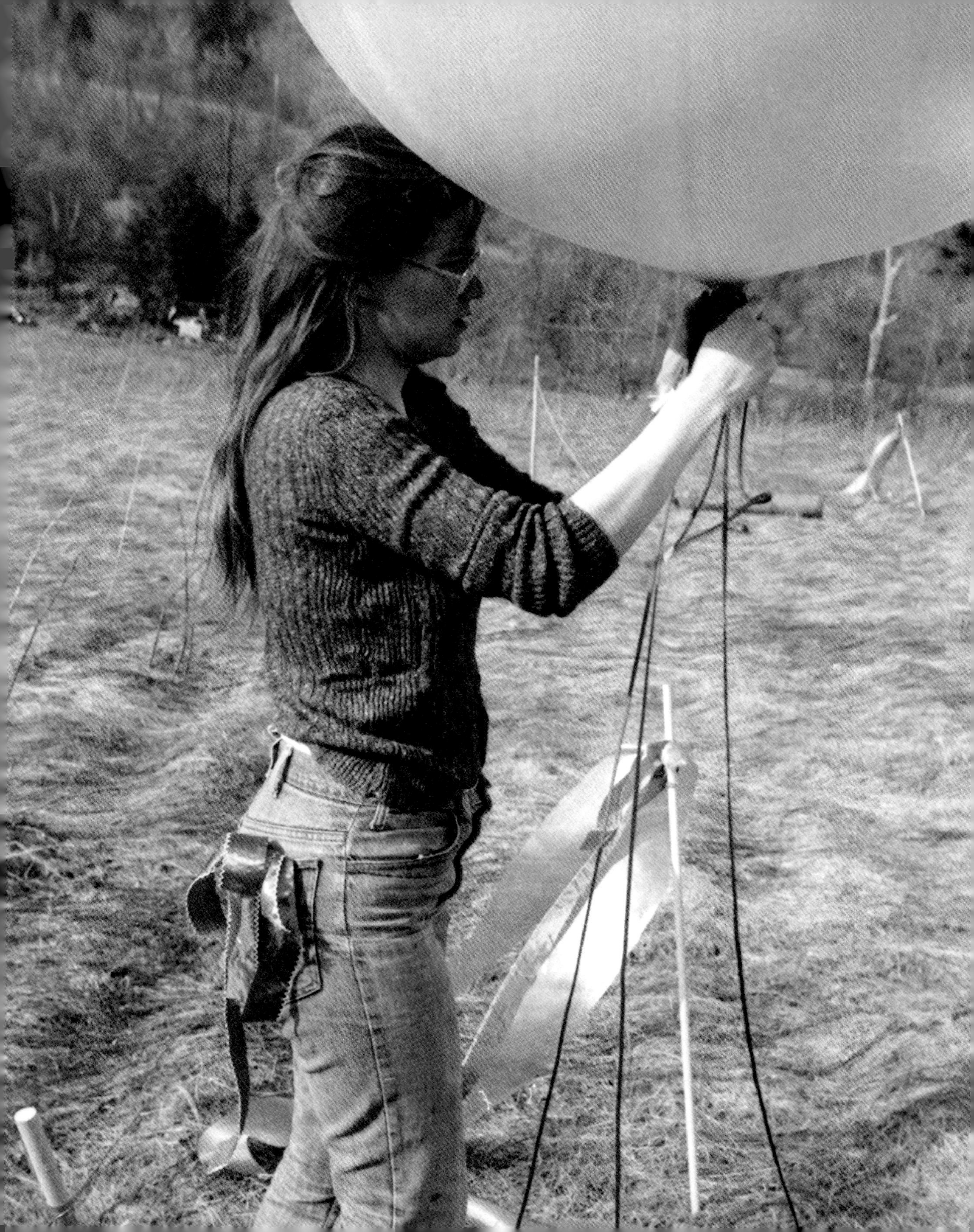

SOME DAYS IN APRIL

Text from artist's book, 1979.

Iris is packed like Pandora's box, old gods, the center of an eye, the whole rainbow sifting down flowers in different colors, even wild by roadsides. Alphard is an opposite, at the bottom of the sky, skimming along the horizon and hardly visible in dirty cities, though it's a bright star in a wide space of sky filled with only dimmer points of light. It's the alpha star in the constellation Hydra, the water snake that waits in the mud with its nine heads for the arms and legs of heroes and warrior queens. Euphrasia was in the middle. She organized nuns to keep a hostel for women who had no money, no place, or any people who'd help them. April 24th was the day she died.

Mary Euphrasia Pelletier was born in 1796 at Noirmoutier in France. She joined the Institute of Our Lady of Charity and founded the Institute of the Religious of the Good Shepherd, nuns devoted to the relief of destitute girls and women. She died April 24, 1868.

To breathe the Hydra's breath was fatal. It grew two heads for each one destroyed. One head was immortal. Heracles weighed it down with a rock, killed it with an arrow soaked in its own blood.

Helen was a real but unused name. She told it to some of her friends but she never used it because it was the same as her mother's. She had children of her own. She used flowers, their shapes, their names, strange facts and old folk-lore about them in her work which was a kind of pictorial sculpture, with words, on the walls of her studio, her galleries, a few museums. I don't know what difference April made to her. I know summer mattered because then she relaxed and sometimes took her children to the country. I saw the flowers she made one summer. She put their names on banners. A few years later she was in a bad accident. She died on the thirtieth of April.

Narcissus is the flower for April in Egypt, in Athens, in Rome, altars and tombs were filled or covered with it. Narcissus is the daffodil, yellow,

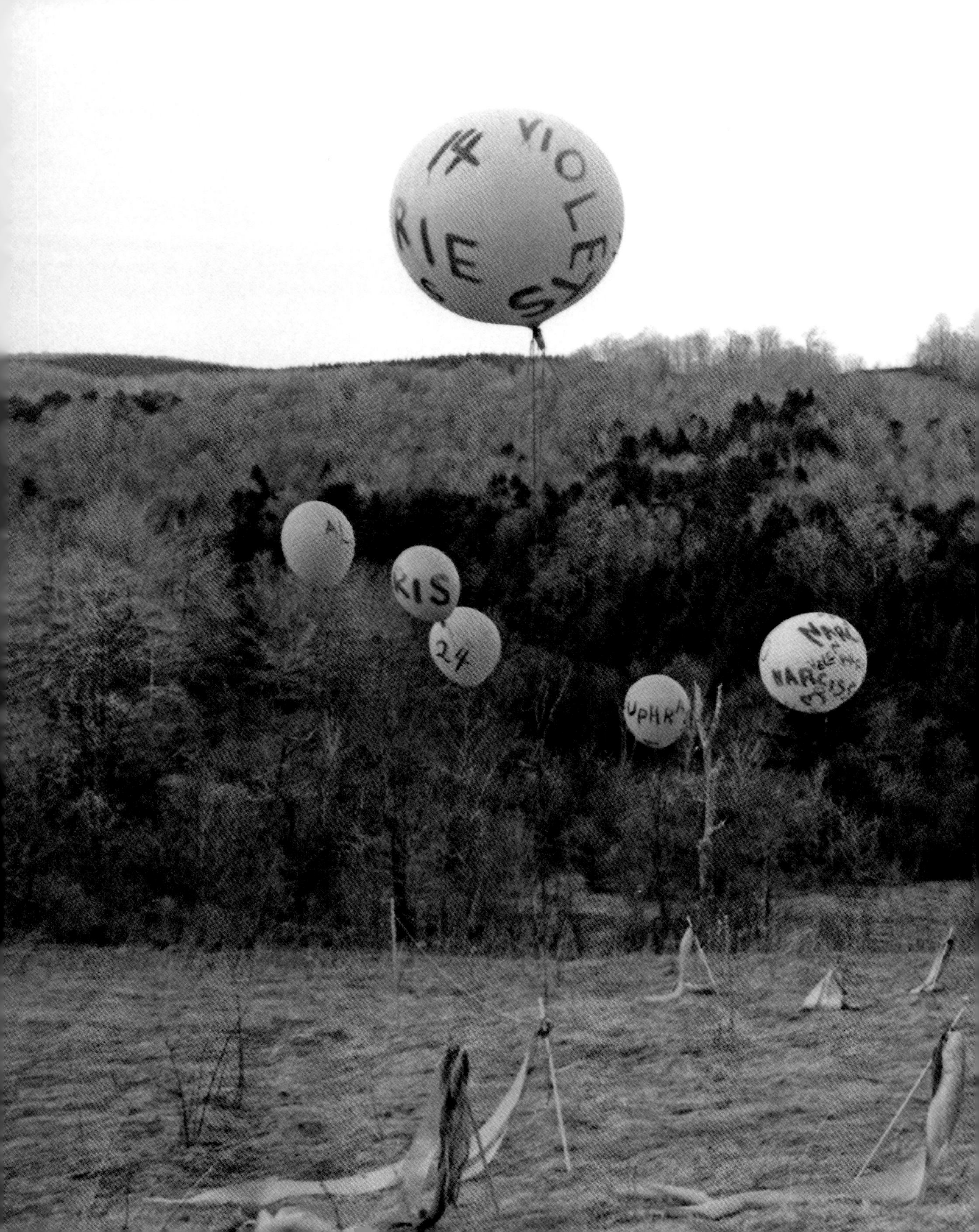
VIOLE
RIE SY
AL
RIS
24
UPHR
NARC
NARCISS

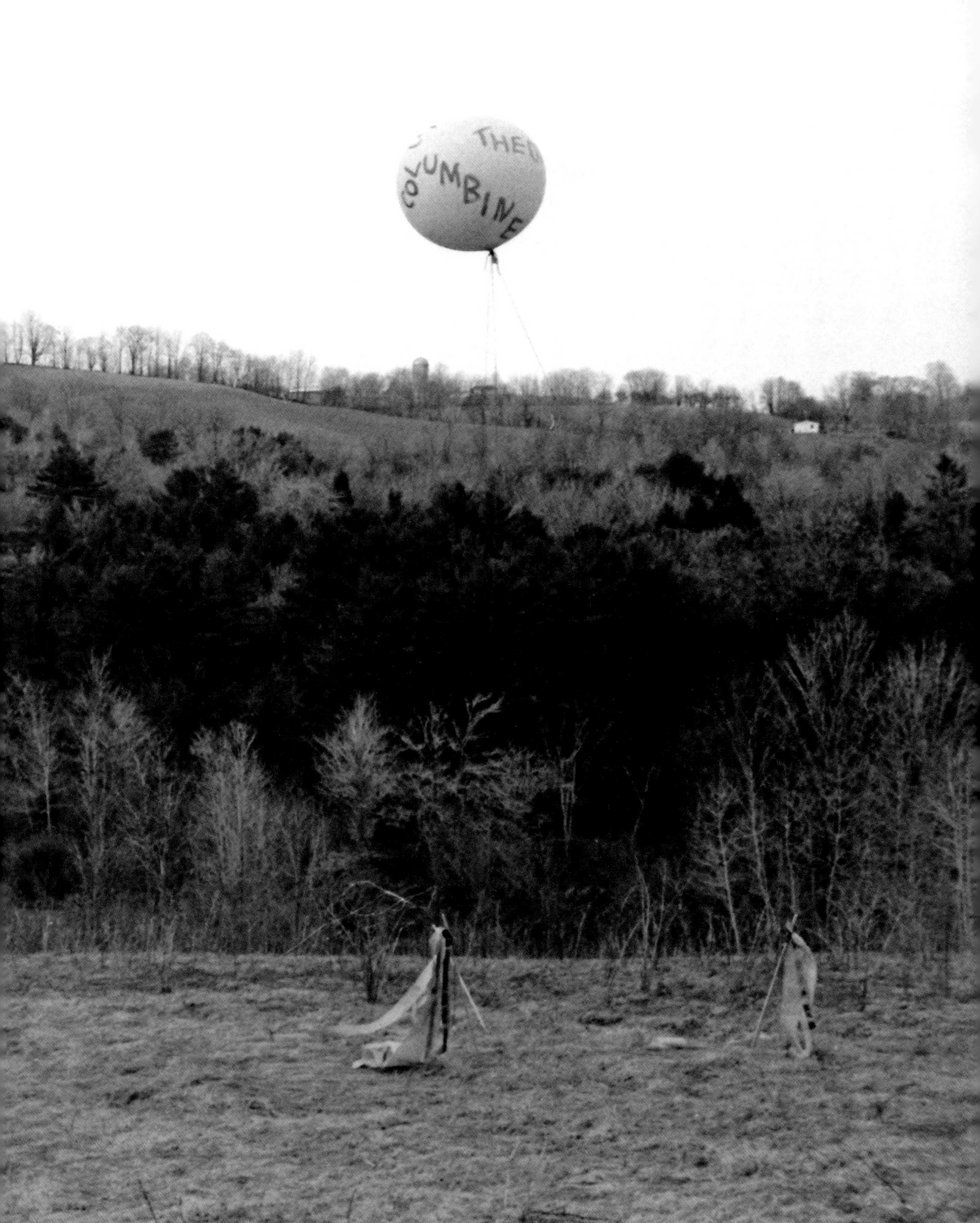
THE
COLUMBINE

white, and yellow and white. Arcturus is blue. It's a bright blue star in a constellation with an outline like a kite, the figure of Boötes who was a charioteer. Arcturus is high in the north like a bright eye watching the weather as it turns from the end of winter around the dim north star to spring before it sets too early to see it in the still present light of the spring evening sun.

Catherine is many women, is nearly the widest European woman's name after the end of Rome. They are still everywhere and different. The old Catherines were mystics, teachers, driven saints, writers, theologians. Then there were queens, nuns. Other women you might never hear about, mothers, aunts, sisters.

April was special because both their birthdays came then. There were presents, small parties on the nearest Sundays, cake after dinner or ice cream. The garden flowers came up; it wasn't so cold; the days got a little longer.

Marie liked violets in the way she liked any brief, impossible thing, for the reasons Teddy, her husband, grew columbine and yellow-orange roses. She wanted to smell like violets. She made lace in patterns called gentian, Parma Violets, les Violettes de Toulouse. She didn't live long. She was sick so long it was good when she died.

Marie had dark brown glasses whose upper edges rose and pointed outwards as though they could fly off. Seven marcasites, small and colorless, caught the light in a row above each of her eyes like jeweled eyebrows in the evening. After dinner, in the yard with the morning glories, her husband would point out the brightest stars or the season's constellations, tell her their names. Every April she would recognize Corona Borealis, the northern crown. At Easter he brought her white lilies.

I remember that they thought of Teddy as a good man because he didn't drink, use rough language, or see other women. He worked hard. They had separate bedrooms after her first mastectomy. He lived two more years. He died all of a sudden, a heart attack. He used to paint watercolors of the flowers in his garden. He painted columbine because he loved their complex but definite shapes, delicate colors, because he liked to grow difficult flowers. He told the people he liked about his flowers. He showed us their barely visible seeds.

Teddy built a telescope from cardboard tubes and lenses he ground himself. He said it was for me. He made the tripod from wood cut from

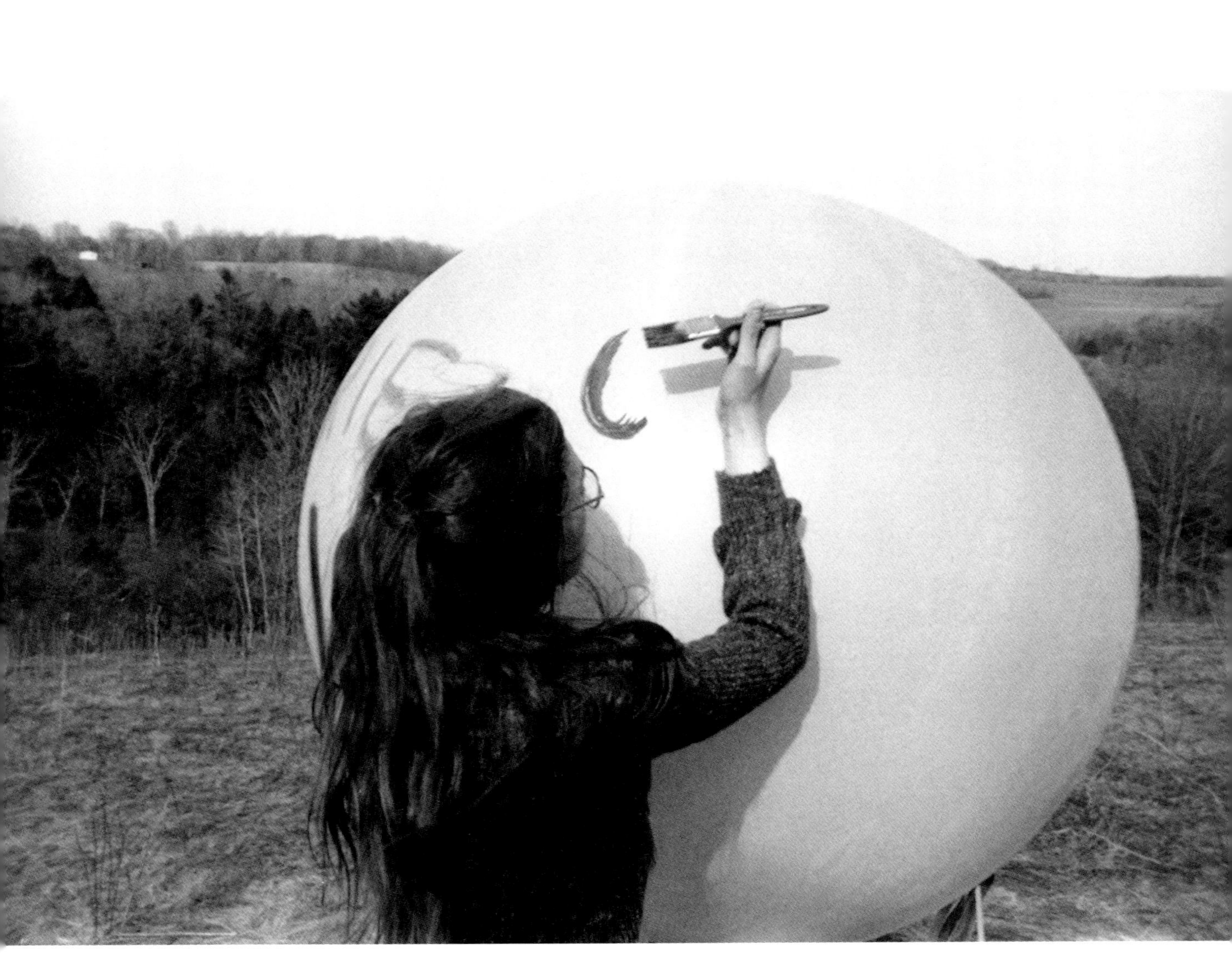

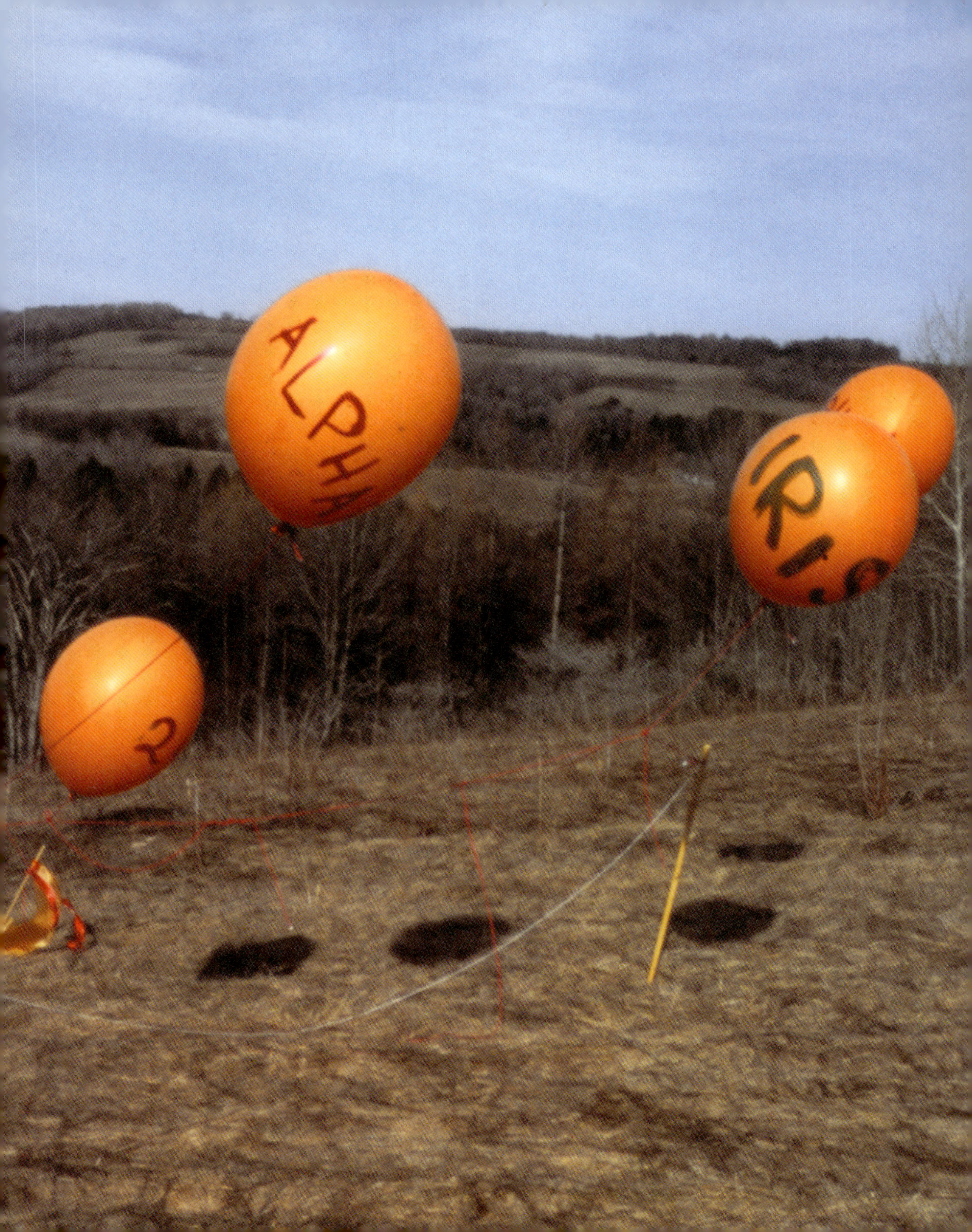

ALPHA
R
2

old furniture we didn't use anymore. When it shook in the least wind he went out and bought one and a telescope too. We learned to find the constellations each season. We looked for double stars where each was a different color. He liked Leo because it signaled spring. Regulus is its alpha star. As it rose earlier in March and April nights he looked for more of his flowers.

These words are here, were there, because I still connect them. You would use other words, or do it another way, or not at all.

Once stars were flowers. Now, anyone can write on a balloon.

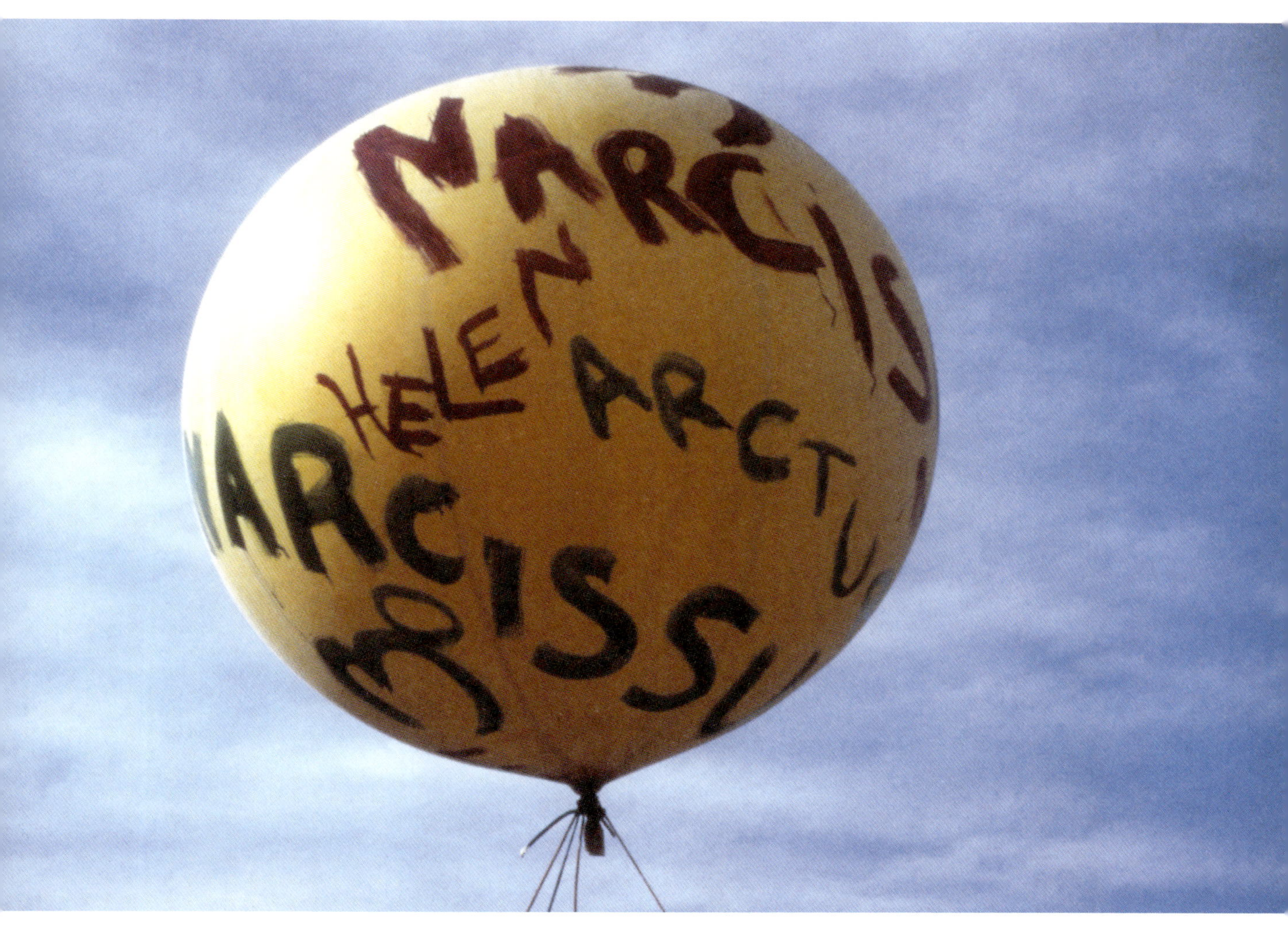

MARCIS
HELEN
ARCT
MARCIS
CISSI

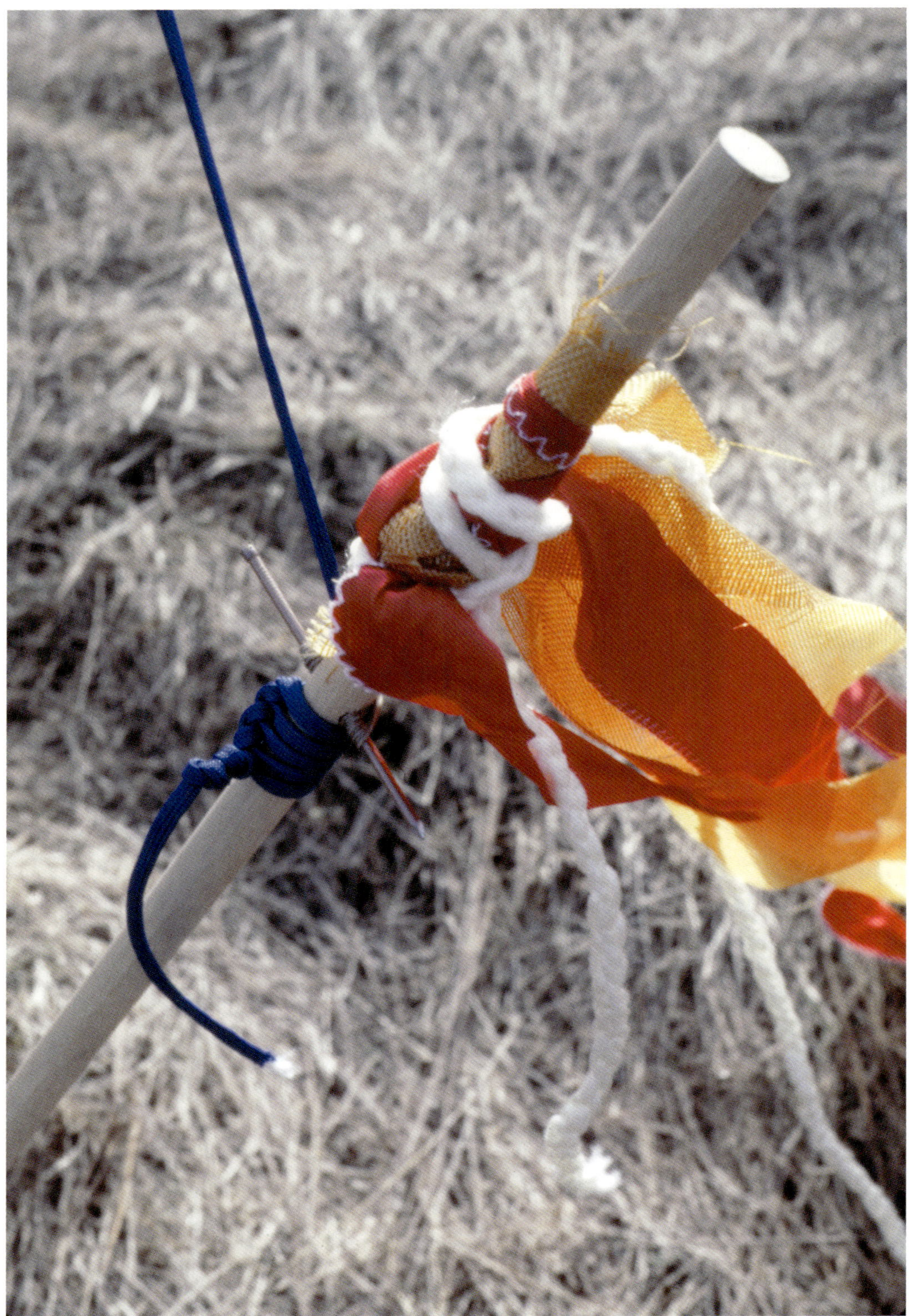

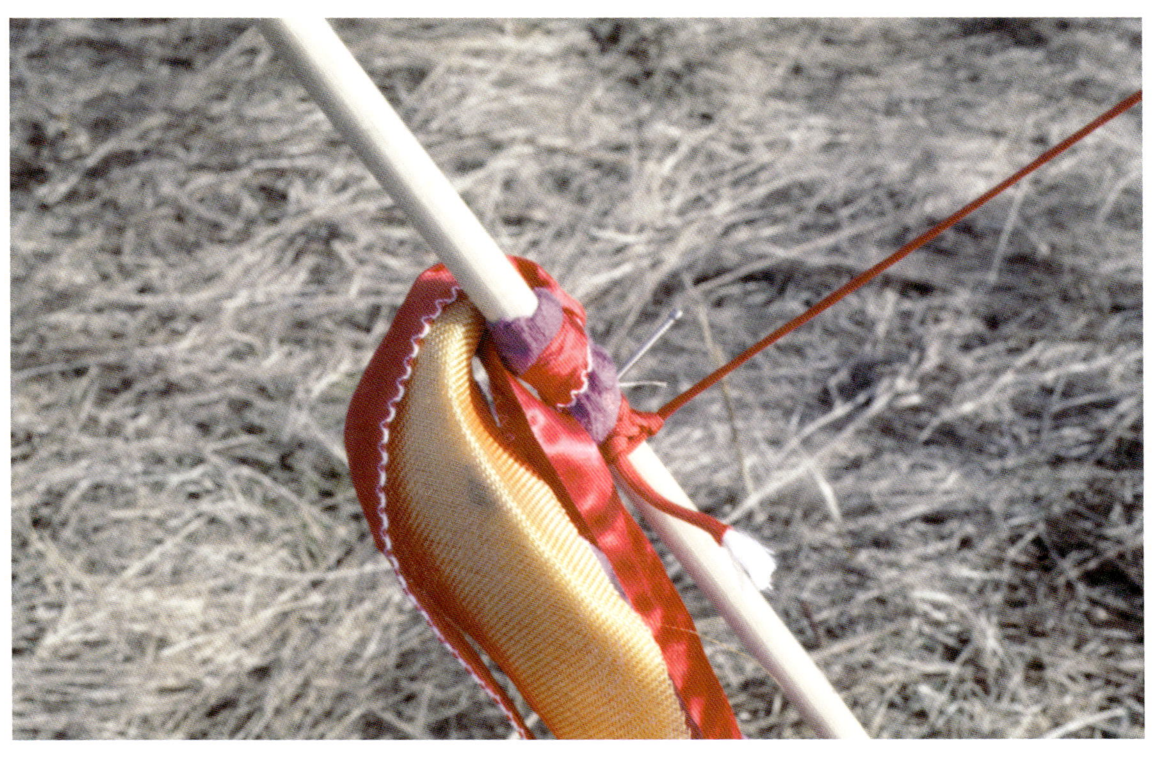

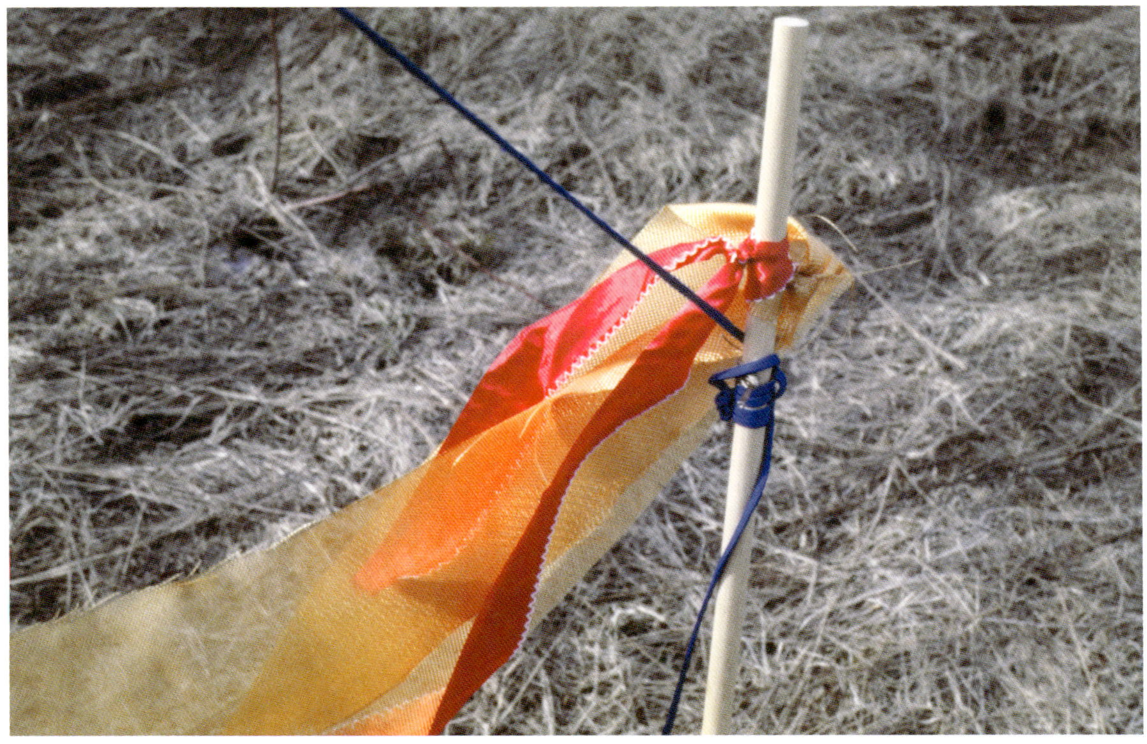

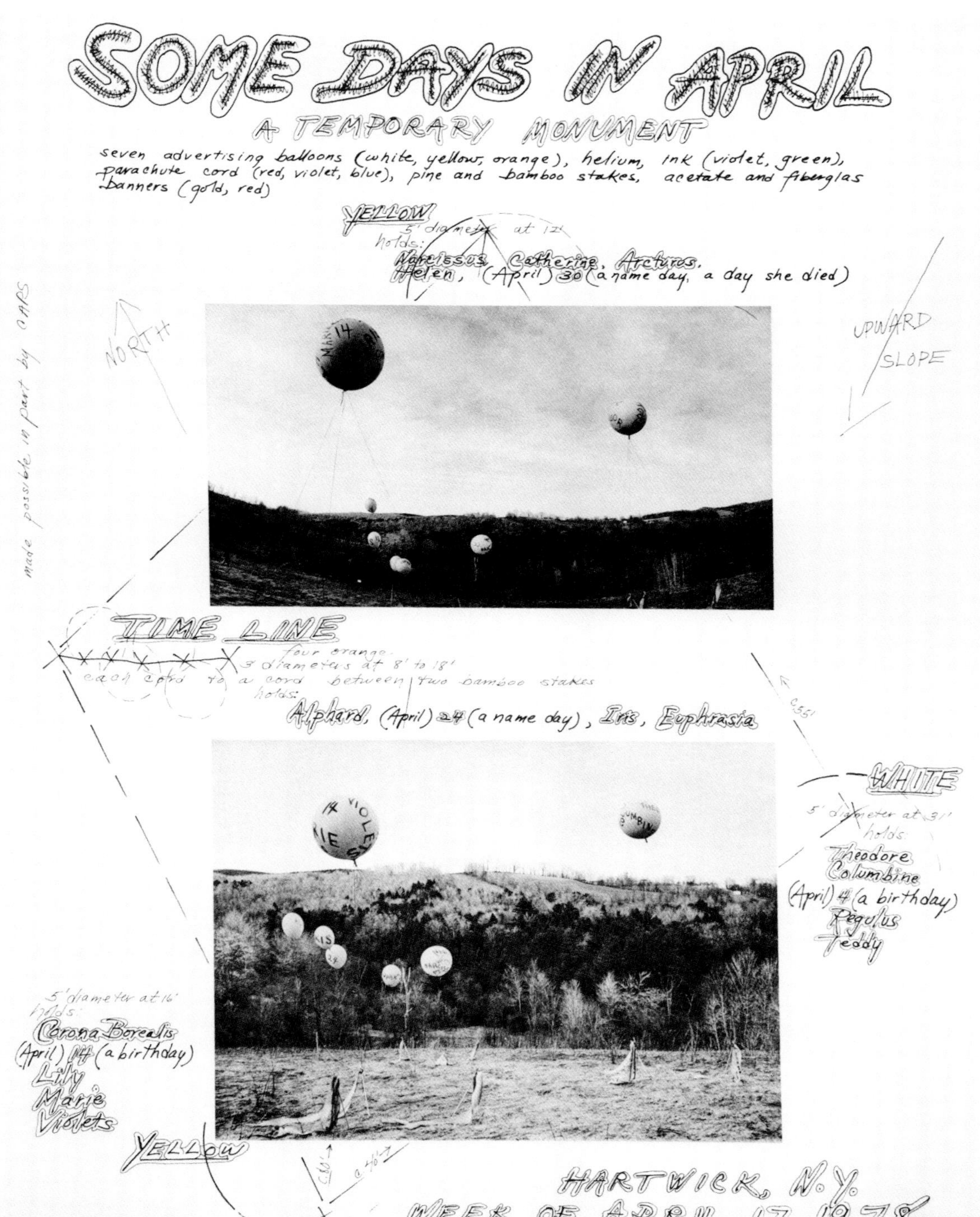

SOME DAYS IN APRIL
A TEMPORARY MONUMENT

seven advertising balloons (white, yellow, orange), helium, ink (violet, green),
parachute cord (red, violet, blue), pine and bamboo stakes, acetate and fiberglas
banners (gold, red)

YELLOW
5' diameter at 12'
holds:
Narcissus, Catherine, Arcturus,
Helen, (April) 30 (a name day, a day she died)

made possible in part by CAPS

NORTH

UPWARD SLOPE

TIME LINE
four orange
3 diameters at 8' to 18'
each cord to a cord between two bamboo stakes
holds:
Alphard, (April) 24 (a name day), Iris, Euphrasia

WHITE
5' diameter at 31'
holds:
Theodore
Columbine
(April) 4 (a birthday)
Regulus
Teddy

5' diameter at 16'
holds:
Corona Borealis
(April) 14 (a birthday)
Lilly
Marie
Violets

YELLOW

HARTWICK, N.Y.
WEEK OF APRIL 17, 1978

© 1978, Rosemary Mayer

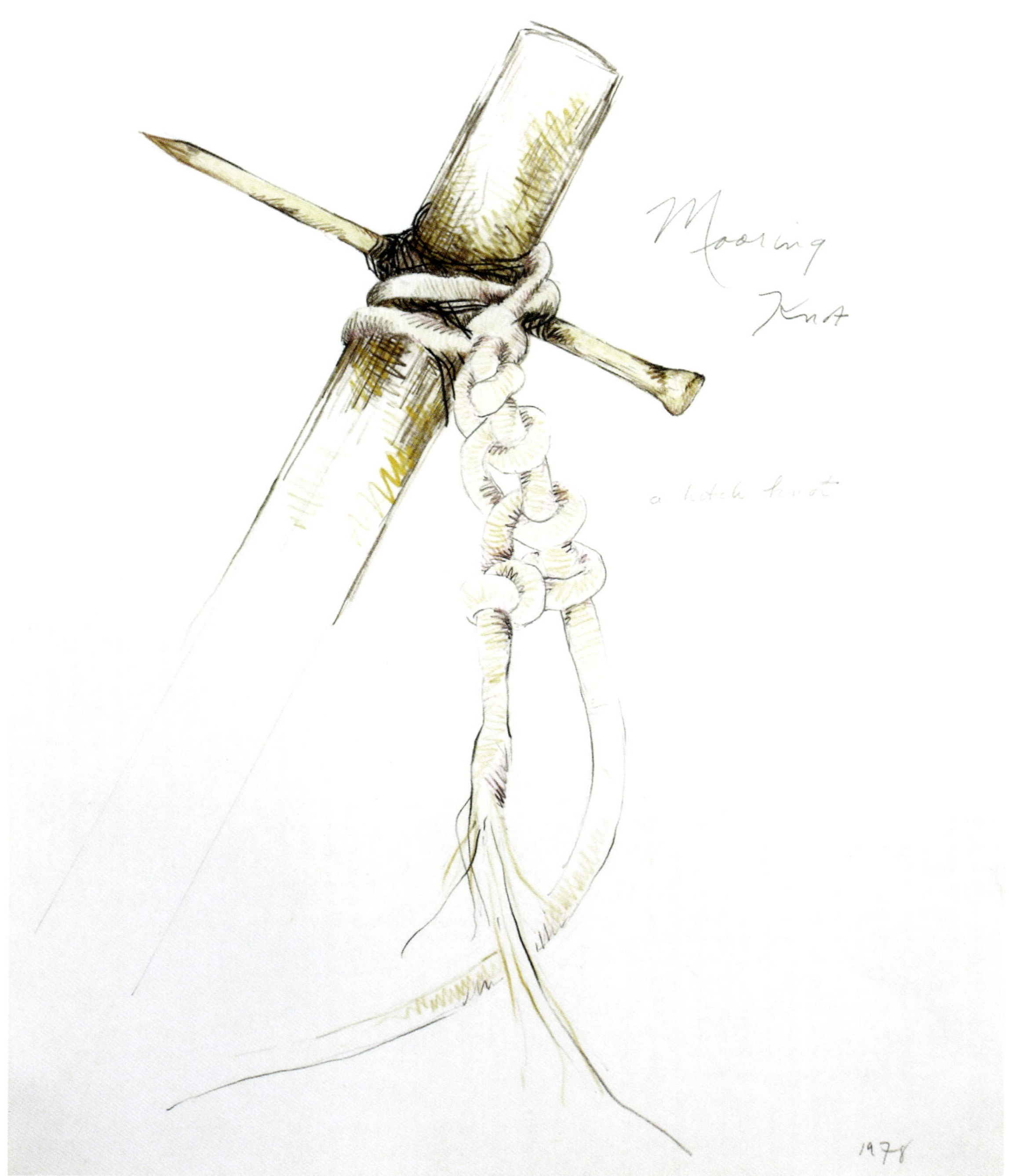

Mooring
Knot
a hitch knot
1978

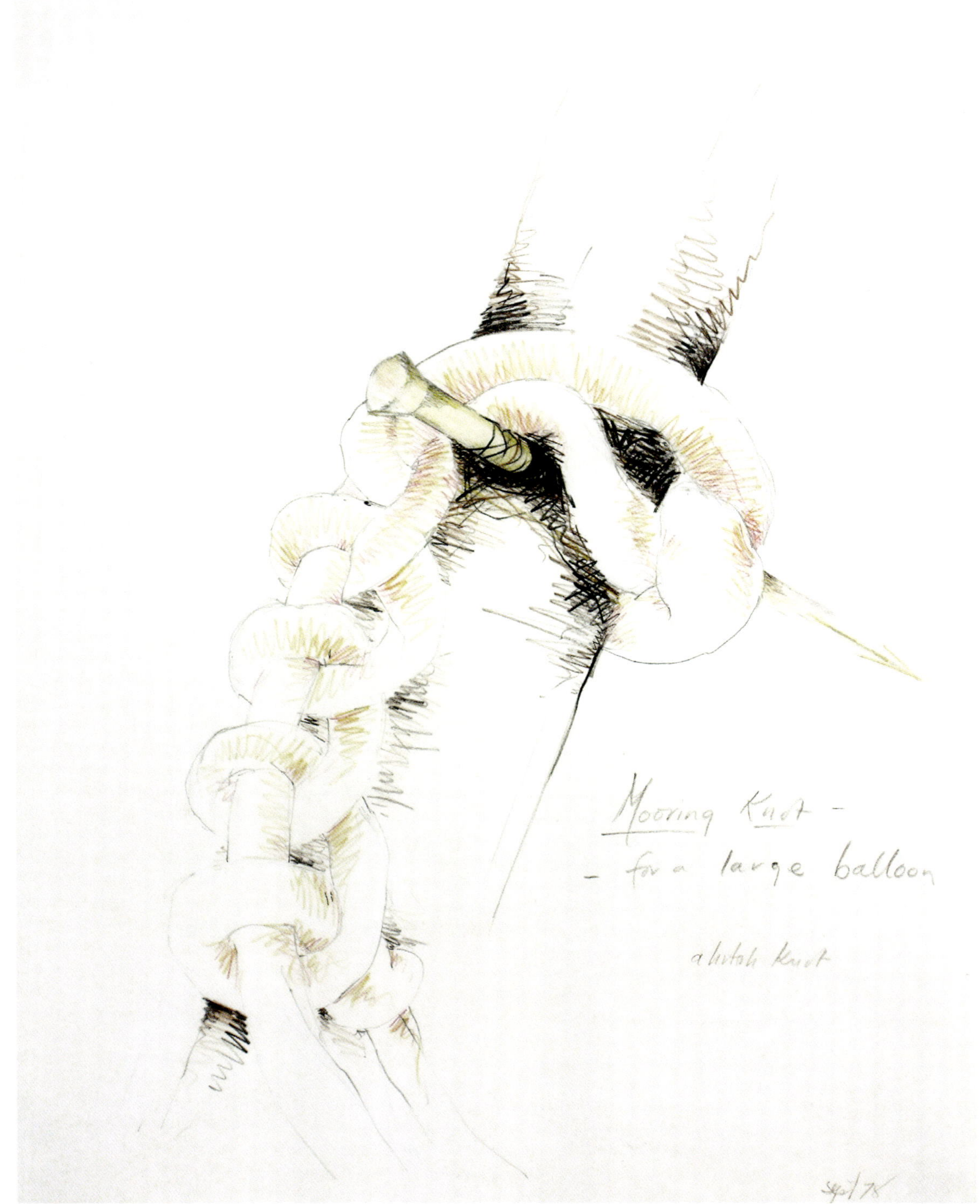

Mooring Knot –
– for a large balloon

a hitch knot

Sept 78

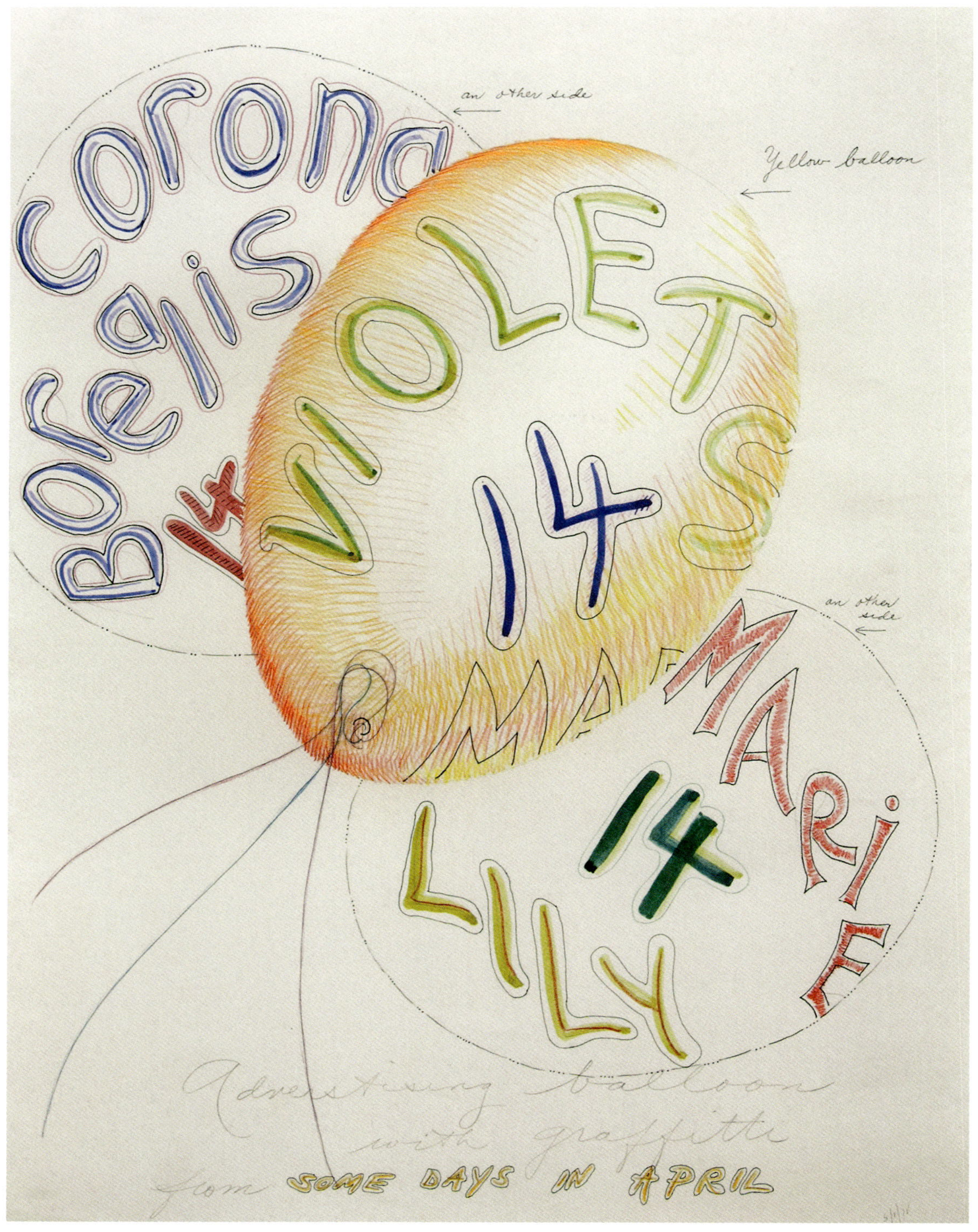

corona
borealis
VIOLET
14
MARMA
MARIE
14
LILY
by
an other side
Yellow balloon
an other side
Advertising balloon
with graffitti
from SOME DAYS IN APRIL

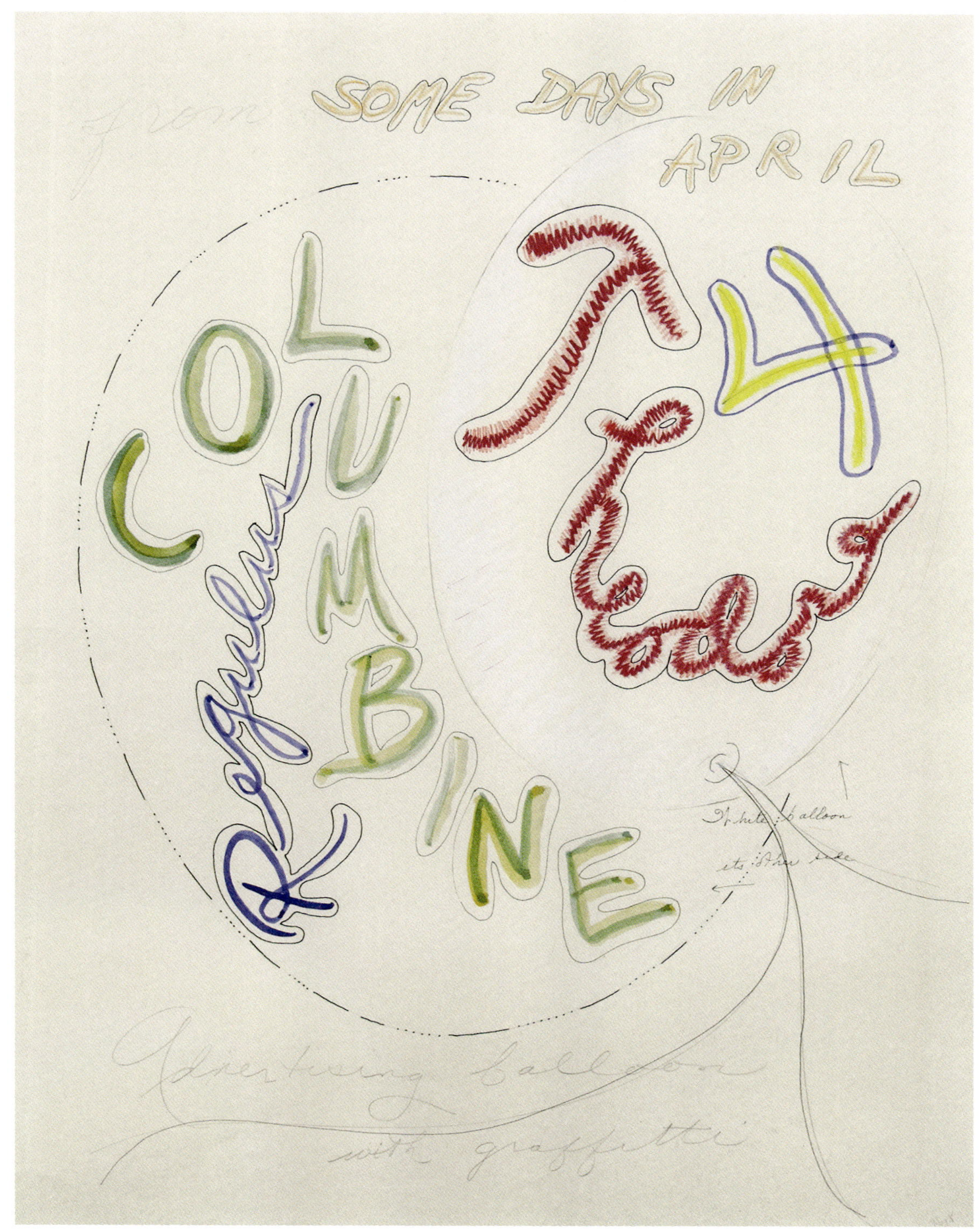
from
SOME DAYS IN
APRIL
COLUMBINE
Regulus
74
White balloon
its other side
Advertising balloon
with graffitti

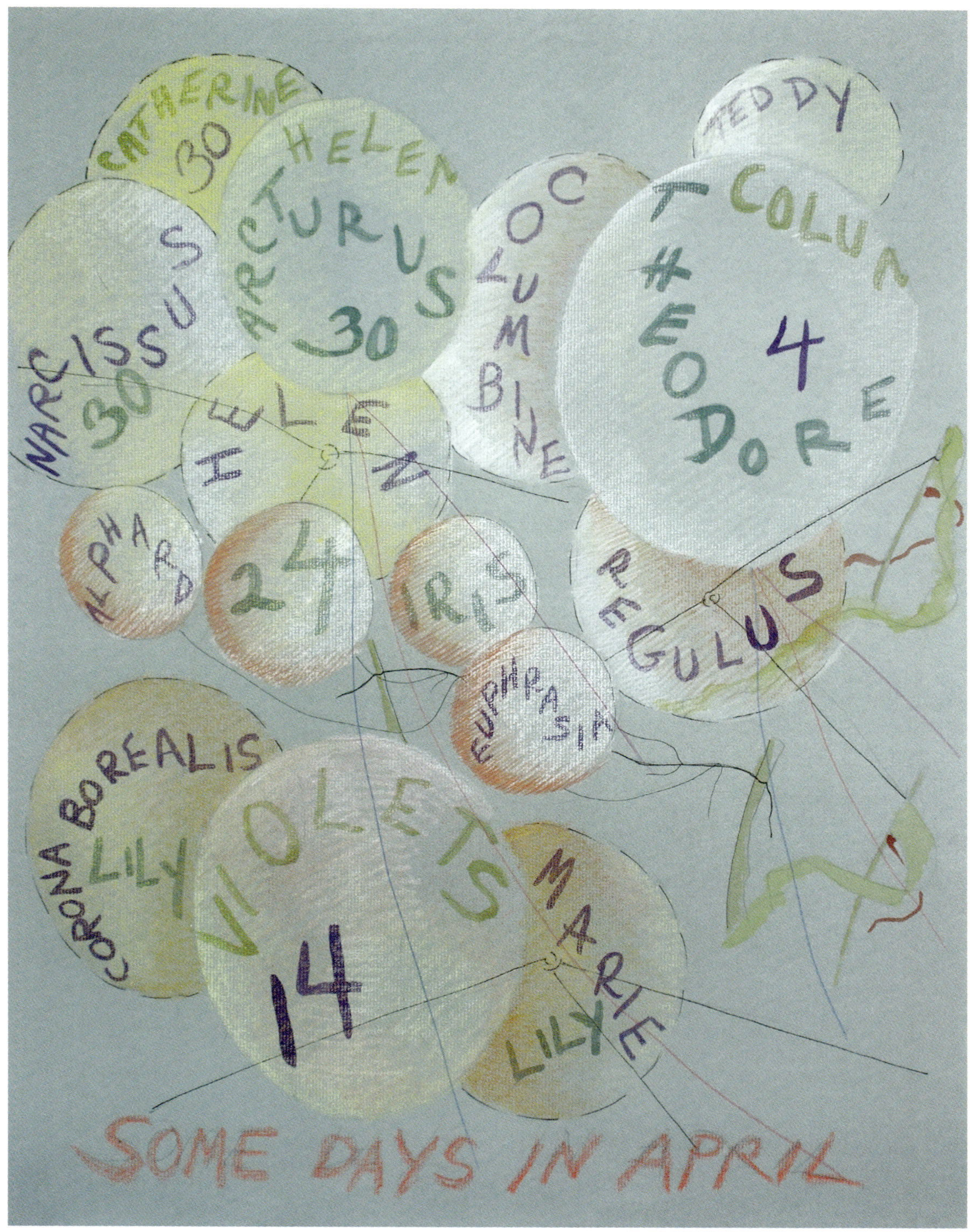

CATHERINE
30
HELEN
ARCTURUS
30
NARCISSUS
30
OCT
COLUMBINE
TEDDY
THEODORE
4
HELEN
24
ALPHARD
IRIS
REGULUS
EUPHRASIA
CORONA BOREALIS
LILY
VIOLETS
14
MARIE
LILY
SOME DAYS IN APRIL

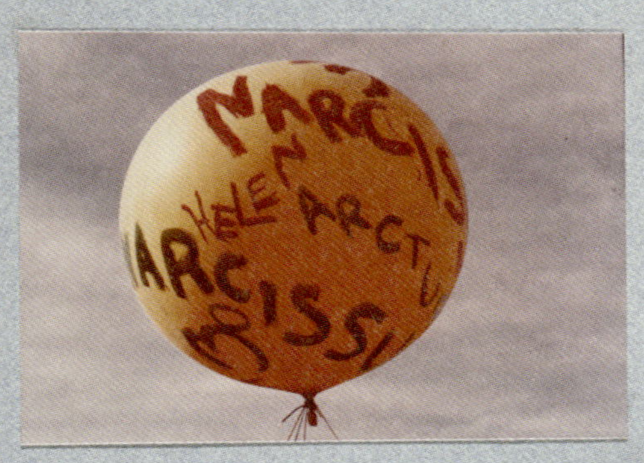

HELEN WAS A REAL BUT UNUSED NAME. SHE
TOLD IT TO SOME OF HER FRIENDS BUT SHE
NEVER USED IT BECAUSE IT WAS THE SAME
AS HER MOTHER'S. SHE HAD CHILDREN OF HER
OWN. SHE USED FLOWERS, THEIR SHAPES, THEIR
NAMES, STRANGE FACTS AND OLD FOLK-LORE
ABOUT THEM IN HER WORK WHICH WAS A KIND
OF PICTORIAL SCULPTURE, WITH WORDS, ON THE
WALLS OF HER STUDIOS, HER GALLERIES, A FEW
MUSEUMS. I DON'T KNOW WHAT DIFFERENCE
APRIL MADE TO HER. I KNOW SUMMER MATTERED
BECAUSE THEN SHE RELAXED AND SOMETIMES TOOK
HER CHILDREN TO THE COUNTRY. I SAW THE FLOW-
ERS SHE MADE ONE SUMMER. SHE PUT THEIR
NAMES ON BANNERS. A FEW YEARS LATER SHE
WAS IN A BAD ACCIDENT. SHE DIED ON THE
THIRTIETH OF APRIL.

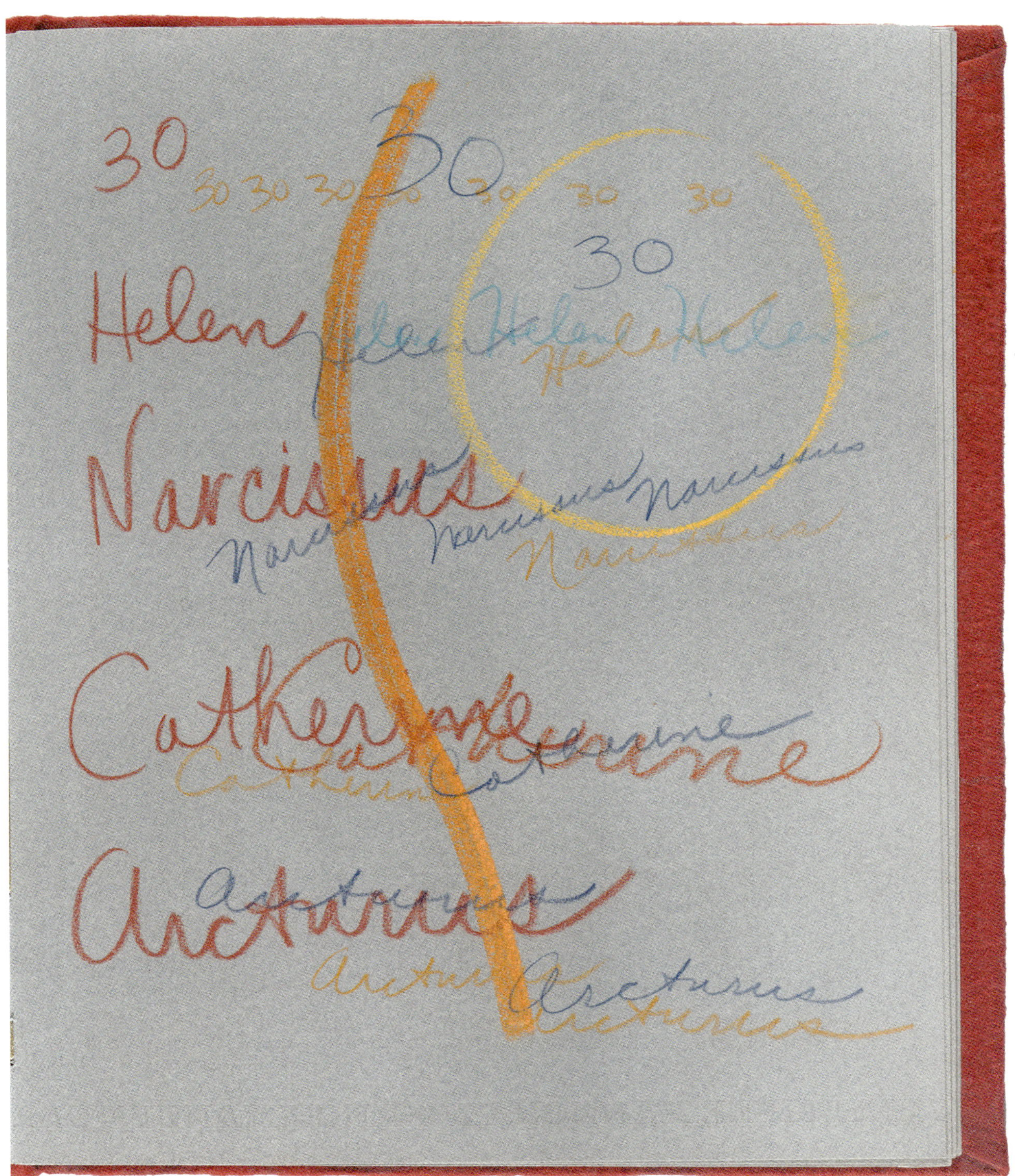

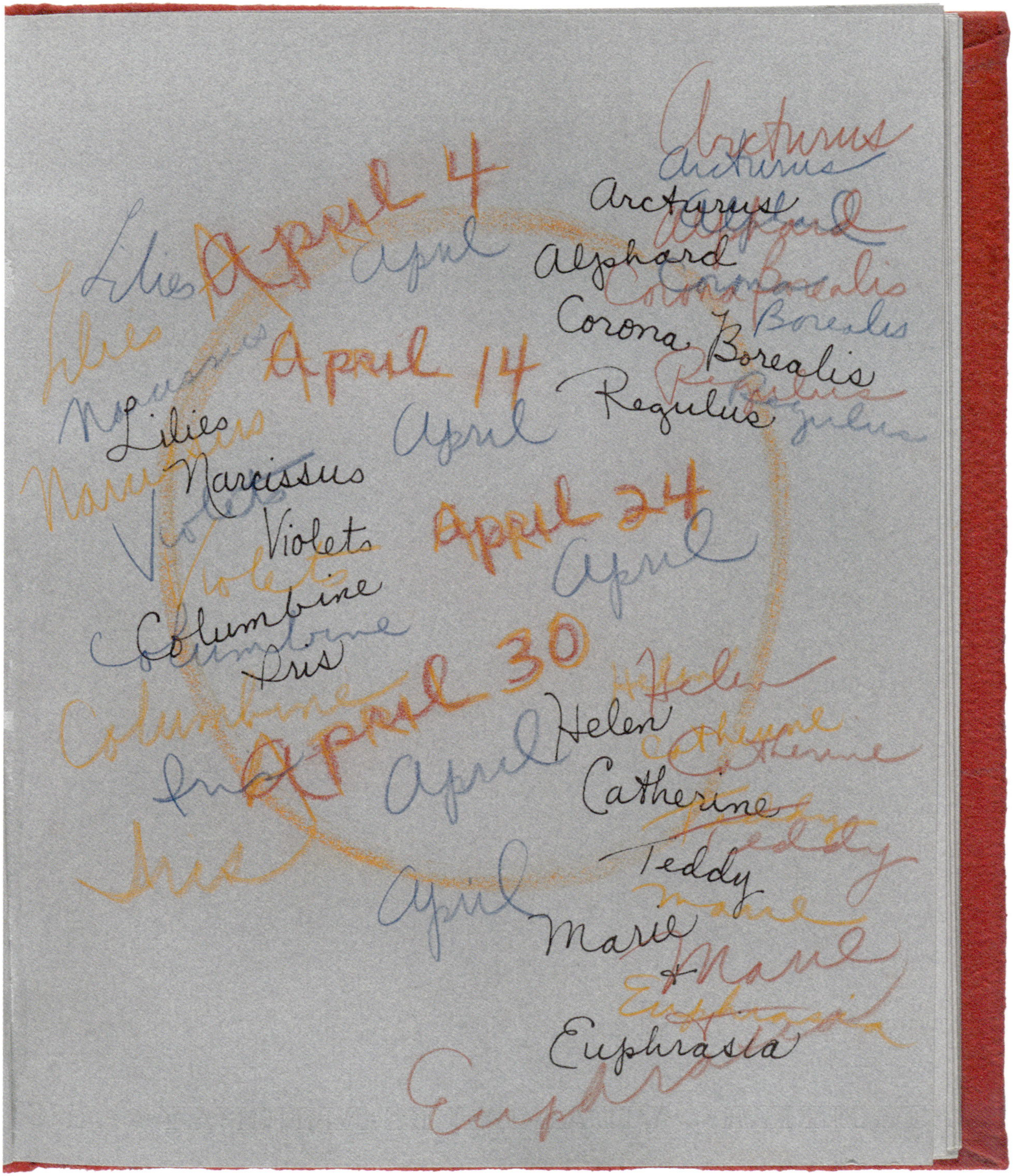

Lilies
April 4
April
Arcturus
Arcturus
Alphard
Corona Borealis
Regulus

Narcissus
April 14
April
Lilies
Narcissus
Violets
Columbine
Iris

April 24
April

Columbine
April 30
April
Helen
Catherine
Teddy
Marie
+ Marie
Euphrasia
End
Iris

April
Euph

THESE WORDS ARE HERE, WERE
THERE, BECAUSE I STILL CONNECT
THEM. YOU WOULD USE OTHER
WORDS, OR DO IT ANOTHER WAY,
OR NOT AT ALL.

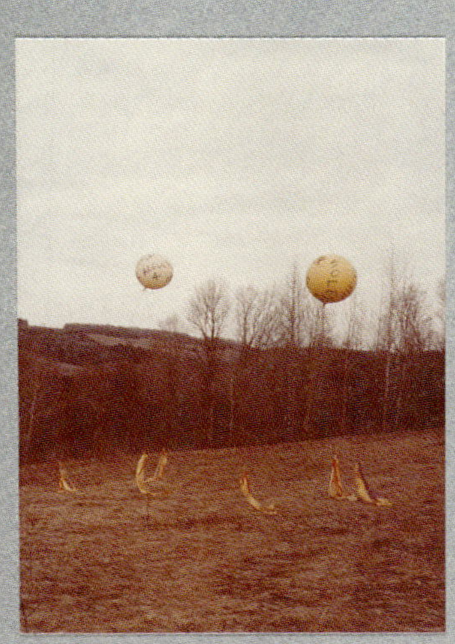

BALLOON FOR A BIRTHDAY

Installed on November 7, 1978
Balloon, helium, paint, rope, and metallic streamers
Rooftop of 461 Park Avenue, New York, New York

Flyer, card, photographs

BALLOON FOR A BIRTHDAY

NOVEMBER 7
CHRYSANTHEMUM
ALDEBARAN
PAUL JOHN MATTHEW

above 461 Park Avenue South
New York City

a work by ROSEMARY MAYER

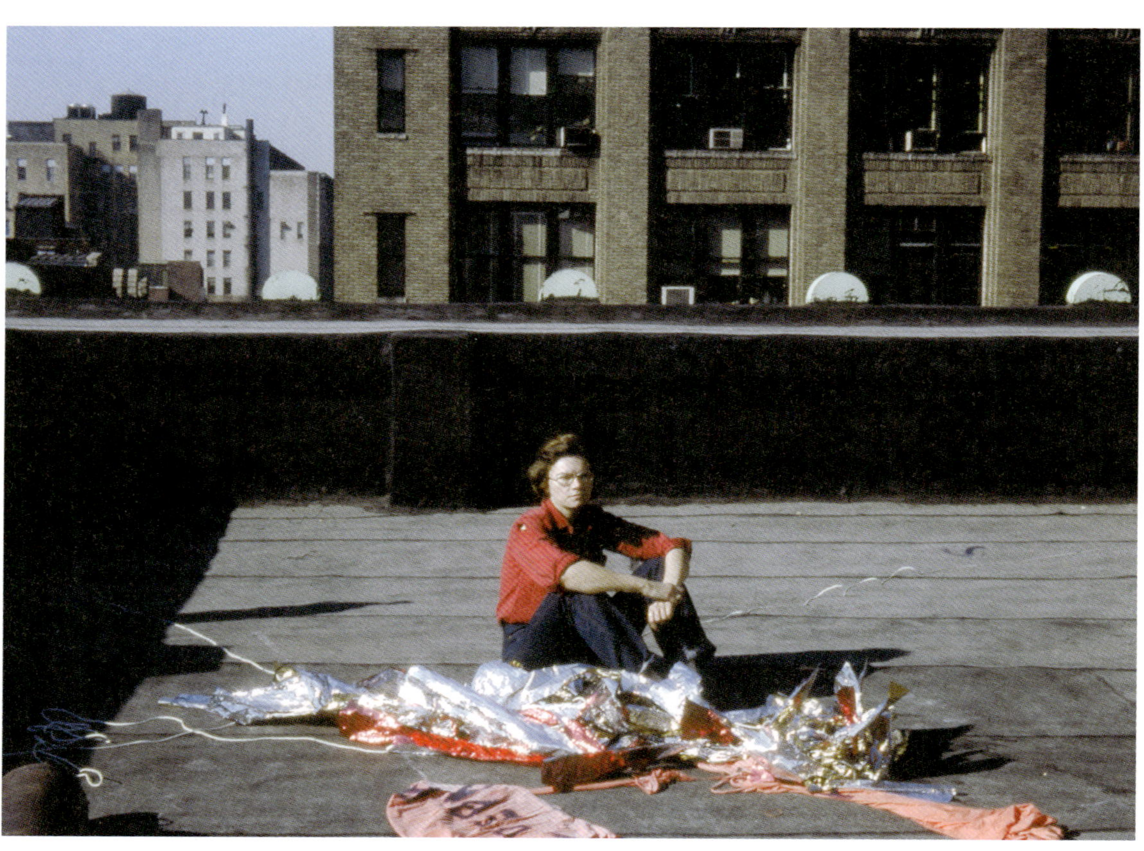

BALLOON FOR A BIRTHDAY

NOVEMBER 7   CHRYSANTHEMUM   PAUL JOHN MATTHEW   ALDEBARAN

The red balloon with words and streamers celebrates

November 7, the birthday of a friend with all of the

names, Paul, Matthew, and John. The balloon connects

the date and the names with chrysanthemums, flowers

blooming in November, and Aldebaran, a bright red star

overhead in November nights.

Once the stars were flowers. Now, anyone can write

on a balloon.

               above 461 Park Avenue South

               New York City

a work by Rosemary Mayer

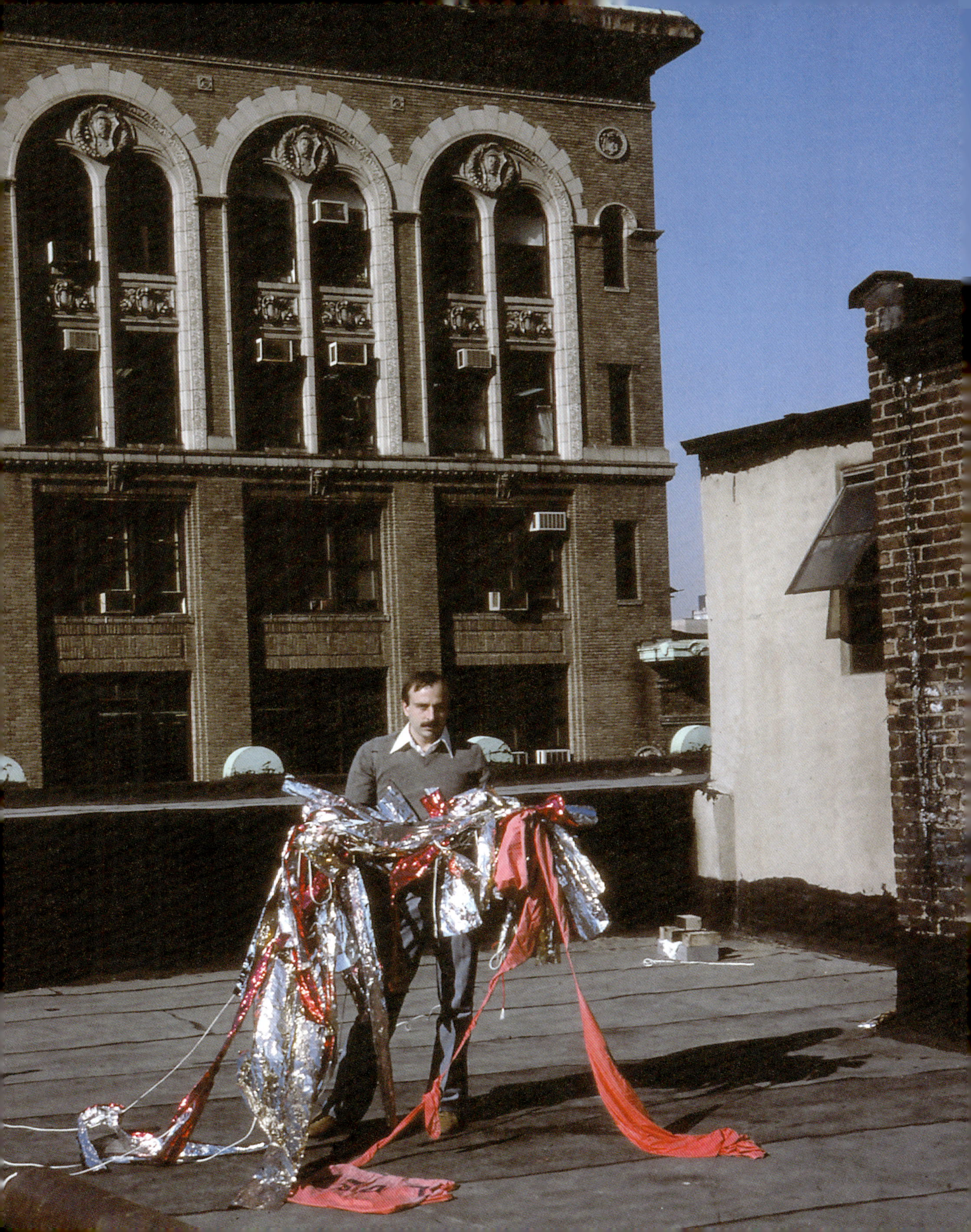

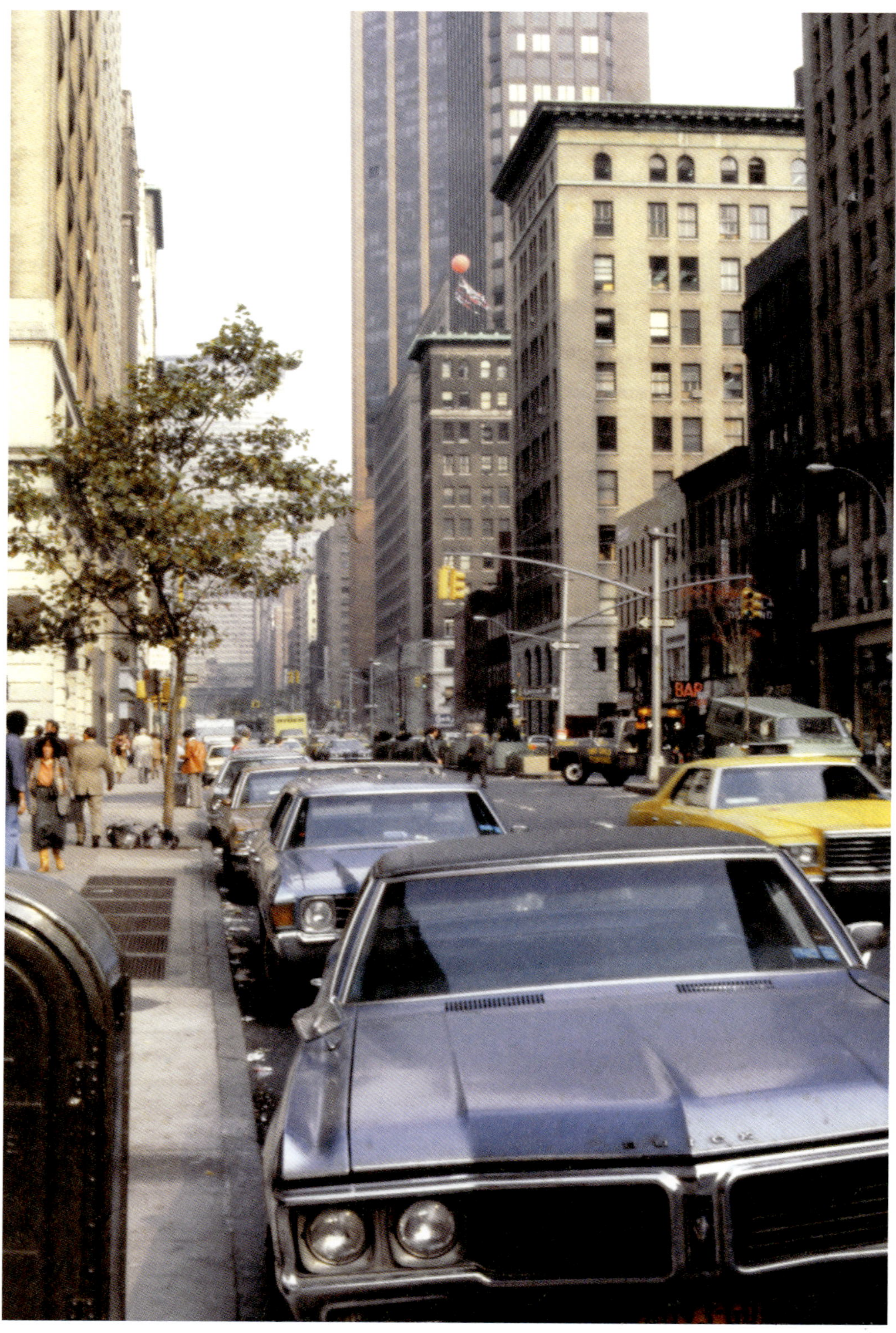

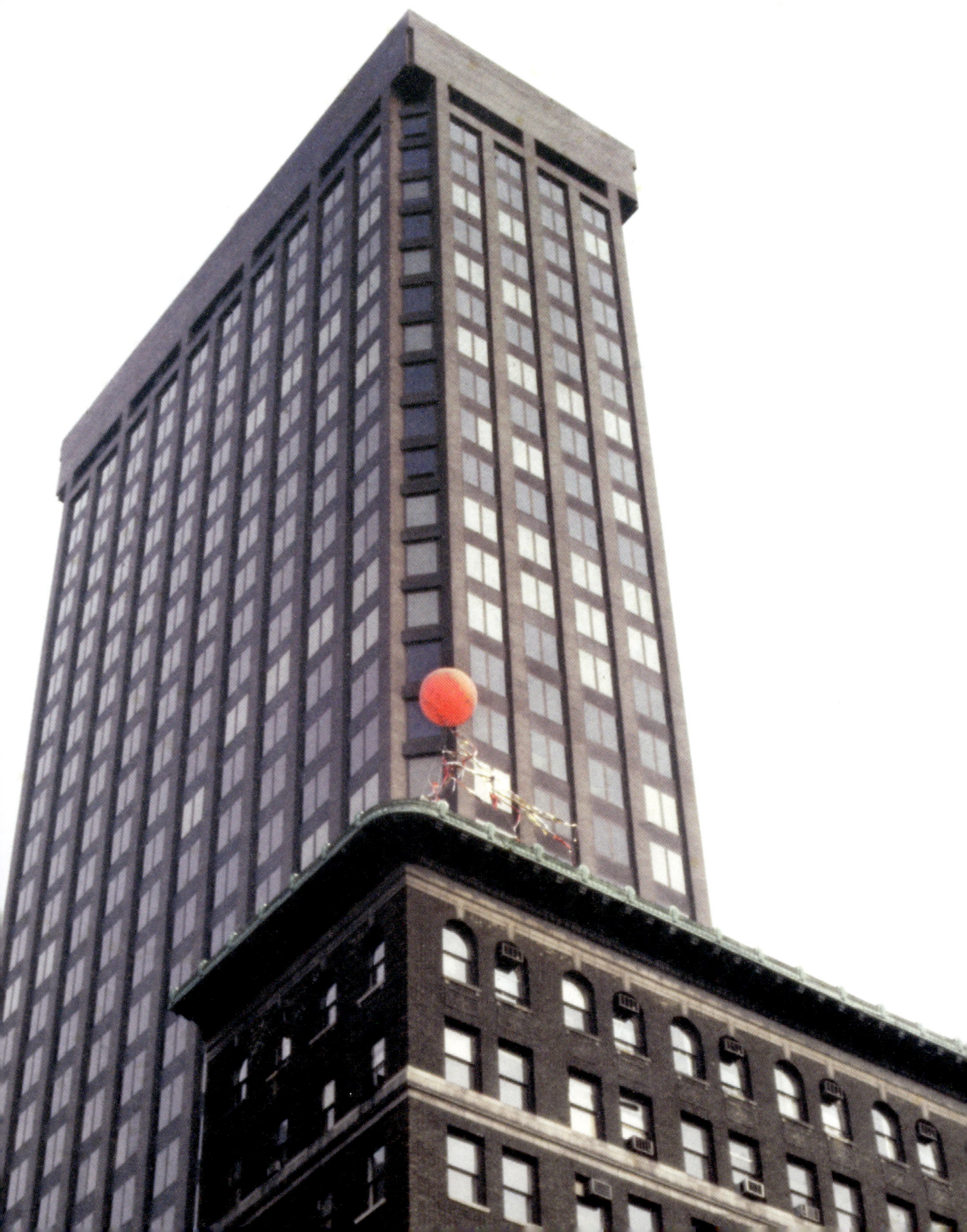

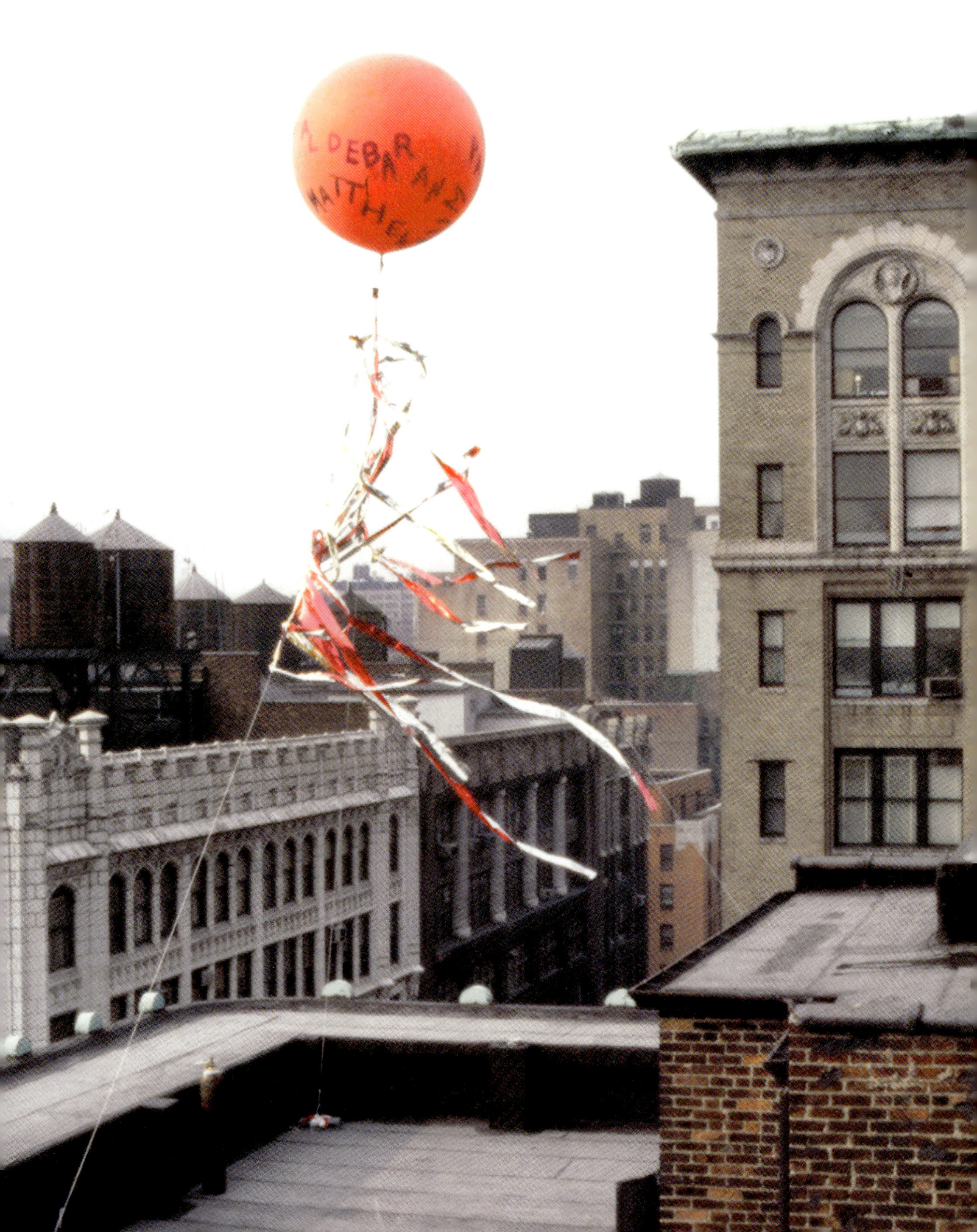
ALDEBAR
MATTHE

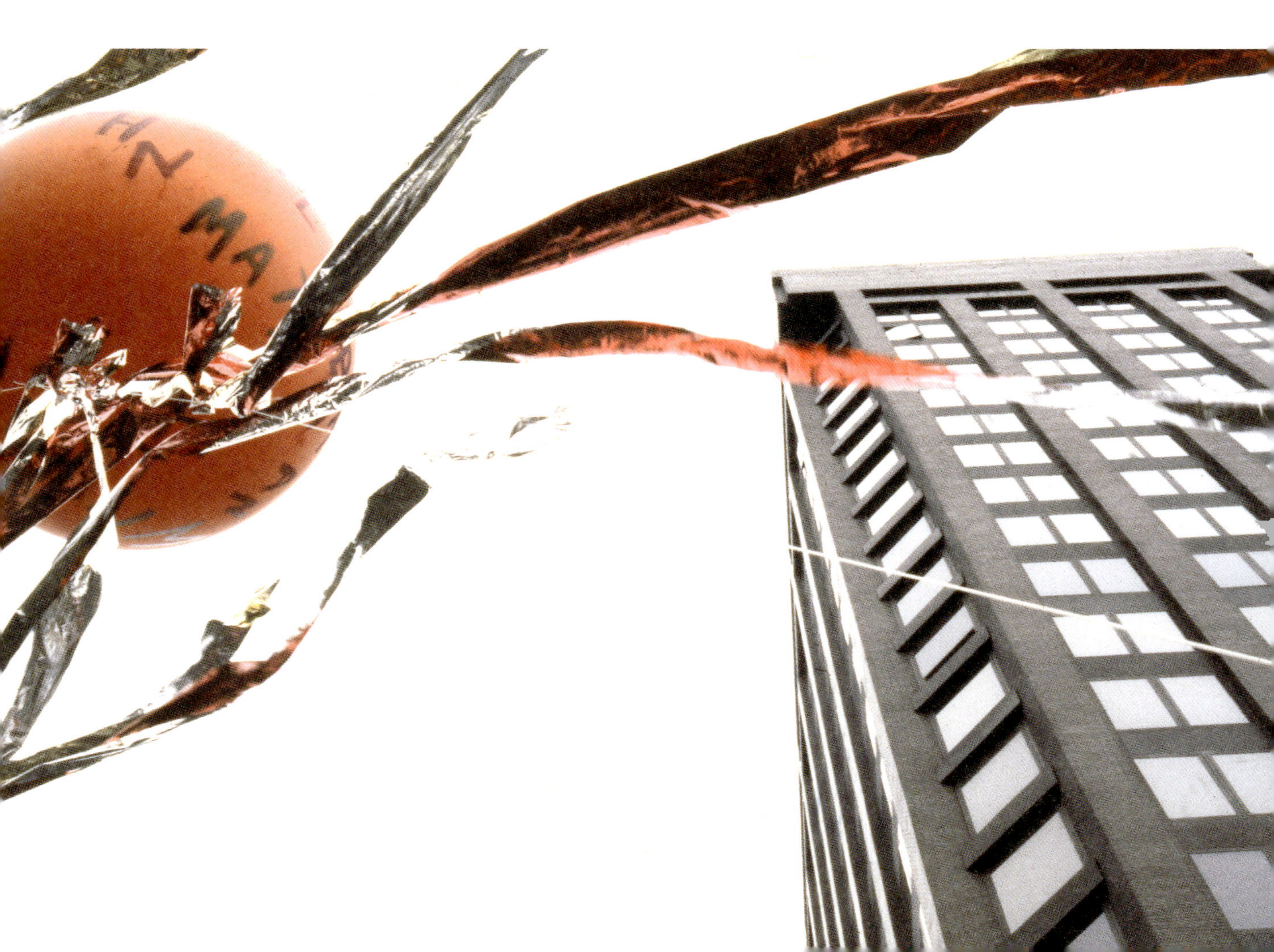

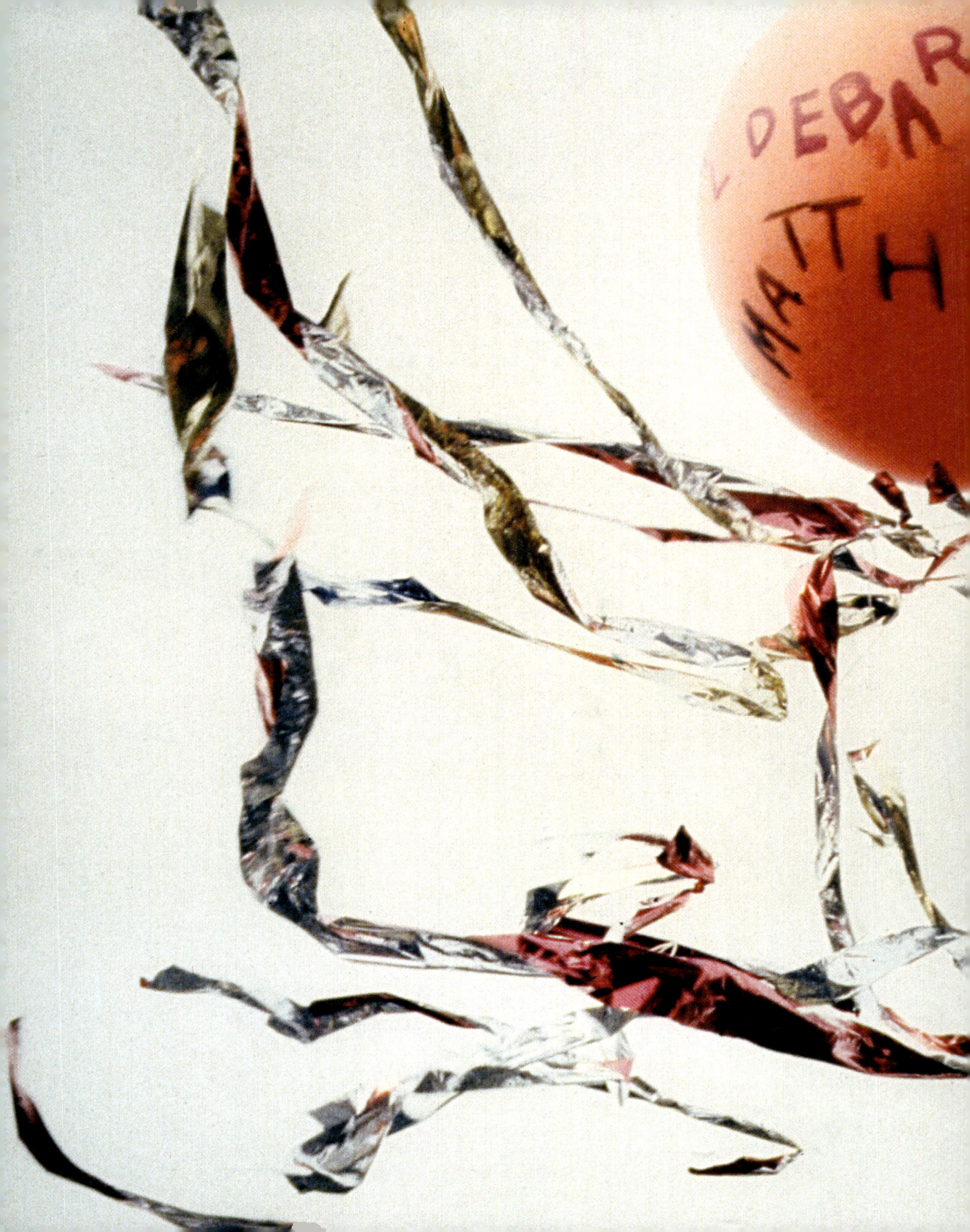
DEBAR
MATTH

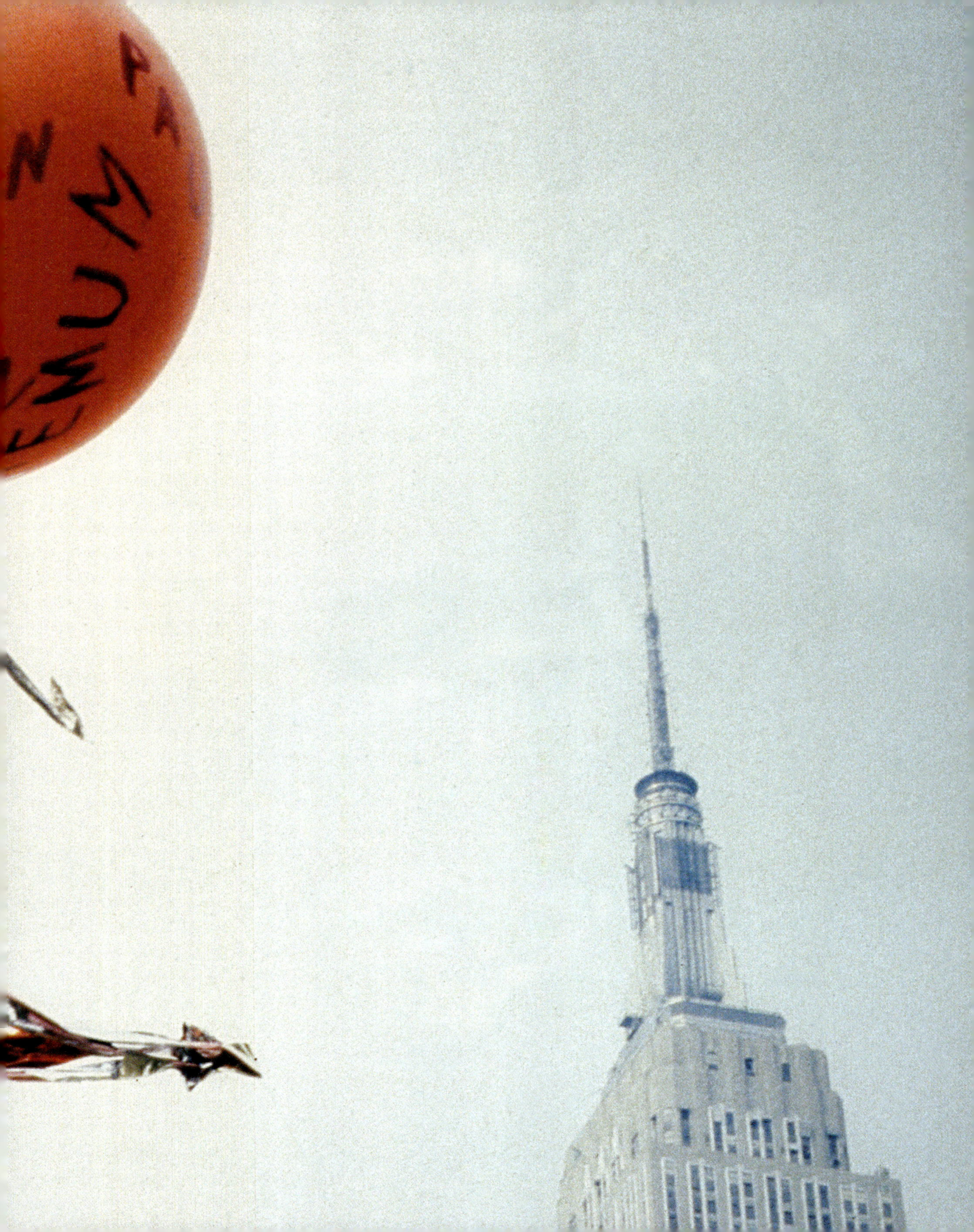
MUM
PA
N

SNOW PEOPLE

Installed during the month of February, 1979
Snow, wood, and paint
Garden of the Lenox Library, Lenox, Massachusetts

Photographs, text, drawings

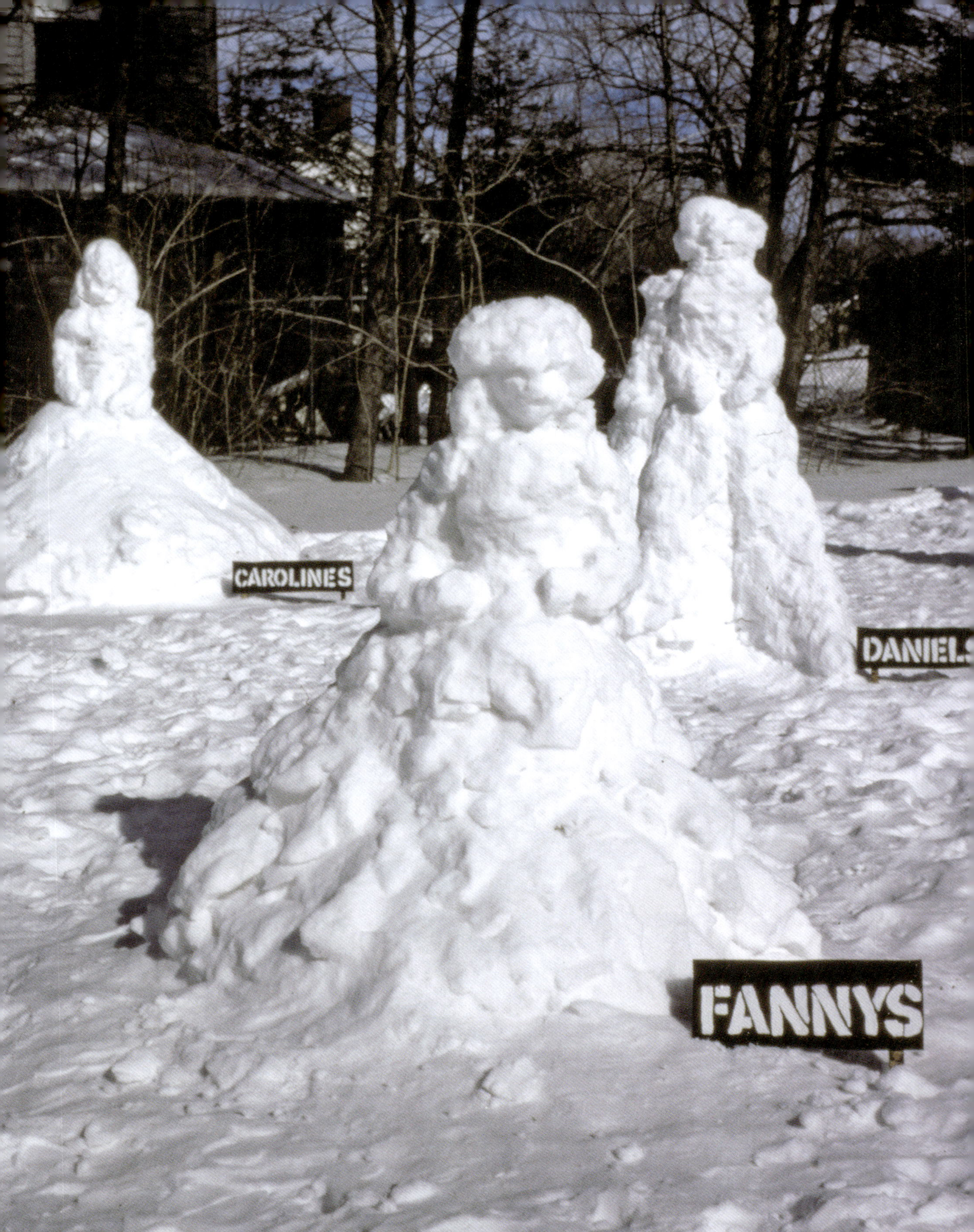

CAROLINES
DANIELS
FANNYS

THOSE

Text published in *WhiteWalls: A Magazine of Writings by Artists*,
No. 5, Winter 1981.

What can I tell you about ghosts? A human figure is the densest sign. Ghosts are fronts, codes for nets of reference spread as wide as words. Balloons can carry words, be deliberate signals for objects forcing connections. Then everything shifts in time and wind and mind.

Once the stars were flowers. Call it August or December the last generation or the next. Light is the time cats have to move in planes of sun on flowered rugs.

Whatever appears gets a name. Hail, sleet, rain, mist and fog fit between clouds and snow or ice on the ground while frost and rime are ices on things which change in sunlight, light from stars, the moon or lamps. The Northern Lights are iridescent pastels like lavender marsh gas over wet sand or gravel which are points between rocks and dust. Enough heat, light, changes sand to glass, a different point along other spectrums, events for different senses. Then there are other planets and different stars.

Always add time. It could be a wooden ladle and the handle will be greasy from jelly boiled out of mosses or the gelatin in bones. It moves in the cauldron. I left that out. If witches and fates weren't on mountains they were by the warm bogs and marshes where fetid clouds of lavender and dim green gases are old breaths.

The moon waxes full. People wax strong or seasons, from one stage to another, thicken or thinning. In a fairy tale, four men steal the moon. They hang it in a tree and let people use its light until they die. Then each one has a moon quarter buried with him. It gets darker. It's a moonless night outside of town, in a small, low-ceilinged room where it's mostly dark around a glass lamp for kerosene or some candles, or a hollow stone or a shell with a wick and fish oil in a room made from adobe or sun-dried bricks. There's a full moon and it lays out a window white on the floor or over the floor and the bed and table until clouds cover the moon, wind changes the flame on the wick.

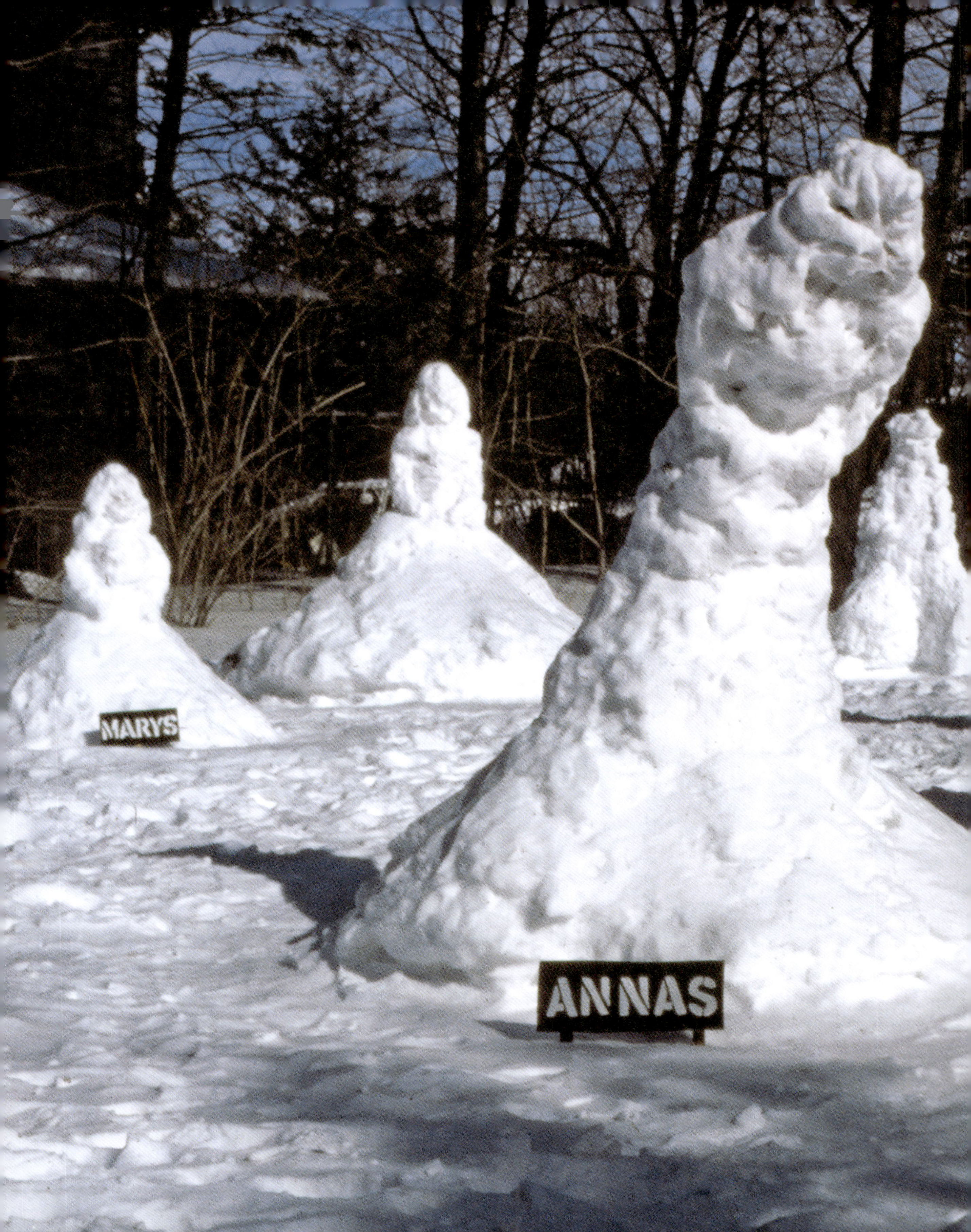
MARYS
ANNAS

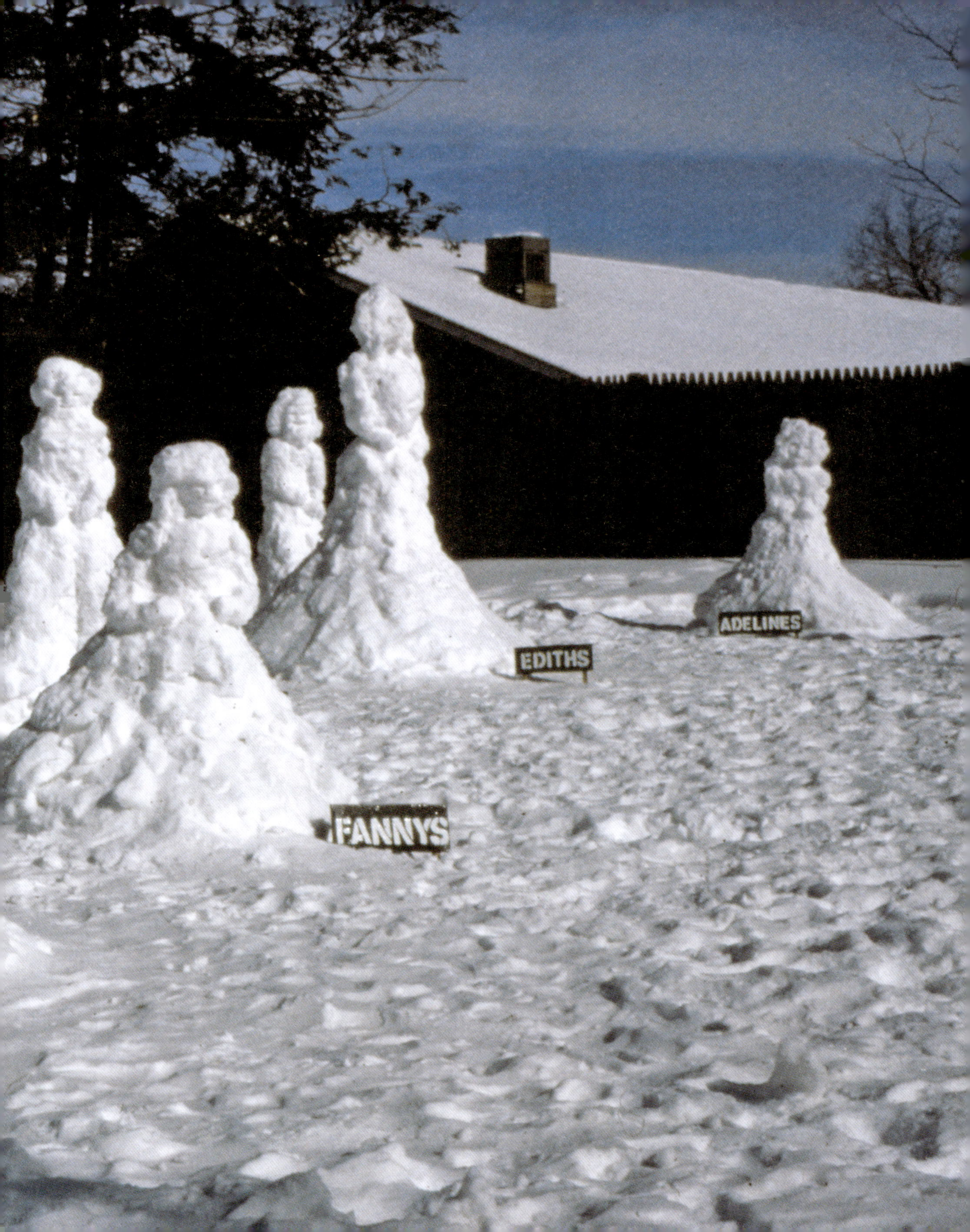
FANNYS
EDITHS
ADELINES

The hottest stars are blue-white. Summer is heat which is a different white in the air than snow in winter. Fall has colors and spring but snow is the most of winter, cold embodied in greyed white, maybe pale blue-violet, but dim and translucent like wax in the figure of a dead queen or a dancer, the death mask of a king or a famous killer. Northern February snow holds the ground, ice for skaters' ponds over whole towns and thick like the cheap glass of old sewing lamps.

You could be Caroline, Edith, or William, have lived long winters with white moons lighting the glassed over ground at night. The moons in January are the Wolf and the Snow Moon. The Wolf Moon's name is for the long shadows of wolves in its light over snow. The last winter moons are the Worm and the Sap Moons. It takes months for sunlight to turn out the leaves on trees. One afternoon it can rain on the tough buds of forsythia. At dawn ice will mark out the shapes of leaves and branches, make frosted arches low with glaze, rimed buds, and bending over roads. Then sunlight beads the ice with water, makes mud by noon.

Ice is food for summer. Once there were houses for ice, sometimes partly underground, to store food in the cold from the last winter. For the ruling classes of the ancient Near East, or for the wealthy in Roman cities, boats packed with ice from the mountains sailed or were rowed down rivers or along the coasts of small seas to load on flowers, fish, or fruit to send to the people who could buy it. That's ice from Earth preserved, bits of the ice caps or the glazes from mountain peaks. The ice on Mars is from different chemicals. Martians are crystalline; their cities are glass. There is no lightning and it never rains.

Glass is forever. That's not true. Glass eyes break; lenses for telescopes crack; crystal decanters can shatter. Glass in Egypt was blue, red, and yellow. The Romans had these colors and purple and brown. Glass breaks faster than snow melts though snow changes fast even if we have catalogues of snow crystal patterns before it leads to high rivers and the mud which can be a toy. It becomes anything when a child at the end of winter begins to play in the damp garden. She can build mud cities, channels for rivers, bridges that replace the melted snow forts, the white figures of people and animals. Children make what they need with whatever they have. They use analogies, fill in stories, supply a history with any missing details.

Medieval glassmakers followed the wood. They worked in isolation,

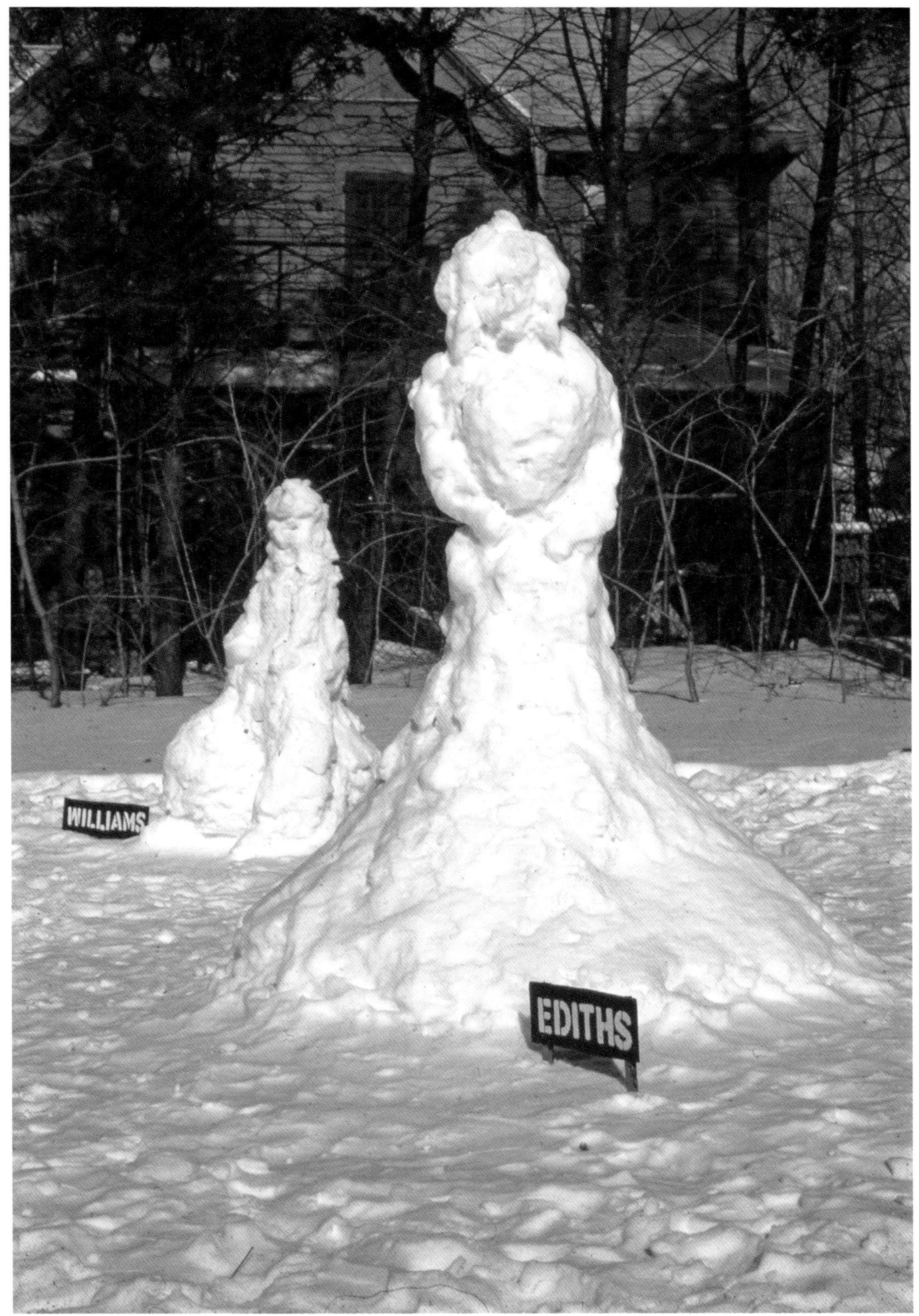
WILLIAMS
EDITHS

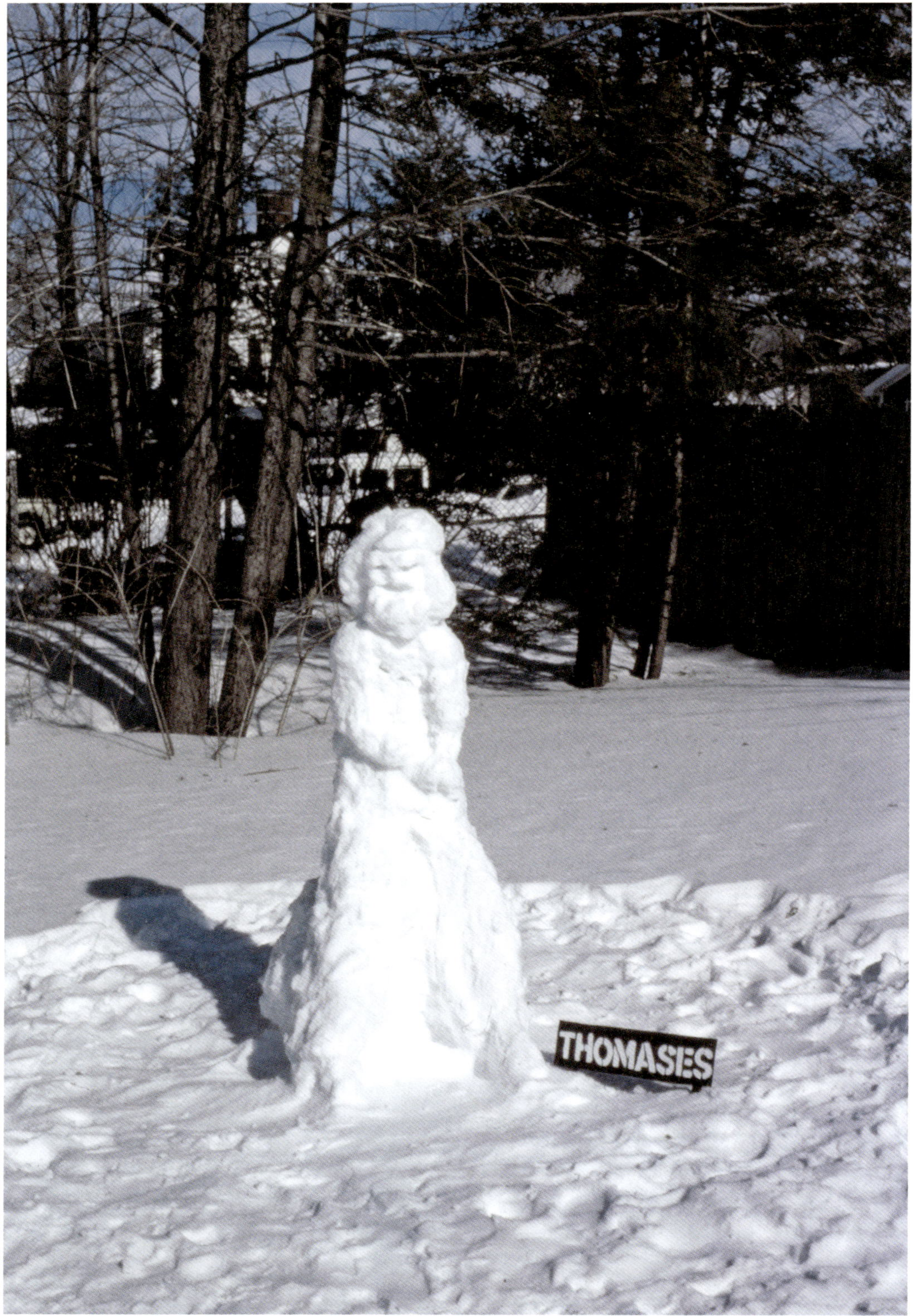
THOMASES

mostly in forests where there was enough wood to heat furnaces and keep them going. The industry of antiquity became a rare and secret craft.

It's like the sun on women's hair in Venice. They washed it in secret solutions, then went up on their roofs with special hats. The hats had no crowns, only wide brims. They parted their hair down the centers of their heads, put on their open hats and waited for the sun to redden the roots of their hair.

We're talking about spring, heat and mud. There was once a theory that spring opened the shrunken seeds of old diseases fought off in fall and winter. April opens flowers, windows and doors. Leaves enlarge to darker greens. You can sleep without a blanket when a May full moon makes a blue-white bed. Once in a summer I saw the Northern Lights. I thought all the clocks were wrong until I realized what it was. It was a yellow-white glow that didn't change. Polar explorers describe curtains of shifting color so enormous you can hear the layers rustle.

Marsh gas is said to be a glow and a fog that seems to be dimly on fire. He said it was lavender and almost not there. It was dusk and the bugs were coming out. Maybe it was the heat accumulated over the long hot summer day but the smell was rotten. He said it was decaying plants and the color and light was the force of their rotting. You never walked in it. Who could be sure of a bottom? It went on for a few hundred yards, lavender, floating in clouds for ten and twenty feet.

The materials that people once burned for light, that kept wicks and torches in flames, left smells or smoke. The rare sweet smells were from beeswax and pale green bayberry. Candlewood was pieces of resinous pitch pine. In the poorest houses they were upright, stuck into the edges of the wood and the ashes on the hearth for light. Lamps were metal containers for oil and a fiber wick. The flame was open. The lamps hung on a small chain from a low beam or they had a bracket into the wall. The burning oil smoked on the wick. The wick crusted over and the light went out.

Tallow candles were made in autumn after the animals were killed. The fat from sheep and oxen was boiled in a kettle, poured into molds. You could use the same molds for the fatty wax boiled out of bayberries.

Paraffin has no taste or smell. Besides little night lights, old vigil lights, it seals jars of preserved food, is part of salves to soothe weathered skin.

Paraffin is cheap; it's the processed decay of plants and animals, a residue from processed oil. It might have been marsh gas. Kerosene has the same source. Glass is a frozen liquid, a metal fused from sand and an alkali. The oldest glass is green.

In this town we're in under Northern Lights, surrounded by southern marshes, with snow, up river, by red sand and ice, with white summers and ice houses, a candelabra with festoons of cut glass pendants is a beautiful thing for the wealthy. There were a few houses and barns and shops, a school, a church, and the fields where people grew food. At night it was dark except for some light behind windows or the moon. There were children, animals, hunting, cooking, sewing, harvesting, preserving food, weaving cloth, making furniture, meals, barns. Lamps were metal and then glass. They burned oil from fish, then kerosene. Candles were made from tallow or bayberries. Rarely there were elegant candles from beeswax, or later, many plain tapers from paraffin.

You can keep a clear idea of the relations between seasons and things, days, people and places. There are always names. Use them and then count. The order of occurrence is always the same though durations might vary. These are names for incidents and stages, even for unusual lengths. The numbers can reach can differ or when you might mark a change, switch to another name. For example, everything's different if you don't sleep. Time is slow and there's no humor and it's too bright. Almost always you can tell seasons because you feel the air. In some there are smells of flowers, damp ground or trees, smoke from chimneys or burning leaves. The sun is high or low in the sky. At night there are lights in windows or none or a moon.

Things happen. It can be hard to point out a beginning, which is another, and, or where, if, any might possibly crest, ebb, or if they ever end. Any situation lacks clarity, places for old words. Open your eyes and listen. That's a trilobite there, on the table, the thin oval, like a flat, black stone. I bought it in Arizona for a dollar. We say it was a live creature, was dead, crushed, buried, changed, gone, found, sold, and now we see it because we know what it is or was.

Pet animals always indoors watch endless events. Babies stare. Glaciers move through a year and for years, slowly or with a great speed, or they did once, breaking in pieces or enlarging, or the pieces enlarge or shrink, or some of them do. A shelf of rocks or a layer of compacted soil becomes denser in millennia or blows away in finer and finer particles

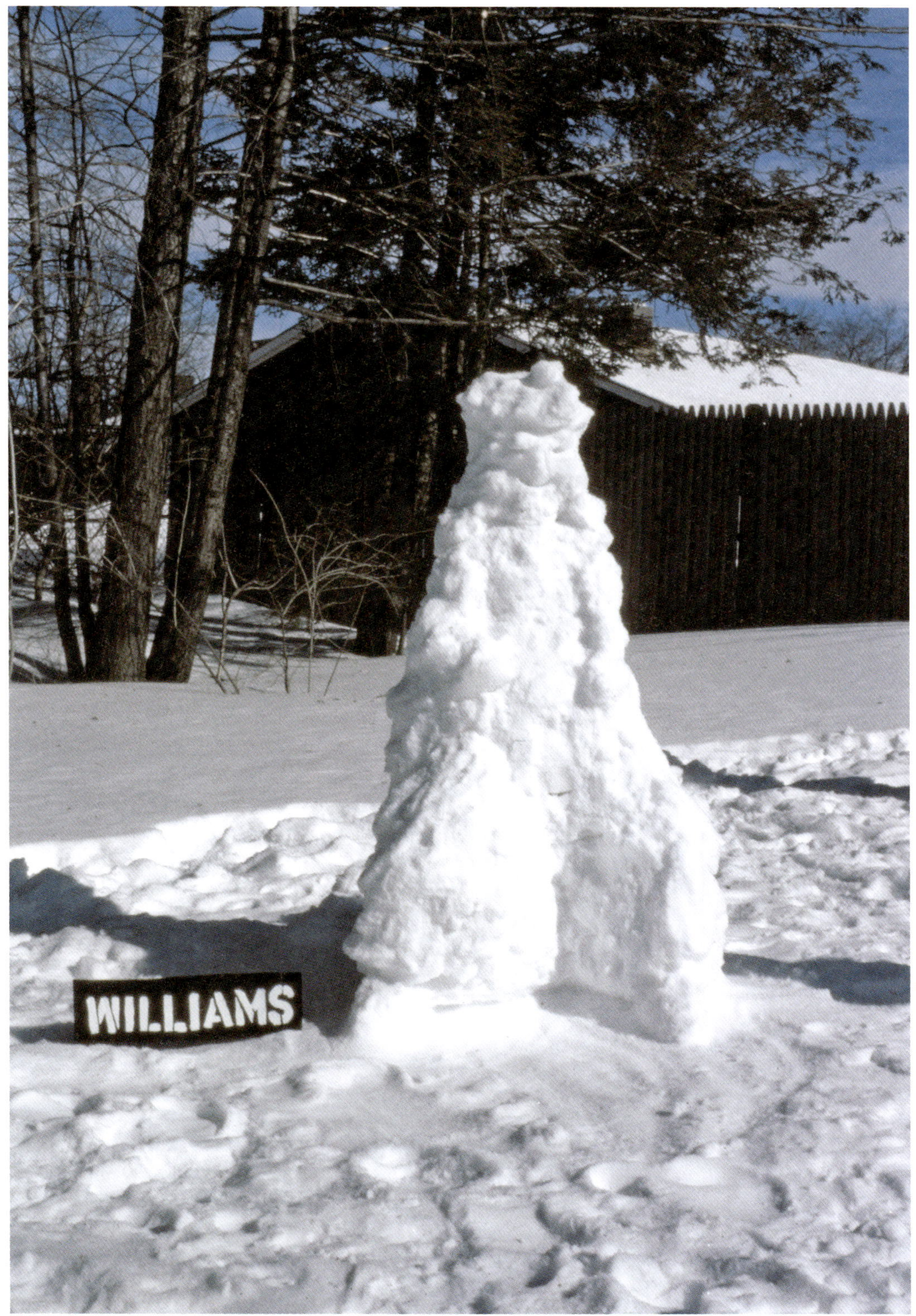
WILLIAMS

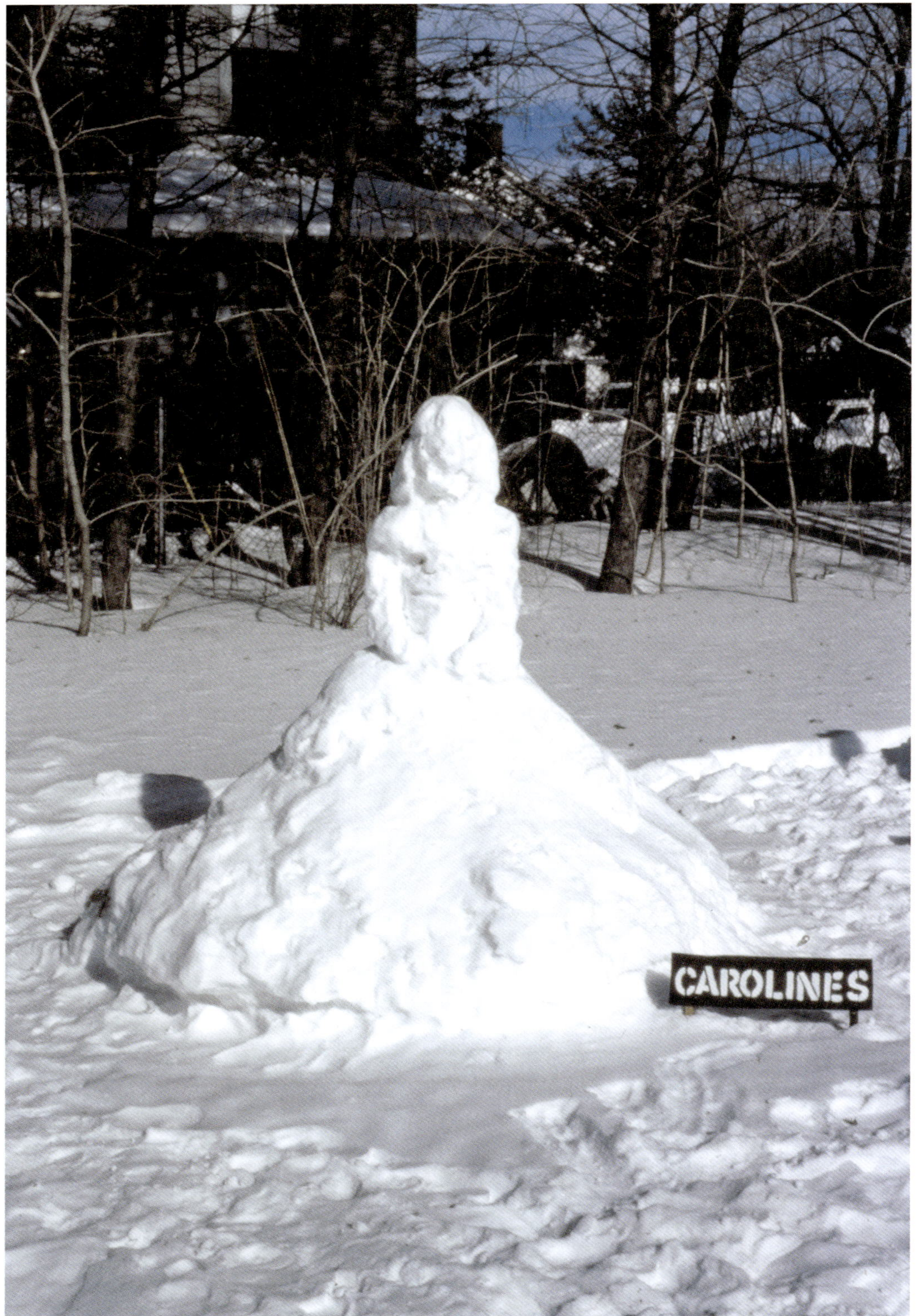
CAROLINES

as slowly as animals change or anemones, more or less toes, new petals or different teeth, or they breathe in water. Or maybe all the charts that put the new forms and times in an order are other cases of leeches or Ptolemy's spheres.

What's Jupiter or Mars? Could be frozen red or yellow balls of striped dust and frozen gases or molten methane and ammonia, or carbon, oxygen and hydrogen powdered so dry a fantasy writer could have you with descriptions of their high, crisp sounds, the red sand whirling up over the edges of craters or mountains with ages in number systems from some other mind. There are clouds and volcanoes on planets and moons even if the colors, the matter, directions, durations, all their aspects are different than any exploding mountains on earth, any tornado still winding in the outer tides of Jupiter or Saturn. Their end is dispersed, could be the background noise, the last detectable resonance, and there's no hint it ends there, any more than there is a point on the edge of a ball of warming gas where the gas stops.

Rocks are markers. They lead back to sand, record movements, heat and cold, pressures over years, forces that make colors or how a material cracks.

Saturn looks brown or yellow to us with a little red. Jupiter is hotter and red and orange and yellow with many moons but no rings. Where we can smell it, watch it, methane is over marshes like a weird breath. Below, packed and slowly returning to the air are countless crushed leaves, bodies, twigs, flowers, teeth, and stamens, that stopped to slowly turn to oil and lavender gases.

Light becomes heat and vice versa. Water and soil, sand, can be anything or snow. Methane could be some other planet or the smell and color of marsh gas. Eventually, somewhere, everything will happen. In the meantime, nearly anything does.

Now I could write out the outlines of a number of lives or connect the figures with objects, see those in particular lights, but I'll leave it. You can hear the tones of their voices, familiar phrases connected to some particular place and time, as you look at their arms and heads and torsos. They're wandering in streets or along the edge of a river or in the woods or a cellar, alone or together or they used to be there. Sometimes they join hands and dance in a circle like a ring of seasons, the rings of Saturn, some planet's orbit.

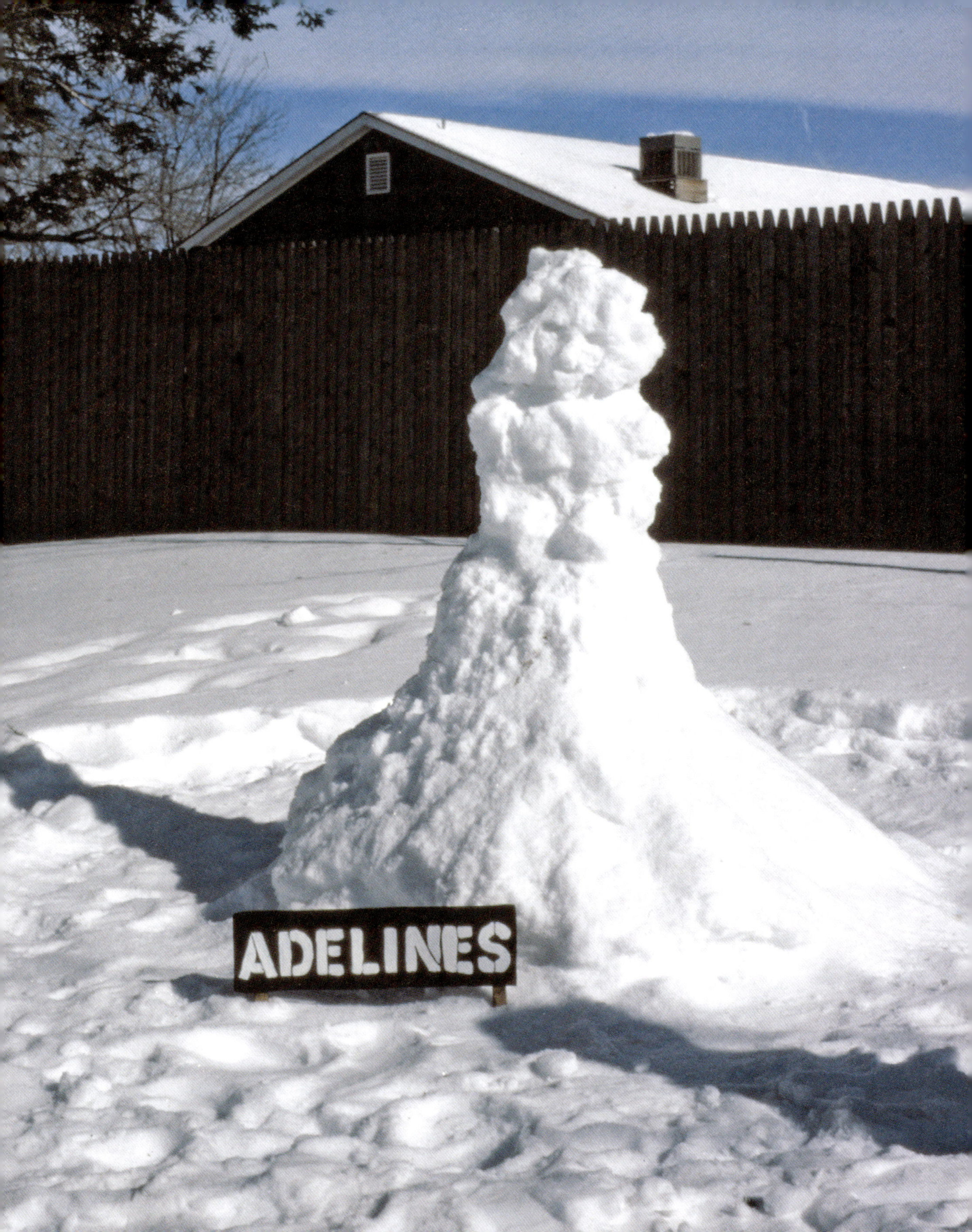
ADELINES

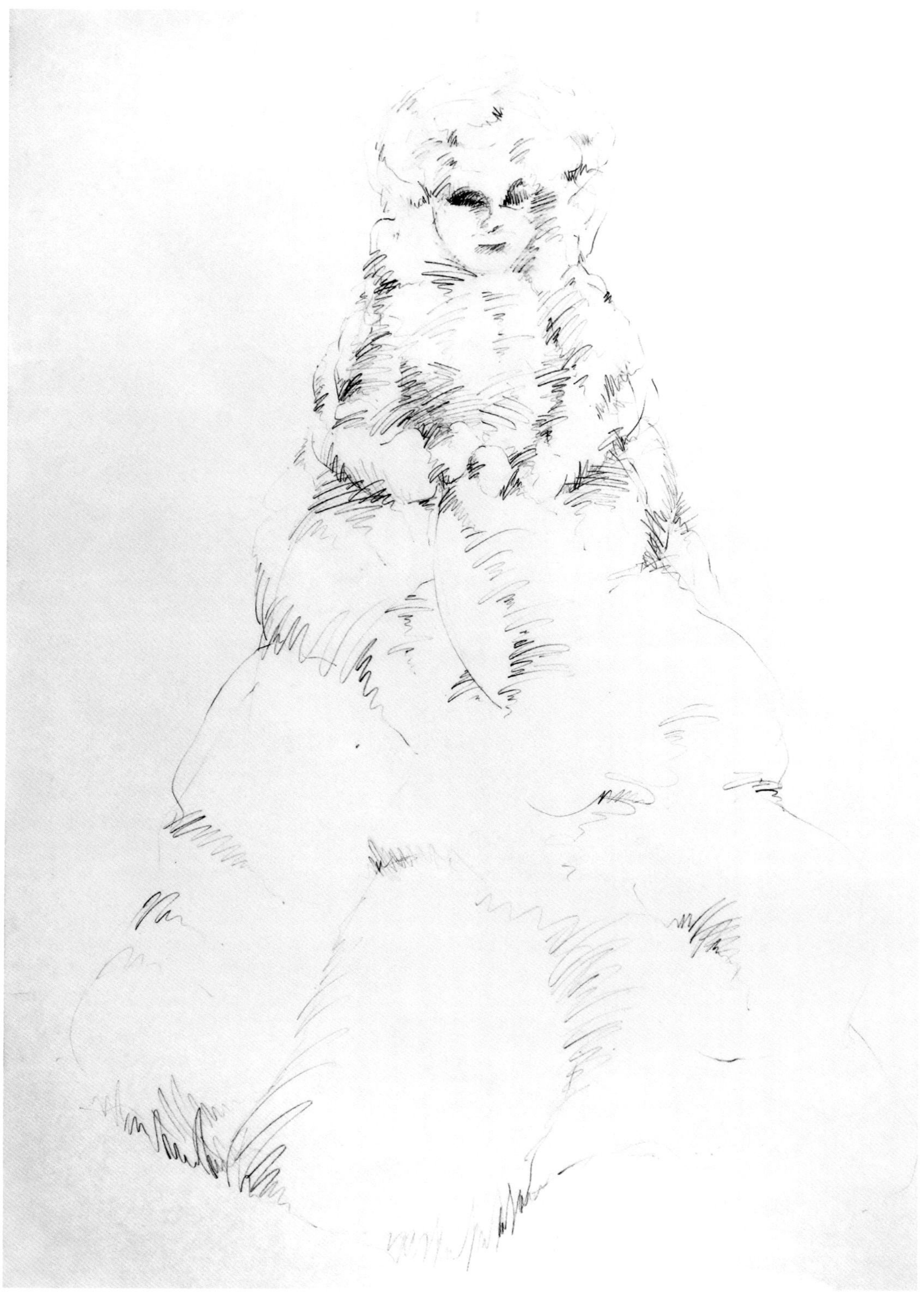

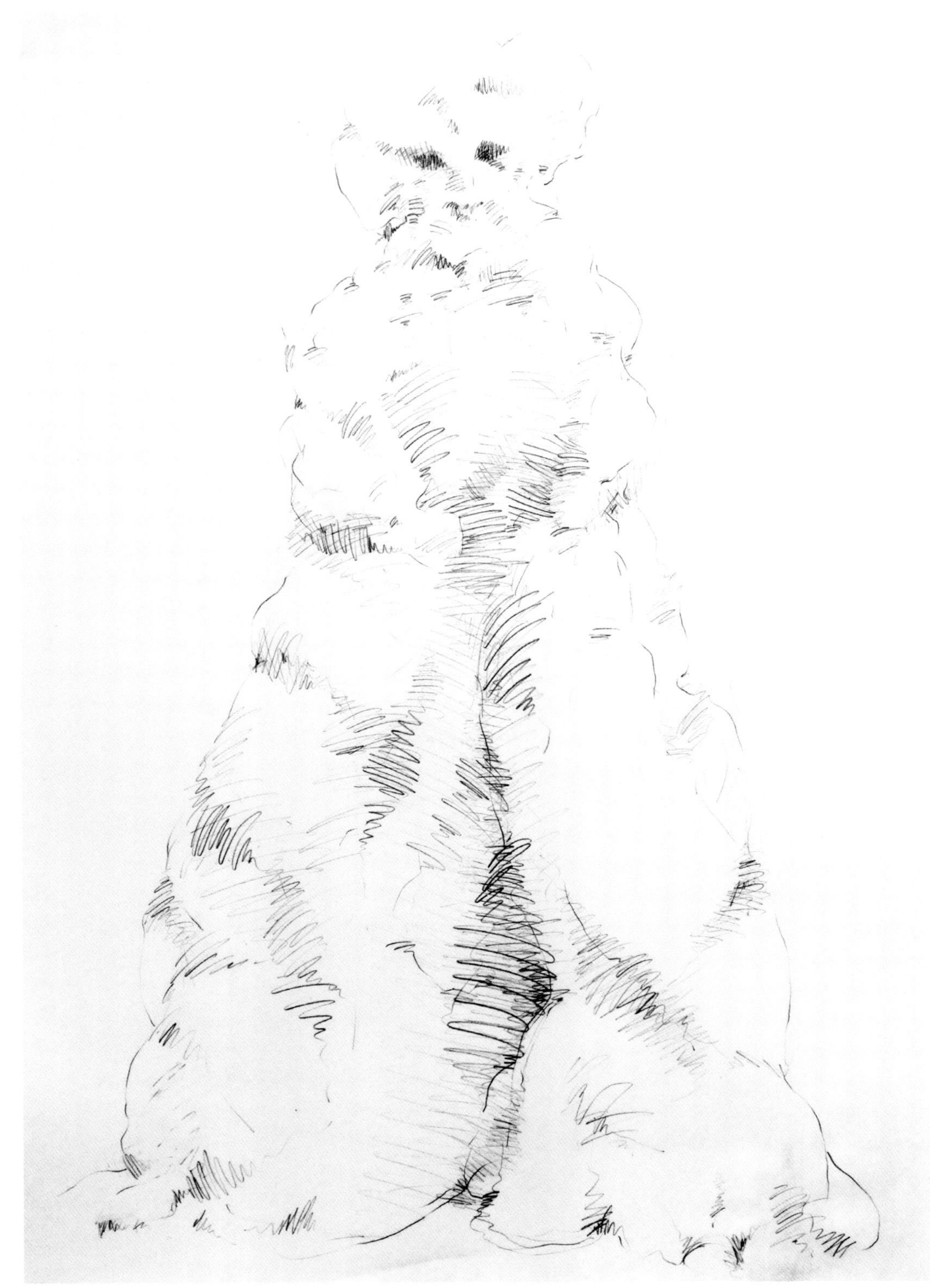

GHOSTS

Installations in 1980 and 1981
Wood, ribbons, paper, and paint
Times Square Show, 201–205 West 41st Street, June 1980
Dialogues, Just Above Midtown Gallery, October 1980
Words as Images, The Renaissance Society, The University of
Chicago, Chicago, Illinois, February 1981
Residency, Tyler School of Art, Philadelphia, Pennsylvania,
March 1981
Hours, Minneapolis College of Art and Design, Minneapolis,
Minnesota, April 1981
Summer Sculpture Exhibit, Arnot Art Museum, Elmira, New
York, Summer 1981

Photographs

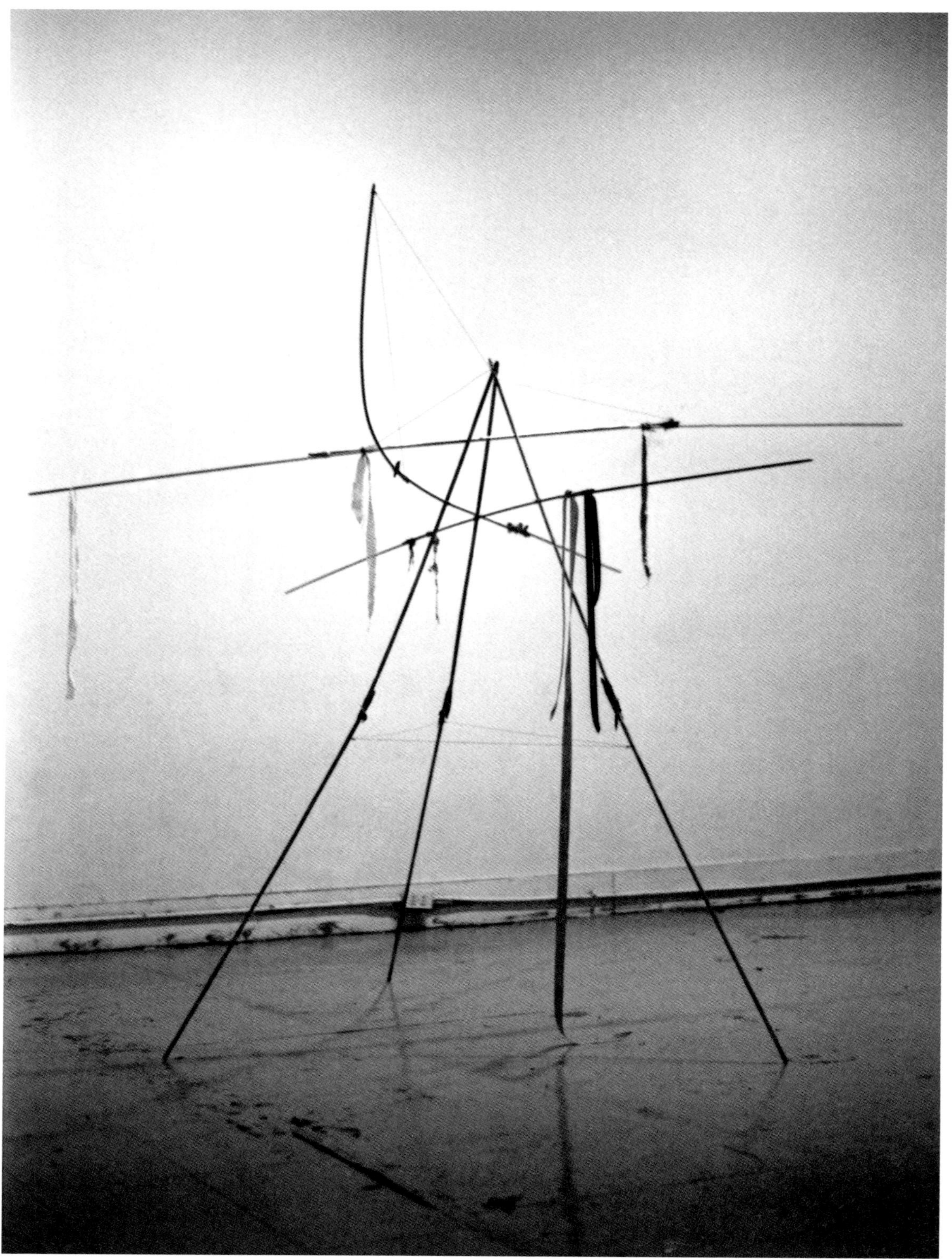

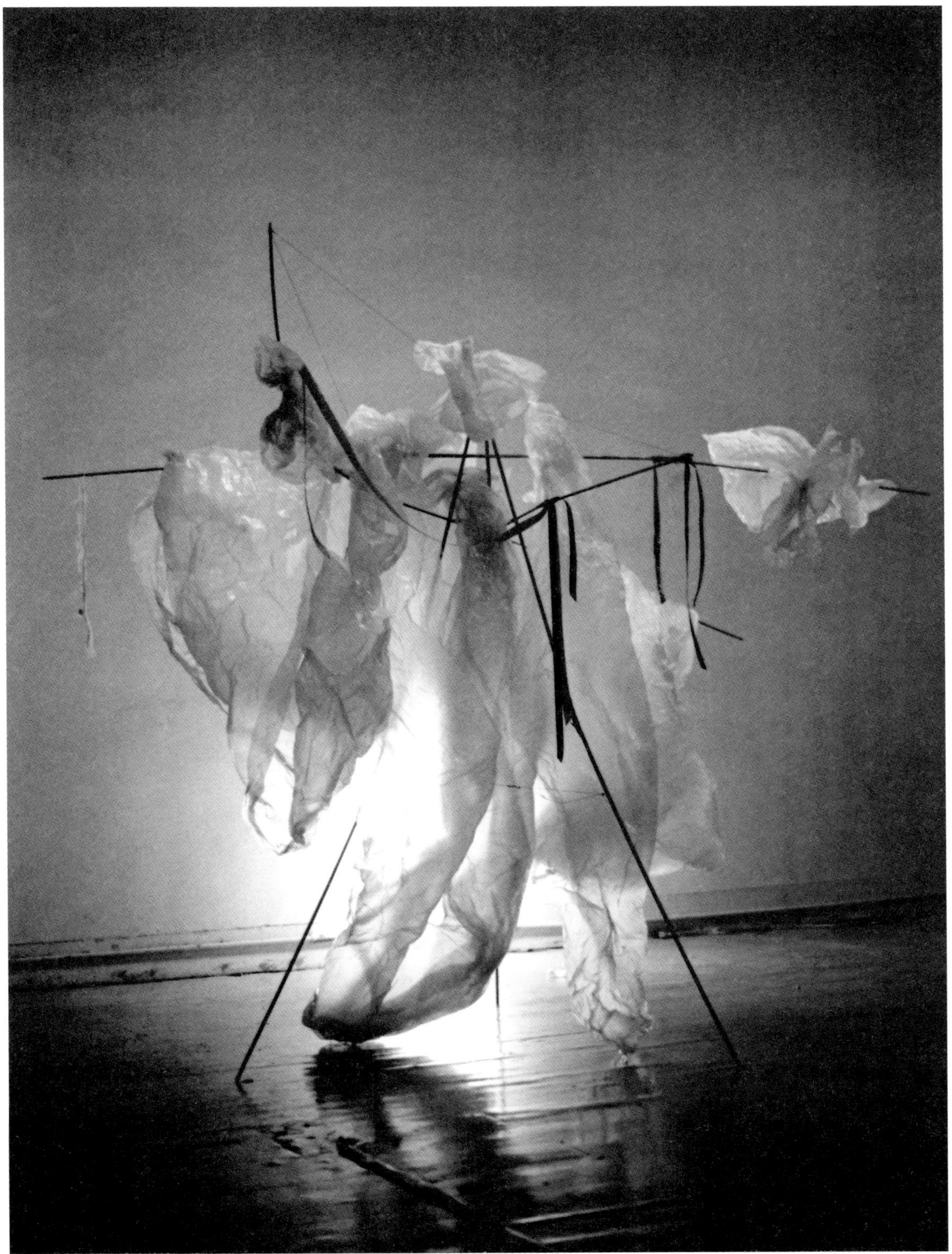

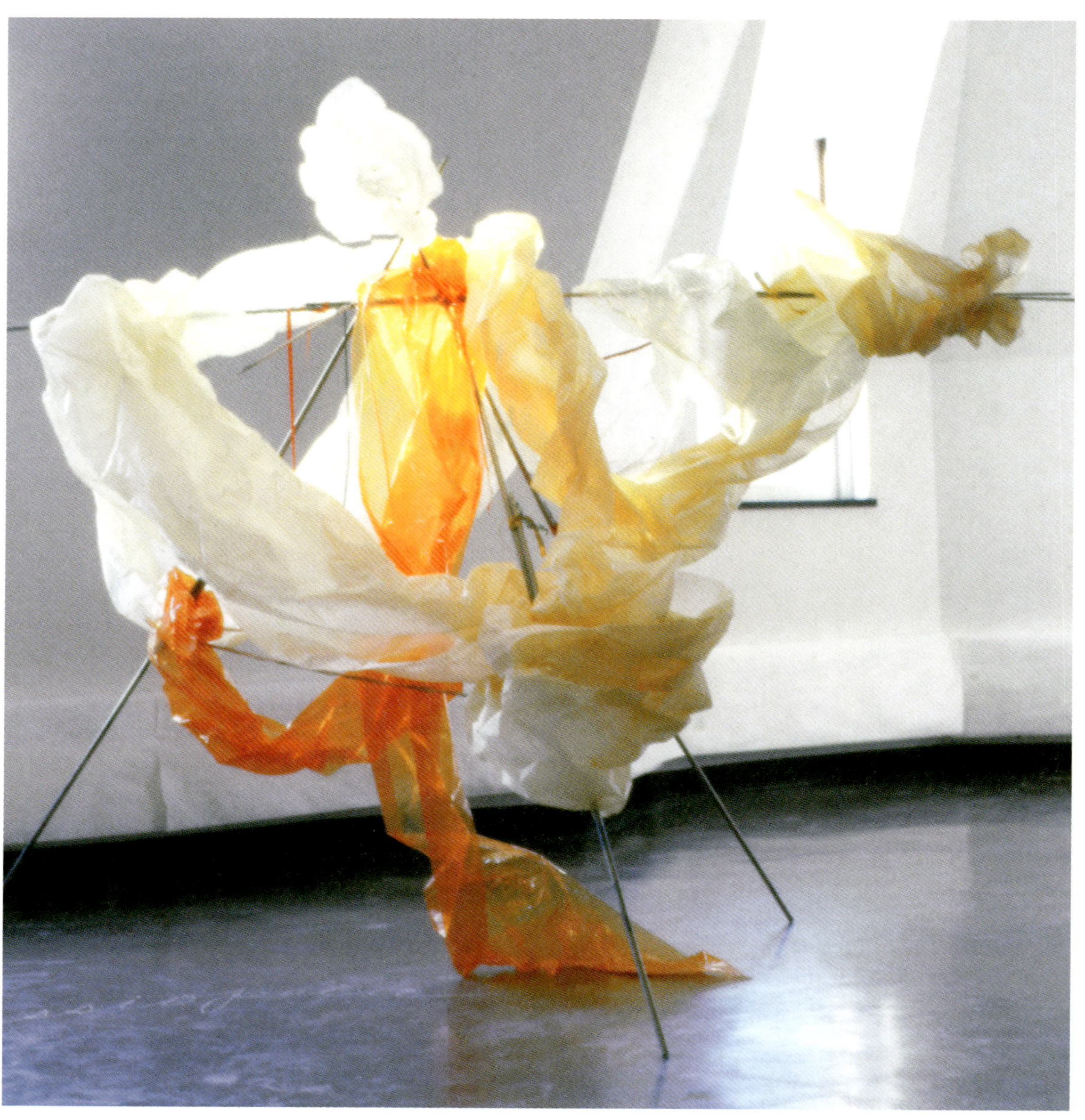

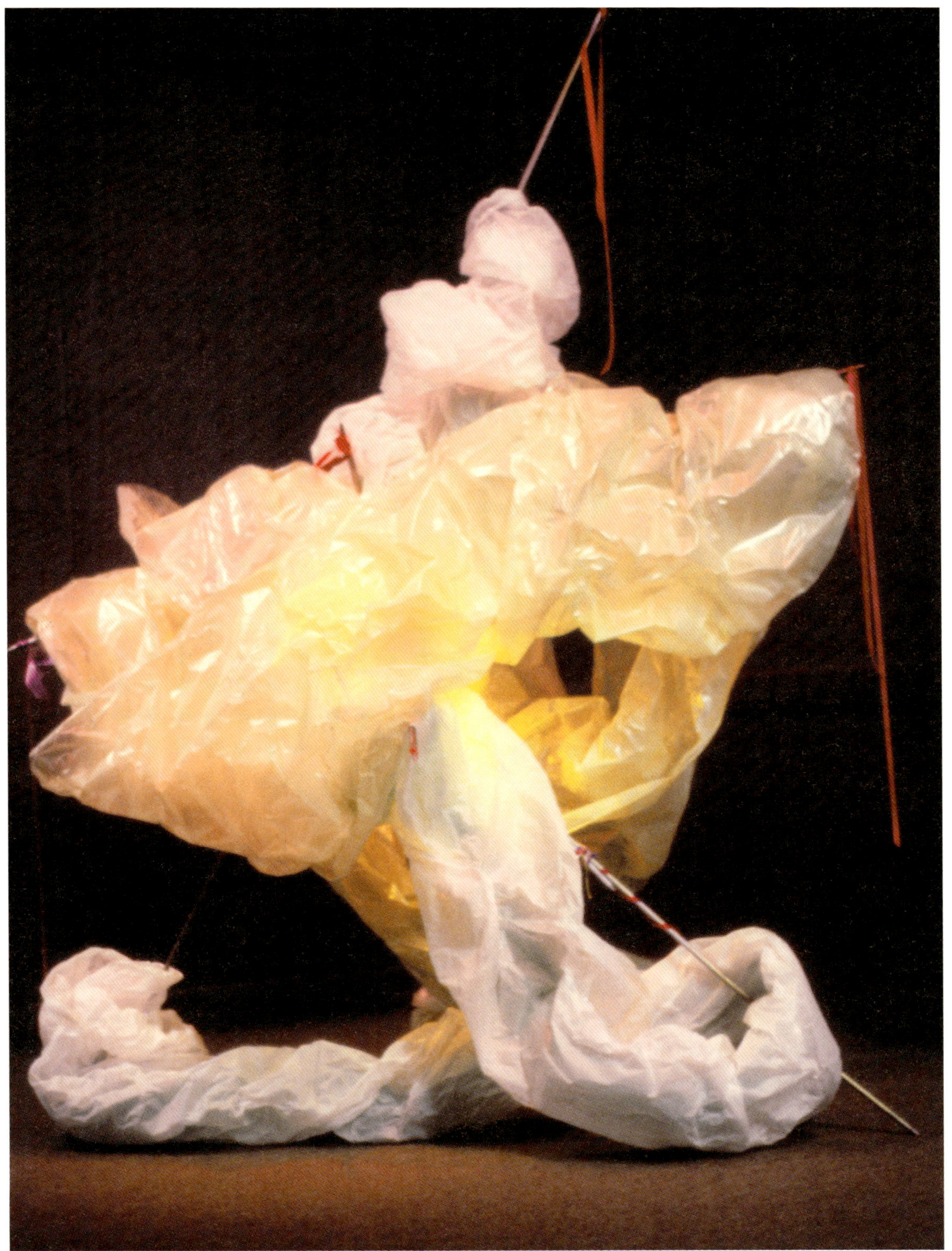

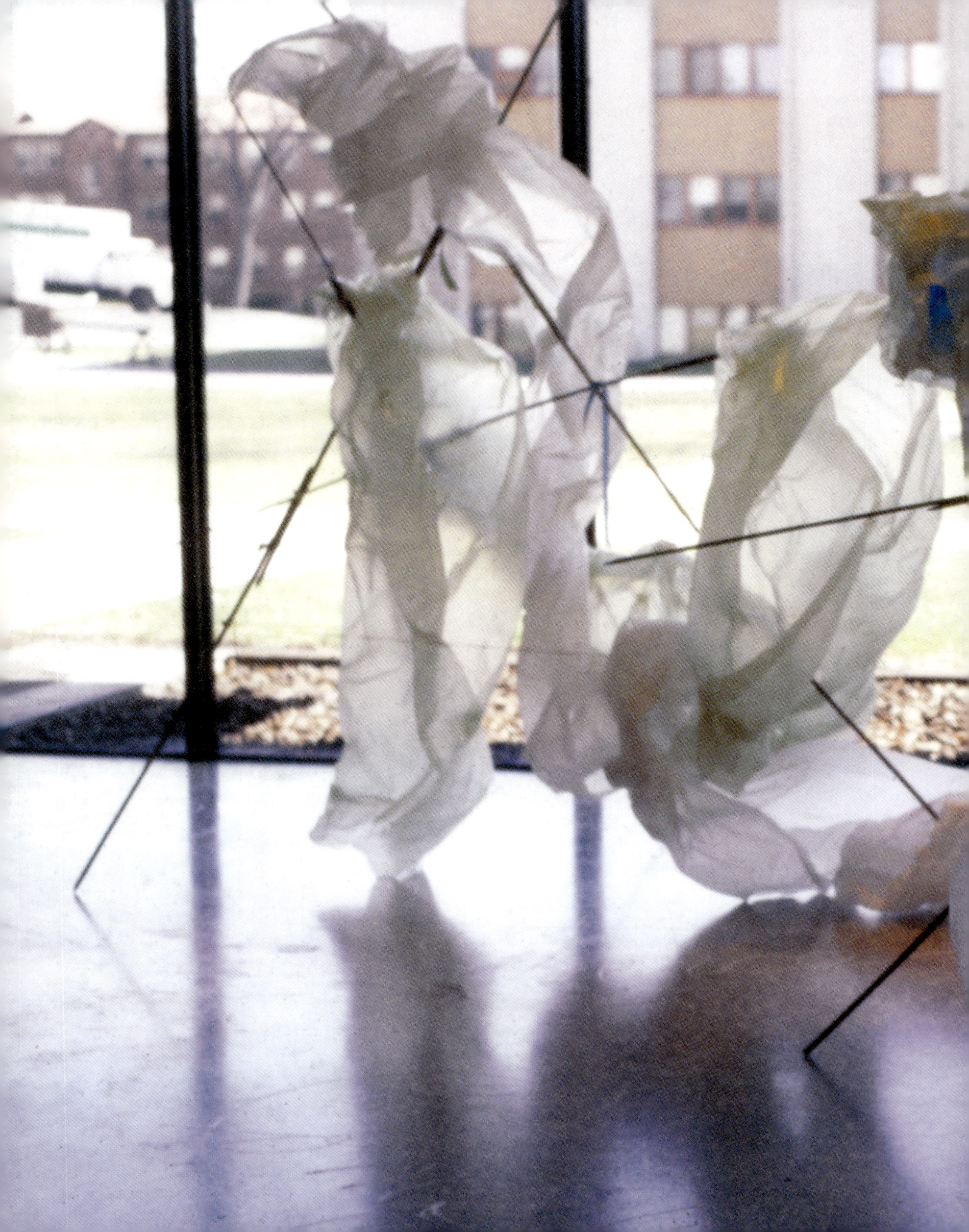

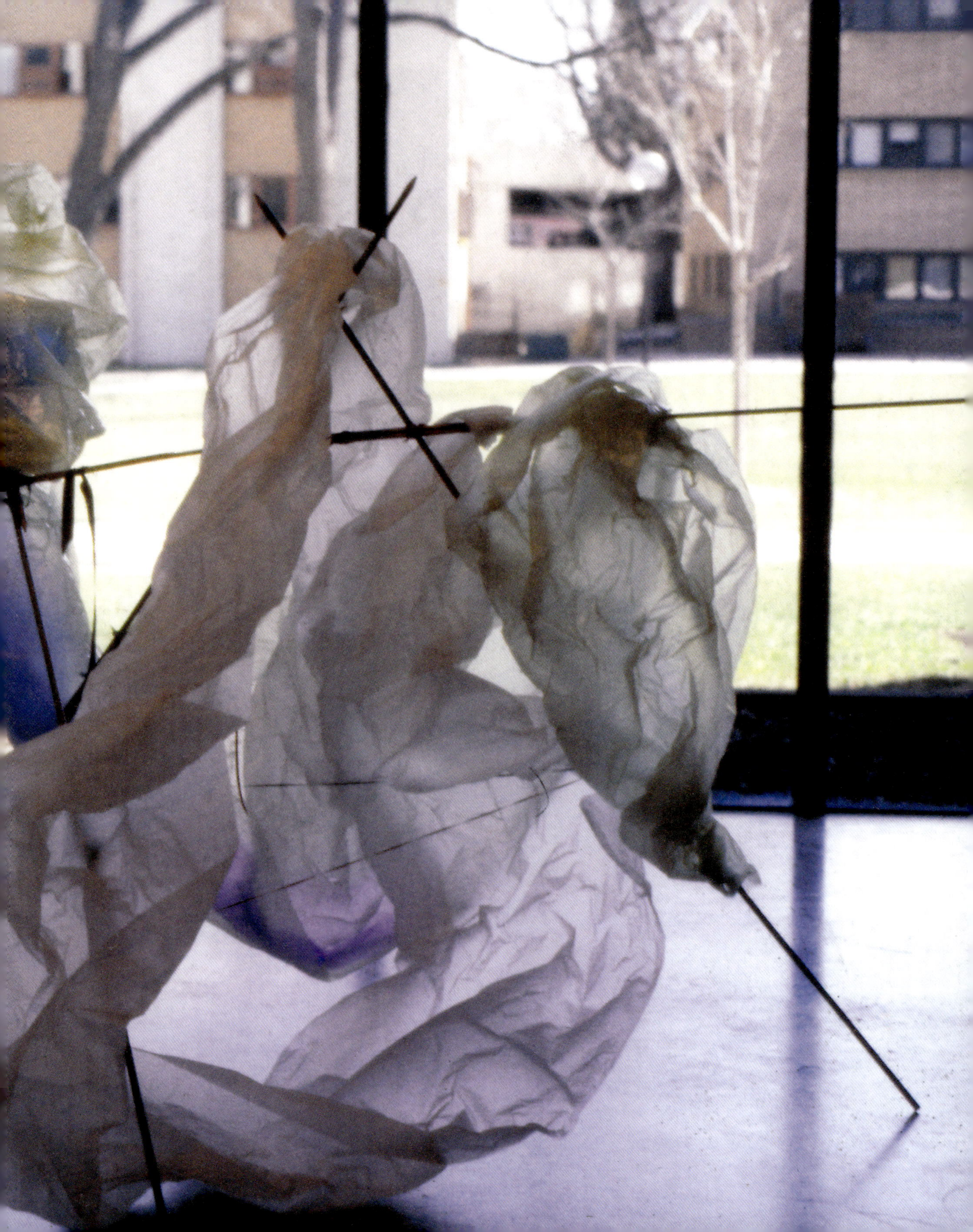

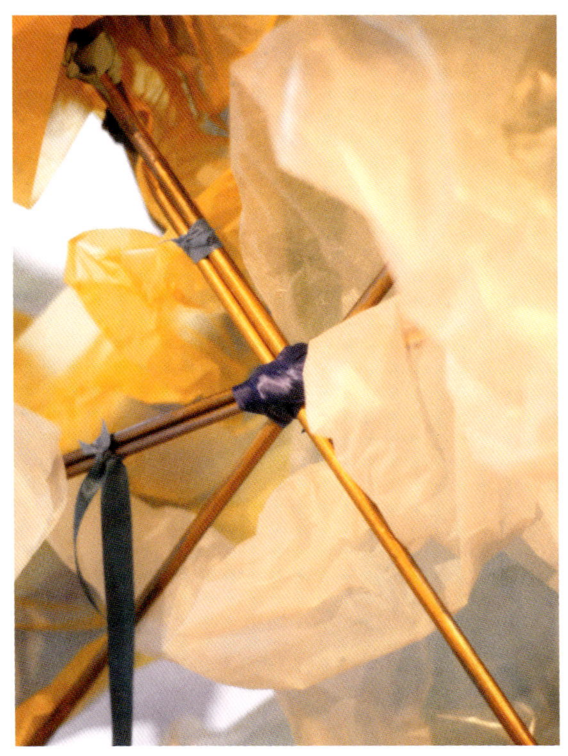
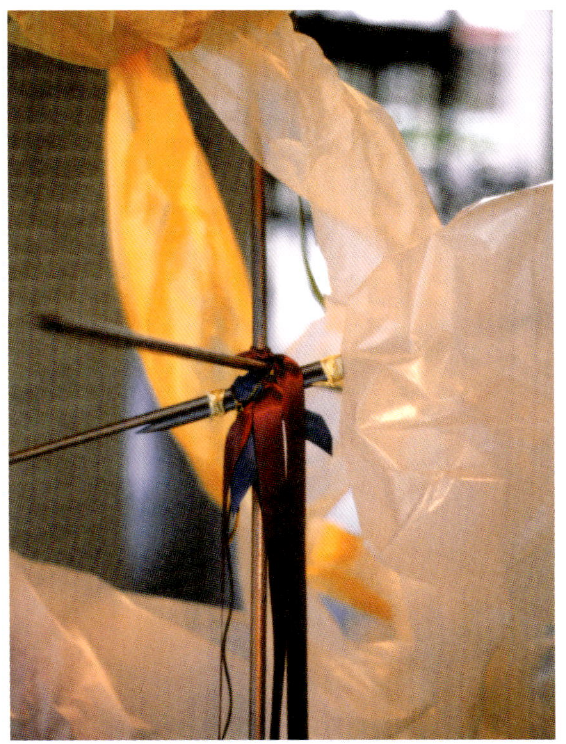
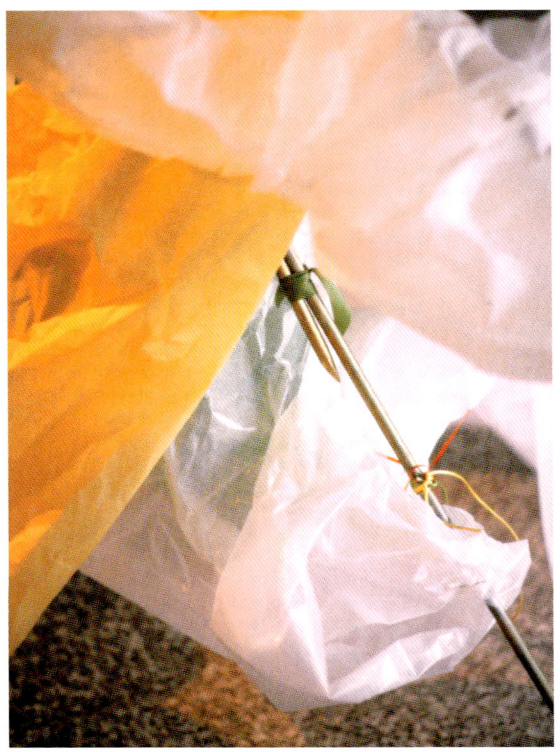
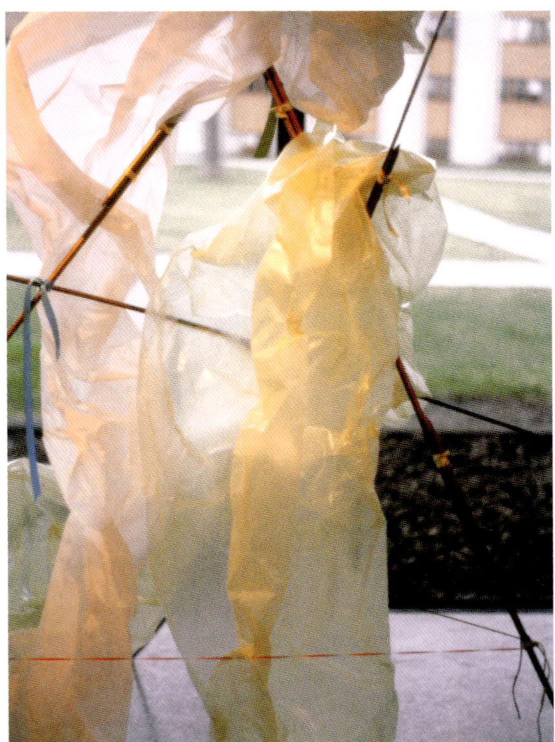

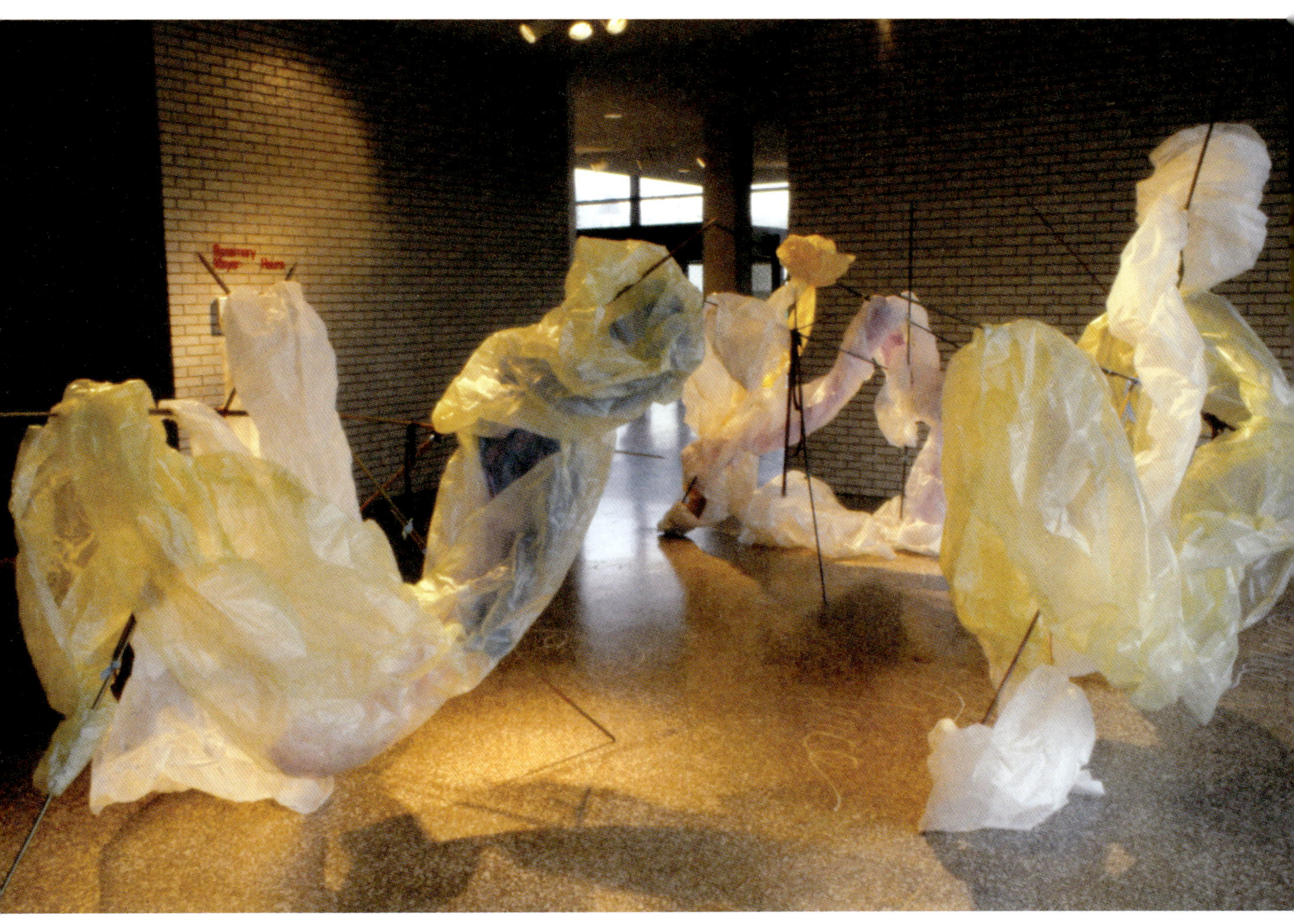

MOON TENT

Installed for the duration of the full moon,
October 2–3, 1982, 6:45 p.m. to 5:27 a.m.
Paper on wood pavilion
Roof of the house of Robert Hobbs, Lansing, New York

Photographs, text, watercolor

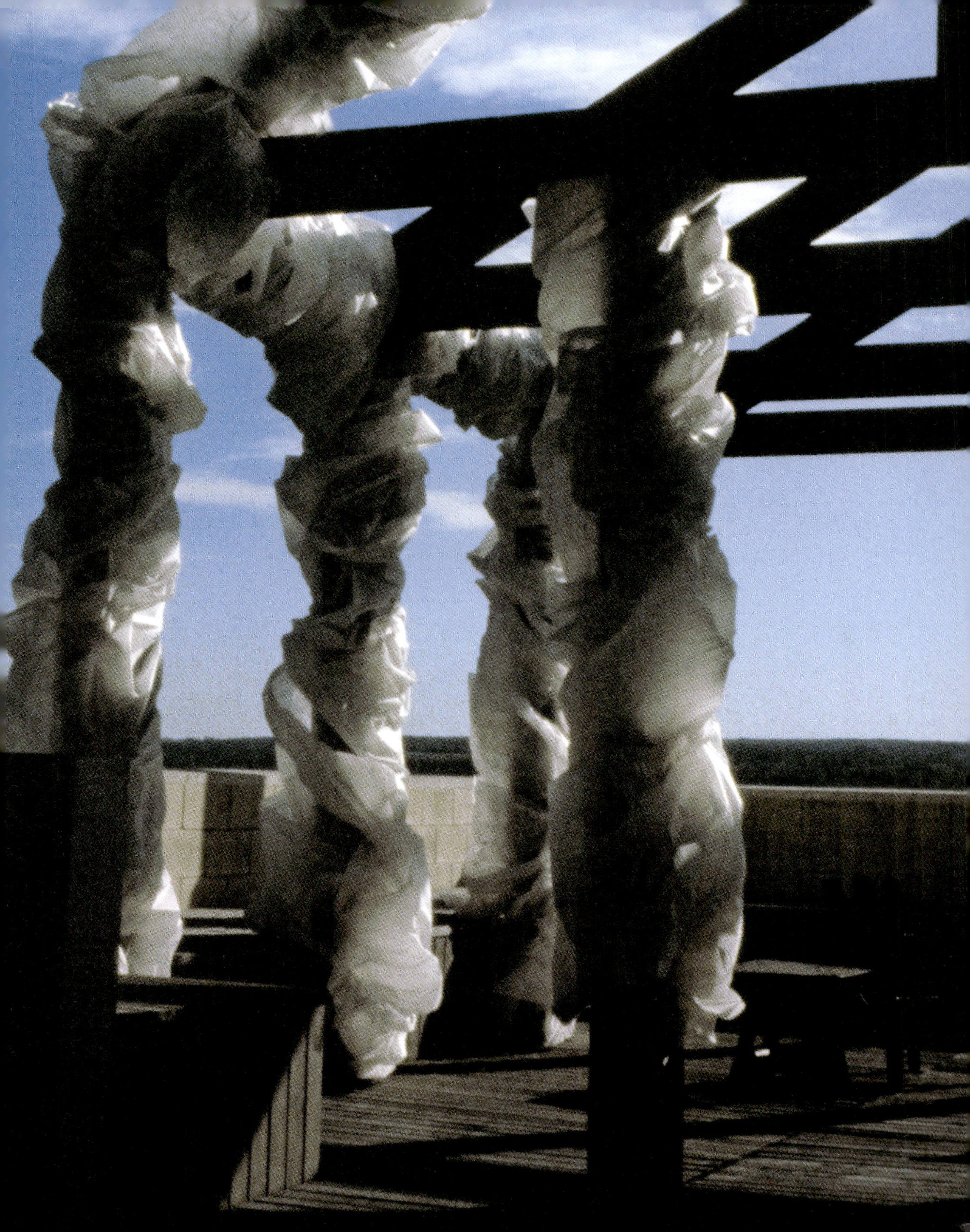

A MOON TENT

Text published in *WhiteWalls: A Magazine of Writings by Artists*,
No. 8, Summer 1983.

The Moon Tent came on a long round in time about light and its possible creatures.

It was a ghost tent, proliferating ghosts and the ghosts of tents in changes of light. It made the absence of bodies present in suggestions of the draping and motion of their clothing. It made irrelevant its actual support structure, turning wooden beams into the caryatids they once would have been. When the moon was up, the dressed beams changed and floated for the people drinking, eating and watching inside, the moon and its creatures.

Light, as anyone knows, is the whole show. In some places, dawn is announced when a difference is visible between black and white threads spread over the back of your hand. In each season and under the different clouds of every night or day, the light is different months and they color our vision different hues if it's June or January, if the clouds are high or low, thick or not even there.

People used to watch the sky, count the days of each moon's thickening to full and waning, or study the clouds for signs of storms or spring or winter. It mattered then for food and warmth or safety. Now it's more often mild aesthetics or old romance, to calm you or bring some excitement. If you notice, it shows your rooms or land in different colors or odd intensities you may not have looked at before. It only makes a difference if you have the time.

To watch the moon you must be able to stay up late. To notice the sun's height in the sky, how it lengthens or shortens shadows, makes different, odd quadrilaterals across the floors of your rooms, you have to have some time. Everything is different in each different light.

When people used to watch the sky and its light intensely, for clues to weather and safety, they celebrated the sure signs of different seasons, maybe to prove they knew what would happen next and thus they would be safe.

In the north of Europe on a day called Beltane in the beginning of May, huge bonfires were lit to mark the return of the sun, the god of fire. Later, scarecrows announced the growing season, flapping in wind in mimicry of human forms. In fall, after harvest, they fell apart in the fields, or maybe sometimes they were taken down so what parts had survived the summer's weather could be used again in the next spring.

Scarecrows are like the guardian deities people used to imagine, solicit, placate, but embodied in tattered forms, the last of the angels and gods of the land.

In winter in the North when the crops or hunted meat is in and stored and there's nothing to do, people amuse themselves making large or tiny figures like themselves. The Inuit made minute men from carved bones jointed with cord or sinew through thin, carefully drilled holes. Five parts—four for limbs and a longer piece for both torso and head, with three holes drilled for eyes and mouth, the nose carved from bone. Dolls for children. Still, in places with long, snow-covered winters, figures of women and men and children appear in the snow. Also sometimes animals. These disappear if the weather turns warmer and for sure they're gone by spring when they've become ghosts of the winter, absent inhabitants waiting to be reformed in the next year's snow.

Scarecrows change in the wind, stand mysterious in disappearing light or at dawn, seem other than you know they are if you pass them under the moon. Snowpeople wait, changing as they melt or freeze, bending, showing a different face or pose with every shift in the light or weather until they're gone. The minds of people now long dead were filled with creatures we would say they never really saw. Books of the dead describe the presence in different forms of the dead, of spirits or gods. It must have been in the changing light that these were seen and then described.

Imagine living, as people once did, with the bodies of all in your family who died before you buried below your floor or just outside whatever shelter you lived in. Imagine presents of food or drink or flowers or some substance considered sacred to the believed-to-be-present spirits of these people who had together produced you. The dead could live when it was thought they did. Like ghosts, flitting in somewhat human form, seen from the corner of an eye, resembling figures known in dreams.

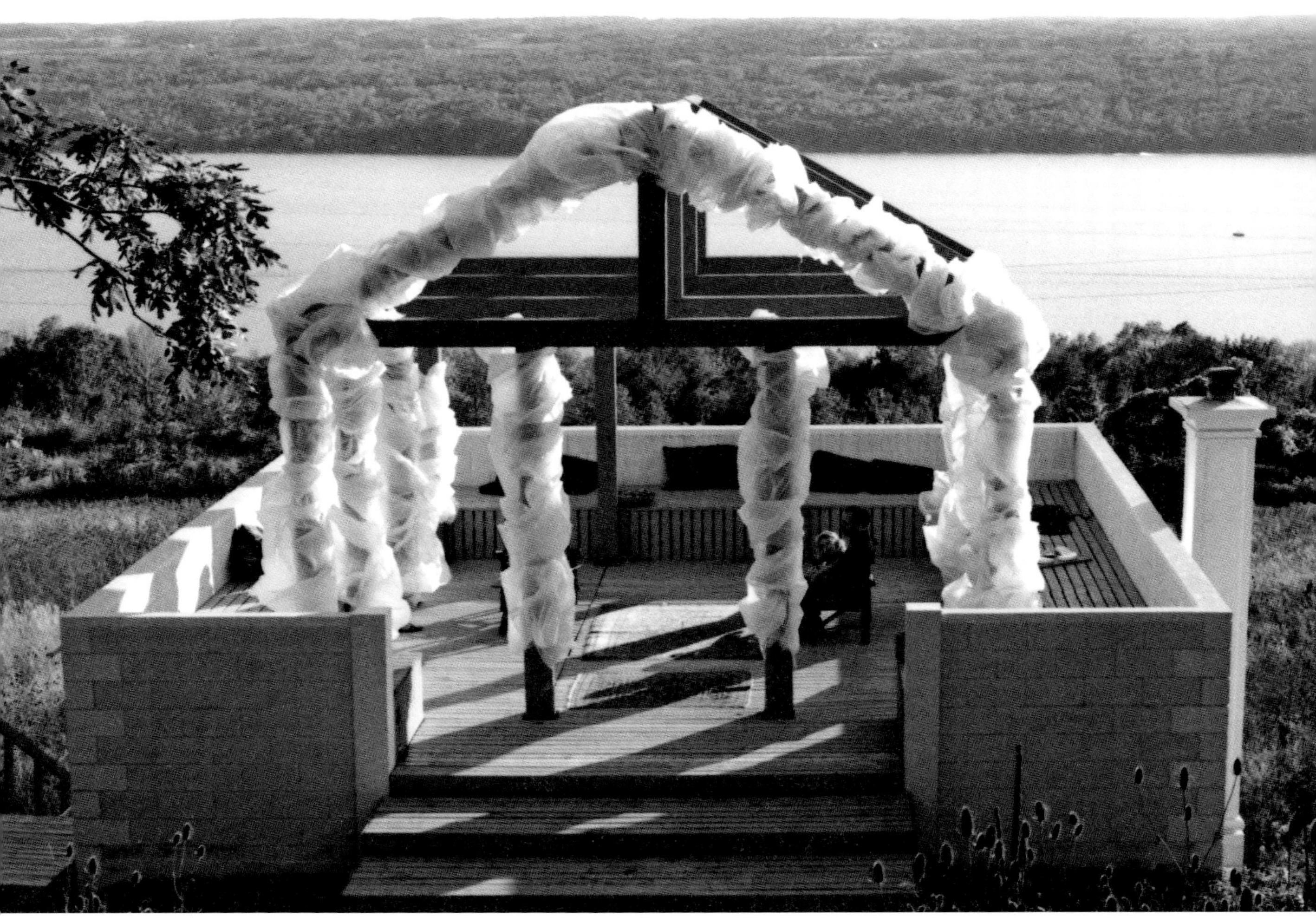

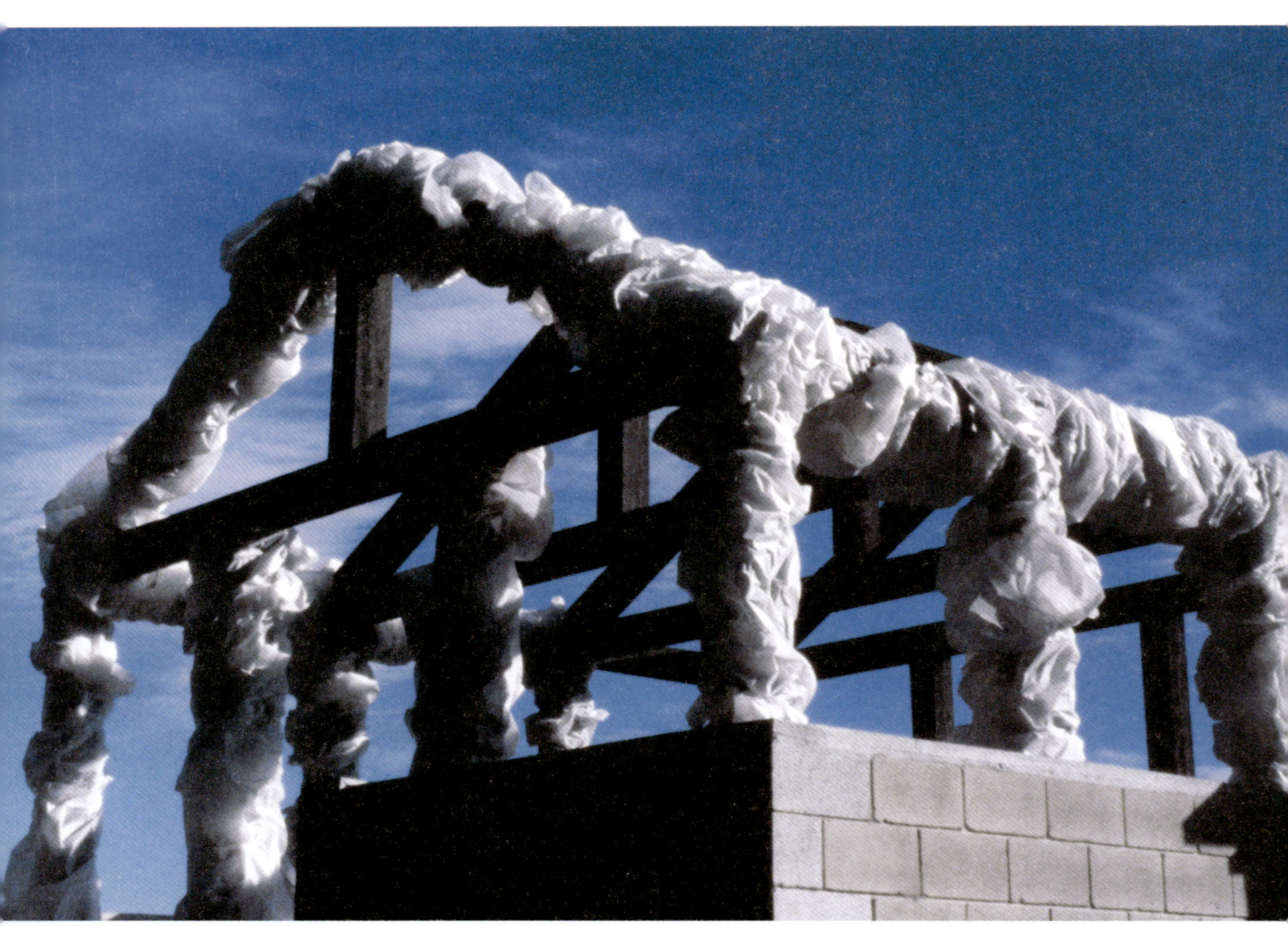

They could glitter, change colors, fade past transparency to disappear.

No one has never seen a ghost. You prefer not to remember. It's easy. They're visible only for seconds and even then they change. They live in the fall of a sleeve or skirt, the shapes in a coat laid over a chair. When the light changes, they're different or gone. Stare at something as the moon or sun rises or sets and see what you see. Any number of things or creatures like what you see in clouds or currents in rivers, or ocean waves. They live one way for seconds or minutes, then have some other form. What you see depends on the way you think.

Buildings have any number of ghosts. Figures in pictures on walls or carved in relief or formed in the round, placed on the roof or at the entrance, or far inside like the gods in temples, saints in churches, or an aesthete's sculpted figures inside or out on the grounds. Caryatids are the ghosts who hold up the roof. They live endlessly through seasons and centuries, slowly losing the fullness of curves, the sharp turn of an elbow, still supporting even when part of the once sheltering roof, or even all of it, is gone.

Where people could barely live on what could be hunted or gathered or grown, where water is scarce, shelter was transient, tents of cloth, or woven leaves or animals' skins. Here, the tents were the ghosts, appearing and quickly gone as the group moved after its needs. Where you raised the tent, how its openings were oriented, whether you surrounded it with a protective wall of brush or bushes, depended on seasons and weather. When nothing more could be found in the place, the tent was packed and moved to assume some other embracing form in another place and season. Even the parts changed. Ropes and cords would be replaced. Holes patched in different cloth or different colors, new swatches of cloth or pieces of hide or woven mats of newly dried leaves made to replace the worn out sections.

Inside it would be dark except near the cooking fire or if there were lamps burning oil. Inside would be food and stories, what happens between people and what they see asleep or in the dark.

Tents were homes and escapes, places of some respite from the search for food and water. Like tents in our camps in the forests or mountains where we go to escape what we have to do. Imagine tents in different colors and forms on the roofs of office buildings or crowded city houses. Places where the wind blows and changes the shapes of hangings, where it would be easy to watch the moon or how shadows change in different seasons.

In old China in autumn people used to celebrate the year's best moon, the West's Harvest Moon, with an all-night feast of food and wine, music and poems. You ate moon-shaped food and drank moon-colored wine on the roofs of buildings on hills or mountains. Anyone who could sang songs or played music or composed on the spot, poems about the moon. There are old statues of Heng-O, the moon goddess, dressed in greens and blue and silver, always dancing, with her right foot raised, holding a moon disc over her head.

To let the moon be seen, a moon tent can't have a roof. And its supports have to float, suggest the draped figures who would have been holding it up, caryatids and the dancing woman who held the moon. People must come and sit or lie down inside, drink or eat, and talk about the absent figures, the moon and its changing light, the space now filled, till morning when everything changes and the tent is dismantled, then gone like a tent moved on in the desert, melted snow figures, or last year's scarecrow.

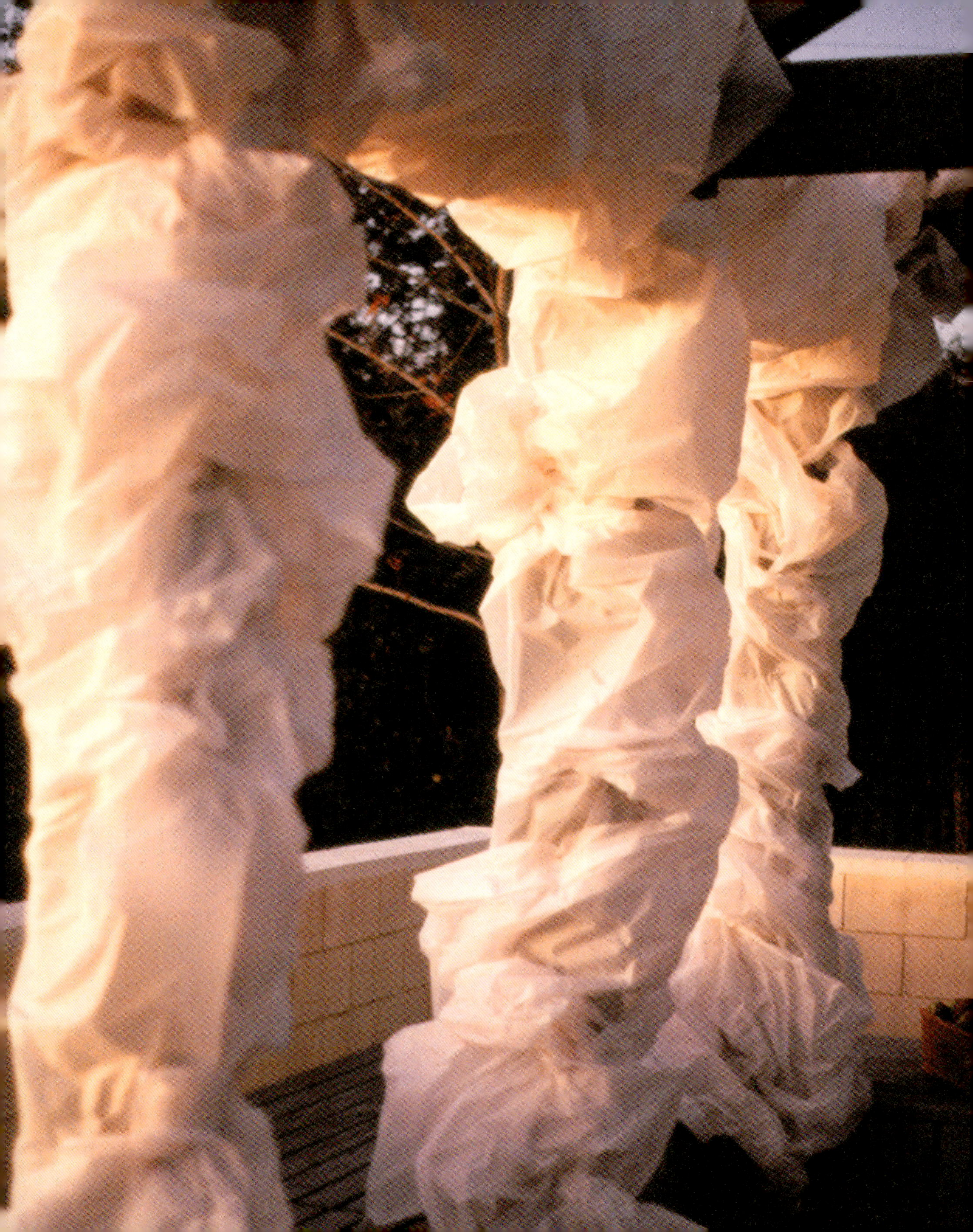

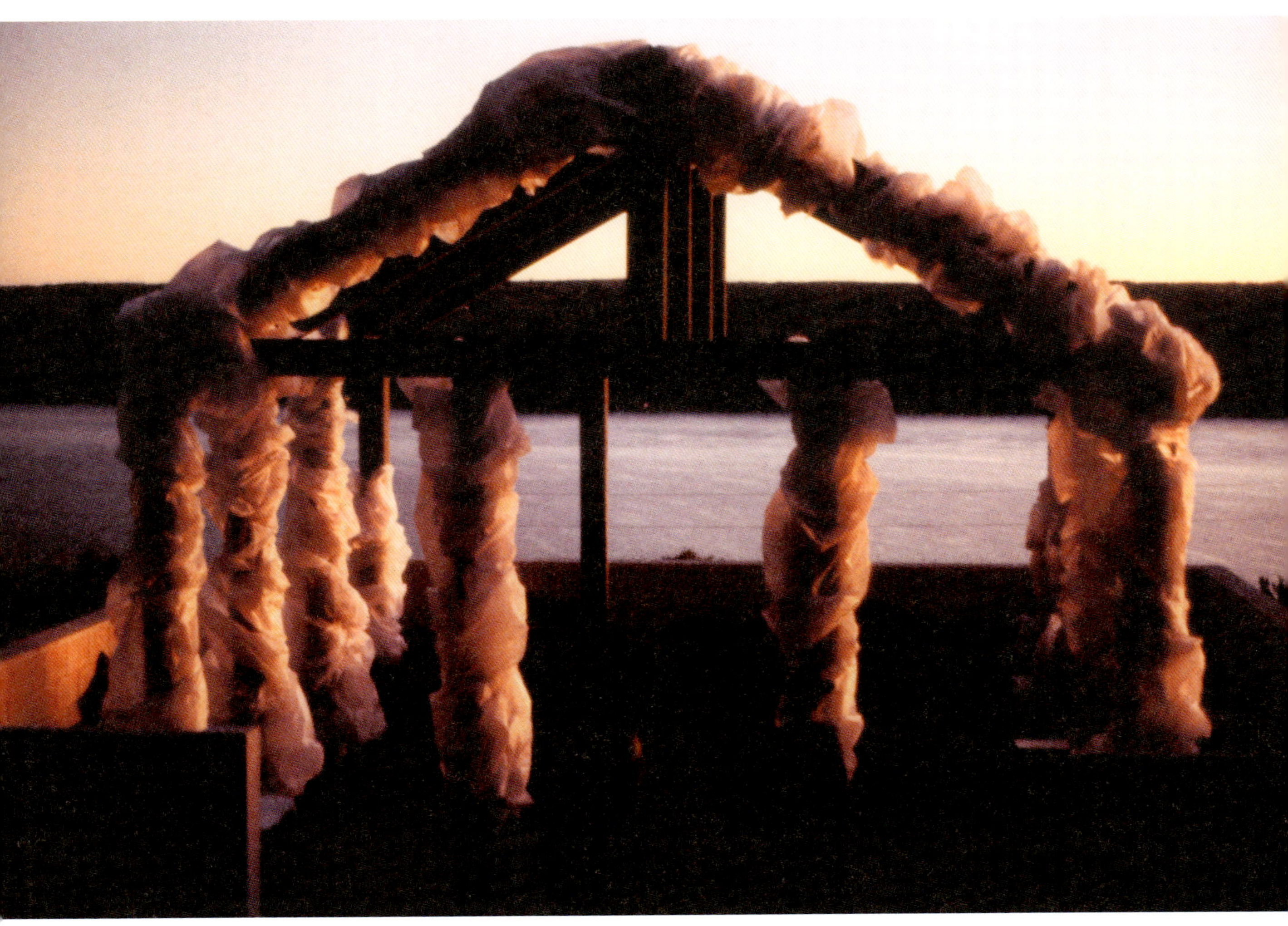

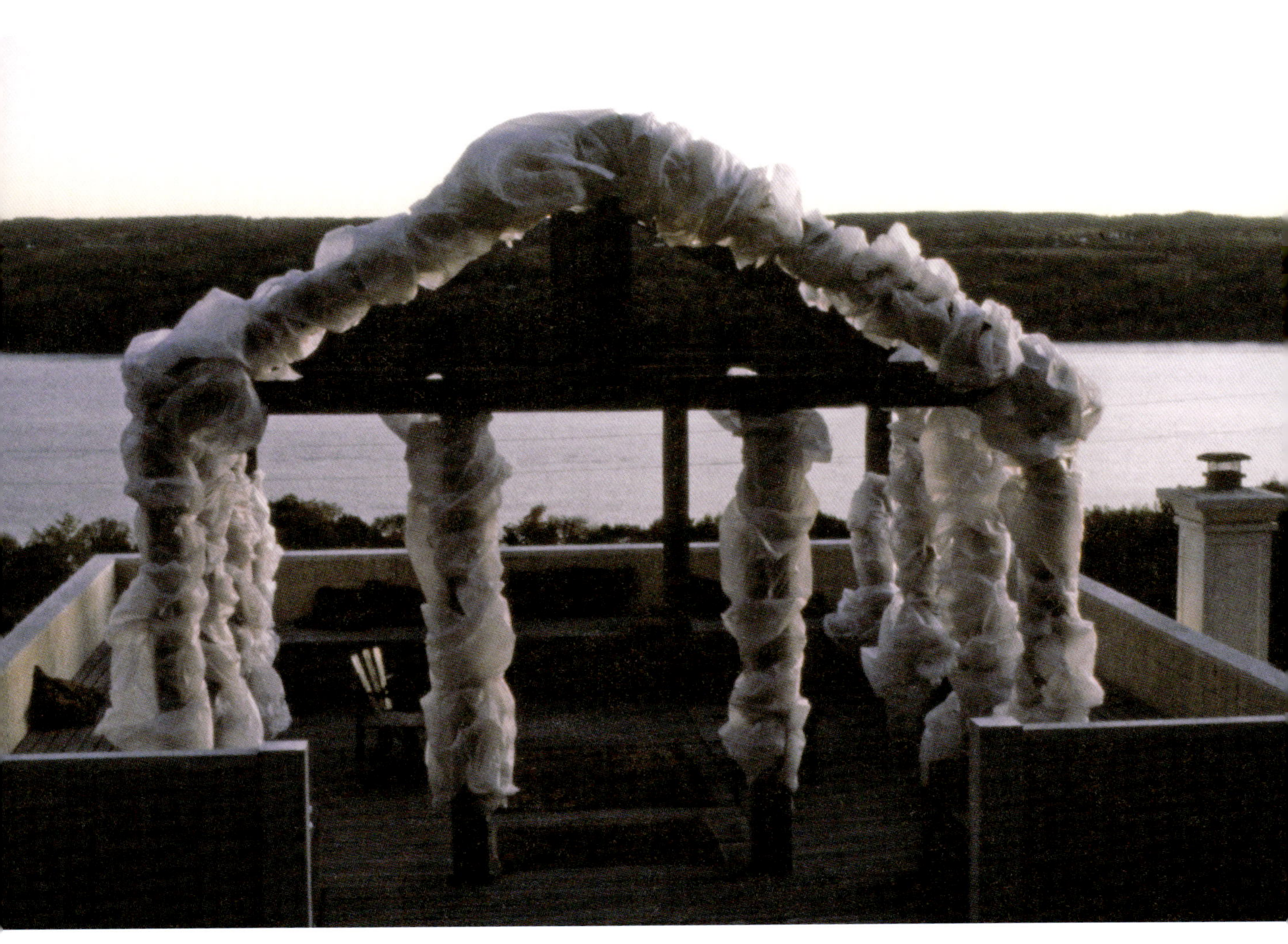

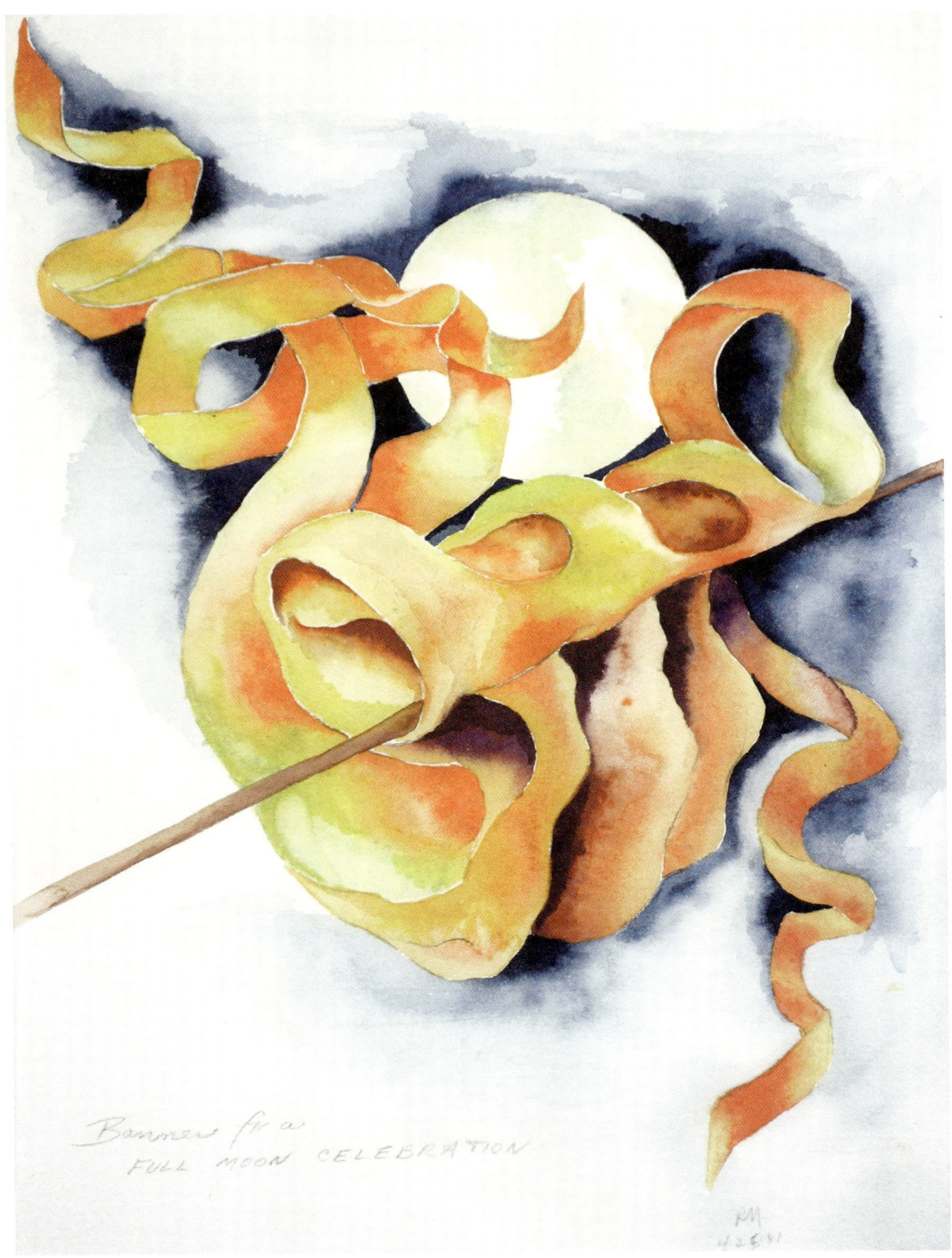

Banner for a
FULL MOON CELEBRATION

Credits

The texts *Spell*, *Those*, and *A Moon Tent*, which originally appeared in *White Walls*, are reproduced with permission from the editors: Buzz Spector, Reagan Upshaw, and Roberta Upshaw.

SPELL

pp. 36, 38, 41, 42, 43, 44, 47, 48–49, 51: Photographs of *Spell* by Eeva Inkeri.

p. 52–55: Flyers for *Spell*, 1977. Photocopied drawing, ink on paper. 11 x 8½ in each (30 x 25 cm).

pp. 56–61: *Spell*, 1977. Artist's book with 39 gelatin silver prints and cut-and-pasted transparentized papers with ink and pastel. Overall dimensions (closed): 20⅞ x 13⅜ x 1³/₁₆ in (53 x 34 x 3 cm). Collection of the Museum of Modern Art. Gift of the artist's estate.

SOME DAYS IN APRIL

pp. 64 and 69: Photographs by Bruce Kurtz.

pp. 66–67, 70, 73, 74, 75: Photographs by Rosemary Mayer.

p. 77: Poster for *Some Days in April*, 1978. Media unknown. 22 x 17 in (56 x 43 cm).

p. 78: *Mooring Knot*, 1978. Colored pencil and graphite on paper. 15⅛ x 12 in (39 x 30.5 cm).

p. 79: *Mooring Knot*, 1978. Colored pencil and graphite on paper. 15⅛ x 12 in (39 x 30.5 cm).

p. 80: *Some Days in April (Marie balloon)*, 1978. Colored pencil and pen on paper. 24 x 18 in (62 x 45.5 cm).

p. 81: *Some Days in April (Theodore balloon)*, 1978. Colored pencil and pen on paper. 24 x 18 in (62 x 45.5 cm).

p. 83: *Some Days in April*, 1978. Colored pencil and pen on paper. 24 x 18 in (62 x 45.5 cm).

pp. 84–87: *Some Days in April*, 1979. Artist's book with pencil, colored pencil, pastel, ink, crayon, printed papers, transparentized paper, and chromogenic color prints. Overall dimensions (closed): 15 ⁷/₁₆ x 13 x ¹³/₁₆ in (39.2 x 33 x 2 cm). Collection of the Museum of Modern Art. The Modern Women's Fund.

BALLOON FOR A BIRTHDAY

p. 91: Postcard for *Balloon for a Birthday*. Media unknown. 4 x 6 in (10.2 x 15.2 cm).

p. 92: Photograph by John Campione.

p. 93: Flyer for *Balloon for a Birthday*. Photocopied typescript. 11 x 8½ in (30 x 25 cm).

pp. 95, 96, 97, 99, 101, 102–03: Photographs by Rosemary Mayer.

SNOW PEOPLE

pp. 106, 108–09, 111, 112, 115, 116: Photographs by Rosemary Mayer.

p. 120: *Untitled (Snow Person)*, 1979. Graphite on paper. 26 x 37½ in (66 x 94 cm).

p. 121: *Untitled (Snow Person)*, 1979. Graphite on paper. 26 x 37½ in (66 x 94 cm).

GHOSTS

All photographs by Rosemary Mayer.

p. 124: Structure for *October Ghost*, 1981. Wood and ribbons. Dimensions unknown. Installed in artist's studio.

p. 125: *October Ghost*, 1981. Wood and ribbons. Dimensions unknown. Installed in artist's studio.

p. 126: *Cassiopeia*, 1981. Wood, ribbons, and paper. Ca. 78 x 84 x 84 in (198 x 213 x 213 cm). Installed in the group exhibition *Words as Images* at the Renaissance Society, Chicago, Illinois. February 1981.

p. 127: *Roses*, 1981. Wood, ribbons, paper, and yellow and magenta incandescent lights. 86 x 76 x 62 in (218 x 193 x 157 cm). Installed at the Arnot Art Museum, Elmira, New York.

pp. 128–29, 131, 133: *Hours*, 1981. Wood, gilding, ribbons, and paper. Group of four sculptures, each ca. 84 x 84 x 84 in (213 x 213 x 213 cm). Installed at the Minneapolis College of Art and Design. April 5–26, 1981.

MOON TENT

pp. 136, 139, 140, 143, 145, 147: Photographs by Rosemary Mayer.

p. 149: *Banner for a Full Moon Celebration*, 1981. Watercolor on paper. 14¼ x 10¼ in (36 x 26 cm).

Acknowledgments

The editors would like to express deep appreciation to Julia Klein, Gillian Sneed, and Farrar Lannon for all their work on this book and to Charles Goldman for connecting us to Soberscove. We thank our family for their encouragement of this and other projects to share Rosemary's work. We are also grateful to Claire Barliant, Sonel Breslav, April Childers, Ashton Cooper, Bridget Donahue, Amanda Beroza Friedman, Katie Geha, Maika Pollack, and Ricardo Valentim for their support of Rosemary's work.

Soberscove Press
Chicago, IL
soberscove.com

Temporary Monuments: Work by Rosemary Mayer, 1977–1982 © 2018 Soberscove Press

Artwork and texts by Rosemary Mayer © 2018 The Estate of Rosemary Mayer

Photographs © 2018 The Estate of Rosemary Mayer

"Pleasures and Possible Celebrations": Rosemary Mayer's Temporary Monuments, 1977–1982 © 2018 Gillian Sneed

Library of Congress Control Number: 2018942495

ISBN: 978-1-940190-21-1
Design: Rita Lascaro
Second Printing in 2022
Printed in Lithuania

Distributed by
ARTBOOK | D.A.P.
75 Broad Street, Suite 630
New York, NY 10004
artbook.com

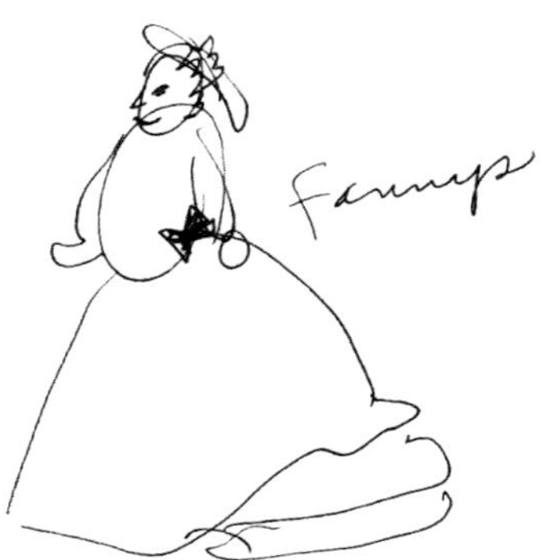
Fannys